KT-392-479

Courts and Transition in Russia

DISPOSED OF
BY LIBRARY
HOUSE OF LORDS

Courts and Transition in Russia

The Challenge of Judicial Reform

Peter H. Solomon, Jr.
and
Todd S. Foglesong

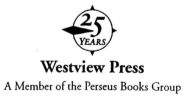

Westview Press
A Member of the Perseus Books Group

All rights reserved. No part of this publication may be reproduced or transmitted in any form or by any means, electronic or mechanical, including photocopy, recording, or any information storage and retrieval system, without permission in writing from the publisher.

Copyright © 2000 by Peter H. Solomon, Jr., and Todd S. Foglesong

Published in 2000 in the United State of America by Westview Press, Inc., 5500 Central Avenue, Boulder, Colorado 80301, and in the United Kingdom by Westview Press, Inc., 36 Lonsdale Road, Summertown, Oxford OX2 7EW

Printed and bound in the United States of America

Cataloging-in-Publication Data available from the Library of Congress
ISBN 0-8133-3776-3

10 9 8 7 6 5 4 3 2 1

Contents

PART FOUR
Strategy: The Agenda for Reform

Tables and Figures

Preface

Most students of democratization and the transition to a market economy in Eastern Europe and the former Soviet Union envisage the development of a strong legal order, if not actually a "rule of law," as a vital and necessary ingredient of liberal political and economic change. Yet these writers have little to say about the processes through which such law and legal institutions develop, not to speak of a political culture featuring respect for law.[1] Clearly, the accomplishment of a "legal transition," from bureaucratic-authoritarian law to at least rule by law (the *rechtsstaat*), is a complicated, multidimensional, and lengthy process, involving institutional and cultural change as well as changes in the laws themselves. At the center of legal transition stand the courts, the bodies that execute the law and, ideally, administer justice at the same time.

In post-Soviet Russia politicians and legal officials alike have recognized the importance of strong and independent courts for the achievement of larger policy goals, and from 1992 have pursued a major program of judicial reform. The authors of this study seek to contribute to the realization of that program. They do this by first analyzing the state and operation of courts in Russia and the progress of their reform since the end of Soviet power, and then on this basis outlining what can and should be done to make courts in Russia autonomous, powerful, reliable, efficient, accessible, and fair. The authors, both Western specialists on Russian law and legal institutions, speak at one and the same time to two audiences—Western jurists, especially those involved in organizations in a position to contribute to judicial reform in Russia; and Russian legal and political officials, the persons whose actions directly shape the nature of courts and the judiciary in their country.

We are all too aware of the delicacy of our position, but hope that our approach to this undertaking will make our analysis credible and useful. In studying courts in Russia, we try to avoid an ethnocentric preference for Anglo-American ideals, such as adversarialism; and to compare the practice of justice in Russia only with practice in other countries, rather than with idealized versions of that practice.[2] In fact, for almost all the subjects covered in this book, we start by addressing the assessments and debates generated by Russian jurists themselves— scholars, practitioners, and officials alike. After all, it is they who know their system best—its strengths, weaknesses, and needs. Of course, on most issues Russian jurists generate a wide spectrum of positions, so that in reaching conclusions about what should be done and what matters most, we are ultimately on our own. Although we may tend toward sympathy with some of the ideals of the radical reformers of Russian justice, we do not accept their positions uncritically. Concern with administrative and political feasibility—that is, making reforms happen—often draws us back from the brink and leads us to moderate positions. But we are surely biased in favor of judicial power; we believe that, all things being equal, a society is well off to have strong, autonomous, and effective courts, to which its citizens can and do bring their conflicts. It is to be hoped that our Western readers will benefit from serious and informed analysis of the realities of Russian justice; and that our Russian colleagues appreciate a view from the outside that is sympathetic, as well as informed.

This study places special emphasis on the development of the regular (or what Russians call "general") courts. It deals only briefly with the *arbitrazh* (or commercial) courts and with the specific problems of the high courts (Constitutional Court, Supreme Arbitration Court, and Supreme Court)—matters that have received extended treatment elsewhere.[3] Instead, we deal here extensively with the relationship of courts and judges to other political and legal institutions and actors, and we pay special attention to the problems of the pre-trial phase of criminal cases (including pre-trial detention) and of the implementation of civil and commercial decisions, especially those rendered by the *arbitrazh* courts.

In preparing this study, the authors engaged in extensive and intensive research. This involved reading and analyzing a wide range of materials—laws and legal commentaries, draft laws and their discussions at various fora public and private, and the full range of Russian legal journals, collections, and monographs, not to speak of writings about law and courts in the major Russian newspapers. The authors individually conducted over an eighteen-month period dozens of interviews with legal scholars, officials, and judges at various levels of the court hierarchy. We developed and administered an in-depth questionnaire for judges on the district courts, especially their chairmen and those heading regional councils of judges. We distributed—mainly through the system of councils of judges—a large number of questionnaires and were pleased to receive some 321 completed questionnaires from busy, overworked, respondents, hailing from all over the Russian Federation. Although we would not claim that our survey meets the scientific standards of survey researchers, we are confident its results are useful indicators of the perceptions and attitudes of its respondents.

Our study begins with a historical overview, first of the state of the courts in the late Soviet period, then of the post-Soviet reform process and its political and economic context. Forming the core of the study are seven sections, each focusing on a different set of issues and developing from it a set of concrete recommendations. Finally, in the concluding part, we examine these recommendations as a group, identify what we see as priorities, and explore how new funds might be spent, what changes in legislation are needed, what court leaders can do on their own, and what Western organizations might contribute to the reform process.

It is our pleasure to thank the sponsor of this project, the Constitutional and Legislative Policy Institute (COLPI) of Budapest, and its chief, Professor Stephen Holmes, for warm encouragement and generous support throughout. Within COLPI Christian Lucky and Peter Komivec rendered critical assistance at important junctures. Moreover, we were fortunate to have as partners the Moscow office of the Centre for Constitutional Research, located within the Moscow Public Science Foundation. We are grateful for the cheerful and professional help that we received from its staff, especially Kitty Gagnidze and Olga Sidorovich.

In conducting the survey of judges we had strong support from the head of the Council of Judges of the Russian Federation, Iurii Sidorenko, and the help of Valerii Rudnev and Kitty Gagnidze. Our Moscow research overall benefited immeasurably from the assistance of Rudnev and of Olga Shvartz. Finally, we would like to acknowledge the cooperation of the judges, legal officials, and scholars who gave us interviews; a list is provided in Appendix D.

On the North American front Boris Sergeev helped us analyze the results of the survey of judges. We also benefited from the research assistance of Tomas Balkelis, Eric Myles, and Aleksei Trochev, in Toronto, and William Scanlan in Lawrence, Kansas.

We would also like to thank colleagues who contributed to this enterprise. Robert Sharlet shared with us his valuable experience in the delivery of legal aid to Russia and other countries of the former USSR. Kathryn Hendley, Eugene Huskey, Sarah Reynolds, and Robert Sharlet provided constructive criticism on earlier drafts of the manuscript, ensuring that the final version was a better product.

Finally we are grateful to Edith Klein of the Centre for Russian and East European Studies, University of Toronto, for editing the manuscript, and to Rob Williams of Westview Press.

Notes

1. See, for example, Juan Linz and Alfred Stepan, *Problems of Democratic Transition and Consolidation: Southern Europe, South America, and Post-Communist Europe* (Baltimore and London, 1996); and Jeffrey Sachs and Katherina Pistor, eds., *The Rule of Law and Economic Reform in Russia* (Boulder, CO, 1997).

2. For a passionate statement supporting this approach, see Kim Lane Scheppele, "The History of Normalcy: Rethinking Legal Autonomy and the Relative Dependence of Law at the End of the Soviet Empire" *Law and Society Review*, Vol. 30, No. 3, 1996, pp. 627-50.

Needless to say, we want to avoid any repetition of the unfortunate experience of Western legal scholars and activists in the promotion of an America-centered legal reform in Latin America a generation ago. See David M. Trubek and Marc Galanter, "Scholars in Self-Estrangement: Some Reflections on the Crisis in Law and Development Studies in the United States," *Wisconsin Law Review*, 1974, No. 4, pp. 1062-1102; James A. Gardener, *Legal Imperialism: American Lawyers and Foreign Aid in Latin America* (Madison, WI, 1980).

3. See, for example, Kathryn Hendley, "Remaking an Institution: The Transition in Russia from State *Arbitrazh* to *Arbitrazh* Courts," *The American Journal of Comparative Law*, Vol. 46, No. 1, Winter 1998, pp. 93-128; Peter Krug, "Departure from the Centralized Model: The Russian Supreme Court and Constitutional Control of Legislation," *Virginia Journal of International Law*, Vol. 37, No. 3, Spring 1997, pp. 725-87.

PART ONE

Courts and Their
Reform in Post-Soviet Russia

1

Judicial Reform in Russia: Politics and Policies

This chapter explores the origins and the development of judicial reform in Russia in the 1990s. It begins with an explanation of why strong and autonomous courts matter for democratic government and market economies; continues with a capsule portrait of the weak and dependent state of courts and judges in the last decades of Soviet power; and concludes with an account of the politics of judicial reform in the new Russian state.

The Importance of Courts

Why should one study, support, and even promote the reform of courts in post-Soviet Russia? The answer is that law matters equally for the development of market economies and democratic states, and that strong, autonomous, and respected courts are necessary parts of an effective legal order.

A market-oriented economy entails countless transactions among private (and also public) actors, and these transactions are based upon confidence that the social environment is sufficiently stable and predictable to make them worthwhile. Two of the most critical elements of this environment are property rights (ownership) and the reliability of contractual relations, both of which must be developed and supported by law. In addition, in modern economies the laws of the state define and regulate the nature and lifespan of economic entities (corporate governance, bankruptcy) and key supporting institutions (banks,

3

financial markets). To be sure, in the absence of effective legal protection of private property or of legal support for contracts, players in the economy develop surrogates (from private guards to private modes of enforcement), but these alternatives do not promote a healthy capitalist system, nor do they supply the degree of stability needed to encourage long-term capital investment.[1]

Effective law is equally necessary for the development of democratic political order. First of all, there can be no real democracy unless there is also a working state, a state that has both credibility among social actors and the capability of ensuring the implementation of most of the legislation adopted in democratic political institutions.[2] Implementation requires a hierarchy of legal norms—in which administrative regulations and individual decisions by officials normally fall within legislative guidelines; and, along with this hierarchy, administrative behavior characterized by impersonal, even-handed, non-corrupt patterns of action. Equally important, democracies require the protection of individual political rights, easy to specify in a constitution but difficult to make real in practice. Such "due process" rights include protections from arbitrary or unfair impositions of state power in the criminal realm, provided by strict limits on the use of pre-trial detention, observance of the principle of presumption of innocence, and the presence of a real and effective right to defense. They include as well freedom of expression, especially in the press and mass media, freedom of conscience, freedom of assembly and political organization, and freedom of movement. All of these essential liberal rights, on which authentic democracy is based, are protected and realized only through a strong system of laws and legal institutions. To be real, rights must have remedies.

As an authoritarian state with a largely state-owned and administered economy, the USSR treated law as simply one of a number of instruments of rule and not even the dominant one. Both political decisions and administrative regulations (at all levels of the political hierarchy) took precedence over law, and even the application of regulations often took an ad hoc form and was strongly influenced by personal relationships.[3] Moreover, the jurisdiction of courts was circumscribed. The range of issues subject to legal regulation by the judiciary was so narrow that little, if any, of this arbitrary rule could be contested and disputed openly, and the resolution of conflicts with the state was driven underground.

The economic and political transitions launched in Russia (and to a degree in other post-Soviet states) in the last decade have demanded a fundamentally different role for law. The transformations in both the economic and political orders, involving significant privatization of productive capacity, the creation of democratic political institutions, and the new commitments to an impressive package of political rights and freedoms cannot be consolidated without a new legal order. But developing legal order where it did not exist is a far from simple matter—made even more difficult by the new weakness of the Russian state.

How does one effect such a "legal transition"? How does one develop the kind of law and legal institutions needed to produce a fair and productive market economy and effective democratic government? It is clear to all observers that the goal of creating a new legal order requires much more than the writing of new laws; arguably, the issuing of laws is one of the smaller factors in the equations.[4] Two other ingredients, though, matter a great deal. They are (1) the development of strong and respected institutions of the law—especially courts; and (2) the presence of powerful constituencies that need and support law.[5] In our view, both of these elements—both "supply" and "demand"—are necessary for the embracing of legal regulation by a society; neither alone will prove sufficient to facilitate the development of even "rule by law" (or *rechtsstaat*). Strong courts and strong constituencies for law may emerge in any order, but both will develop more quickly and fully when they can interact with one another. Which comes first? In the abstract, one may prefer one sequence, supposing that if the demand for law becomes strong, then the supply of law and legal institution will easily follow. But in the real world it is difficult, if not impossible, to generate demand for law through social engineering. What is possible is to pursue the other sequence and take measures to make courts strong, reliable, and fair. In so doing, one might well expect that the development of such courts will raise public regard for them and the later embracing of legal regulation by major social groups.

In short, there is no better focus for persons seeking to promote law in post-Soviet Russia than the courts. And, as we shall demonstrate in great detail, the challenge of reforming the courts in Russia is enormous and multidimensional, calling for investments of many kinds—political, financial, intellectual, and administrative.

The Soviet Legacy

For most of the Soviet period—including at the start of judicial reform in 1989—courts in the USSR were weak, dependent bodies that lacked public respect, and the career of judge had low status and few rewards. Why?

To begin, the jurisdiction of the courts in the USSR was limited mainly to the enforcement of criminal law and the resolution of civil disputes relating to divorce and alimony, housing and inheritance, and labor issues. Since 1930, courts had not dealt with constitutional matters. Their role in reviewing the legality of the actions of government officials was so narrow that most complaints were directed to the procuracy, the administrative agency charged with enforcing legality in public administration (as well as with criminal prosecutions).[6] Further, the courts played but a small role in the resolution of commercial disputes, as conflicts between state-owned firms were handled by the officials of the state *arbitrazh* (a set of tribunals wholly separate from the court system).[7] Even within the criminal realm, courts had no role in the crucial pre-trial phase, lacking, for example, the power to take or review decisions about pre-trial detention.

The rules and realities of criminal trials also reflected badly on courts and judges. As in other countries of the inquisitorial tradition, so in the Soviet Union trials served to confirm the evidence set out in the written file from the preliminary investigation (on inquest) and to impose sentences. Even these limited functions judges could not perform free of constraints, as they faced pressures to avoid acquittals and to sentence according to the policies of the day. Records were kept of a judge's performance, noting such indicators as "stability of sentences" (i.e., the percentage that withstood change upon appeal), and these records influenced the course of the judge's career. Within the courtroom the judge had to pay special heed to the concerns of the procurator, for that official had responsibility not only for conducting the prosecution but also monitoring the legality of the proceedings.[8]

Rather than being independent, judges in the USSR were exposed to multiple lines of dependency—one horizontal and two vertical. Within the localities in which they worked judges depended upon local political officials, including the Communist Party bosses, for the provision of personal benefits (such as apartments, vacations) and for extrabudgetary support of the courts (maintaining and repairing court buildings, provision of cars). In addition, the local Party leaders had a voice in the judge's continuation in office, including a say in his or her periodic renomination for "election" and the right to initiate a recall. Most judges felt sufficiently obliged to their local patrons to cooperate with their needs—whether responding to the occasional intervention about a case or maintaining appropriate records.[9] Still, in the last decades of Soviet power, judges felt even greater dependency upon their two vertical masters—the Ministry of Justice and the higher courts. The Ministry of Justice, and its departments in the regions, administered the courts by controlling their budgets, distributing bonuses, handling complaints, monitoring delays, and writing the performance evaluations on which judges' career advancement depended. The higher courts supervised by holding training courses, convening conferences on judicial practice, conducting disciplinary proceedings, and using their considerable appellate power. While judges everywhere dislike being overruled, the prospect of reversal had special consequences for Soviet judges. Indeed, their records on "stability of sentences" weighed heavily in their performance rating, potential bonuses, professional reputation, and future careers—both likelihood of promotion and possibility of not being renewed after the expiry of the current five-year term. Moreover, judges reversed too often faced disciplinary proceedings and, on occasion, recall.[10]

Another sign (and cause) of the low status of the courts and judges was financial. The Soviet government was famous for its capacity to target resources to its priority concerns, and it was all too clear that the administration of justice was not one of them. Typically, the buildings occupied by courts throughout the Soviet period were among the most modest and worst maintained public buildings—a matter of constant complaint. The salaries provided to judges and budget for court staff and expenditures were barely adequate—exposing judges to rely upon the generosity of local officials, and occasionally to fall prey to corruption. Another sign of the judges' low status was the meager provision of benefits, which in the Soviet system mattered greatly. Thus, the majority of judges in the 1970s and 1980s lacked apartments of their own.[11]

Finally, judges in the late Soviet period had a weak sense of professional identity. For one thing, judges received little, if any, special training before starting at their posts; familiarity with the courts came mainly from earlier experience (of some new judges) working as secretaries in the courts. Opportunities for mid-career training (special courses) existed but were on the whole episodic and superficial. For another, judges had none of the institutions that would have fostered interactions among them and made them into a community. There were no associations of judges, no special journal for judges, and no research institute devoted to problems of the courts and the administration of justice. To be sure, judges in many regions had opportunities to gather in the capital city for conferences, but these were typically organized by Party bodies or justice officials to make judges aware of the current priorities in the struggle against crime, which was viewed by many governmental officials as a prime responsibility of the courts.

It is hardly surprising, in the light of this brief description of the situation of courts and judges in the late Soviet period, that the public did not hold courts in high regard and that judges themselves had low self-esteem.[12] Many governmental officials displayed a condescending attitude toward law, and their actions reinforced the low status of the courts in the public eye. By the 1980s reliance upon bureaucratic regulations (in preference to laws) had become a tradition in Soviet public administration, and observation of the hierarchy of legal norms conspicuous by its absence.

Gorbachev's policy of glasnost, which lifted the veil of secrecy from most of the shortcomings of the Soviet system, enabled journalists (such as Iurii Feofanov and Arkadii Vaksberg) to write frankly about the courts, and it soon became public knowledge both that Soviet courts lacked power and respect and that judges in the USSR depended on a multiplicity of patrons. This knowledge gave journalists and legal scholars alike the opportunity to build support for judicial reform. At the same time the Gorbachev leadership, considering political and economic reform, saw the utility of strengthening the role of law, in part as a means of gaining compliance with reform initiatives. As a result, the Party resolutions of July 1988 on democratization called for the strengthening of law (through the creation of a "socialist *rechtsstaat*"), and with it some reform of the courts. In the three years that remained before the breakup of the USSR, efforts were undertaken to expand the jurisdiction of the courts, to make judges independent of local political power, and to improve the position of the accused in criminal cases.[13]

The main expansion of the jurisdiction of the general courts concerned the civil realm, and especially judicial review of administrative acts. By 1989, citizens could bring suits to the courts about allegedly illegal actions of government officials in many areas of public administration. Both constitutional and commercial litigation saw modest beginnings, but in bodies outside the regular court system. The Constitutional-Supervisory Committee to vet the constitutionality of the laws of republics and union was created, but it was attached to the legislature and part of its jurisdiction was only advisory. From 1988 commercial disputes involving private firms required adjudication, but until 1991 most of them were handled not by courts but by the state *arbitrazh*, which had in the past dealt exclusively with conflicts among state firms. There was discussion in 1990–1991 about giving courts the power to review decisions about pre-trial detention, but this was realized only in 1992.[14]

To break the dependence of judges upon local power Soviet legislators approved in August 1989 a new system of appointment. For judges at the lowest-level regular court, the so-called people's courts, ten-year terms replaced the previous terms of five years, judicial nominations had to pass muster with a qualification commission composed of judges, and the appointments made had to be approved by the regional Soviet, itself supposedly detached from local political concerns. While this new system of staffing the courts did not satisfy reformers who sought for judges the protection of terms for life, it proved useful in exposing the dangers of compromise. Deputies of the regional soviets sitting on the committees reviewing judges' credentials quickly assumed the right to criticize their actions and dictate results in particular cases! Other measures adopted to insulate judges from political pressure included criminalizing attempts to influence judges and the approval in principle of developing trial by jury.[15] Perhaps the most famous achievement of late Soviet judicial reform was the extension of right to counsel to the pre-trial phase of criminal proceedings. Long a goal of Soviet specialists in criminal procedure, the admission of counsel for cases not involving juveniles came for the most part only at the end of the preliminary investigation, unless the procurator in the cases decided otherwise. But as of 1990—after considerable political struggle—the accused gained a right to counsel starting no later than 24 hours after arrest or charging (whichever came first). Shortage of defense counsel and insufficient arrangements for their compensation limited the implementation the new rights, but they remained important and represented a step toward the reduction of the accusatorial bias in Soviet (Russian) criminal justice.[16]

The judicial reform measures adopted in the Soviet period, which at the time seemed an important beginning, were quickly overtaken by more radical measures. Debate about fundamental change in Soviet courts and criminal procedure developed during 1990–1991, a period of uncertainty during which the ideas for radical judicial reform in Russia emerged.

The Politics of Judicial Reform in Russia

The years 1991 through 1993 represented an unusual time, when it proved possible to entertain and even achieve radical changes in the judicial arena. During the last year of Soviet power, 1991, the government of Russia was engaged in a competition with the government of the USSR, seeking both to seize the initiative in the reform process generally and to gain control of institutions and areas of policy. In the judicial realm this had the result of opening an extraordinary window of opportunity for the promotion of radical changes. The window stayed wide open in 1992 and 1993, as the politicians governing the new state remained willing (if not committed) to adopt measures that marked the beginning of major gains in both the autonomy and power of the courts. By 1994–1995 changes in the political climate and economic realities limited the realization of the radical agenda, but the momentum of judicial reform continued, with leading judicial officials developing their own moderate agenda and striving to achieve it. As of 1998, there were many obstacles to the reform process, including the financial weakness of the Russian state, reflected in miserly budgets for the courts and small capacity to fund new initiatives; and the political clout of law enforcement agencies, whose leaders were bent on opposing some key changes in the criminal justice realm. But both scholars and officials alike, despite the ongoing struggle just to keep the courts functioning, still saw themselves as engaged in a larger project of institution building and improvement.[17]

During July 1991, when the government of Yeltsin's Russia was winning its battle with that of the USSR and Gorbachev over both the degree of reform and control of institutions, the Supreme Soviet of the RSFSR approved a law replacing the state *arbitrazh* bodies on its territory with *arbitrazh* or commercial courts. These new courts marked an official recognition of the new economic relationships that were developing with the creation of private business and the privatization of state firms—and the need for courts to adjudicate their disputes. Barely a week later, the Russian Supreme Soviet adopted a law creating for the RSFSR a Constitutional Court—an innovation that the government of the USSR had been unwilling to entertain (having settled in 1989 for a Constitutional-Supervisory Committee of limited jurisdiction and power).[18]

Probably the greatest milestone in Russian judicial reform during 1991 came with the approval by the Russian legislature in October of the equivalent of a "White Paper" on the reform of the courts—a document known as the "Conception of Judicial Reform." Written by nine radical reformers in Moscow (mainly scholars, many of them specialists in criminal procedure), this hundred-page manifesto, the "Conception," encapsulated what we call the radical agenda of court reform and anticipated most of the achievements in judicial reform recorded during 1992 and 1993. Here are a few of its highlights.[19]

To develop judicial independence the Conception supported a new system of judicial appointments and careers, featuring tenure for life; placing the power to discipline and remove judges solely in the hands of their peers; and guarantees of non-monetary benefits, such as housing and access to health services. The Conception also endorsed the provision of full and adequate financing of the courts from the federal budget, the arrangement of courts above the district level in geographical units not corresponding to the boundaries of regions and republics (an idea so far rejected), and the development of corporate institutions of the judiciary. To enhance the power of the courts, the authors of the Conception sought to broaden their functions to include wide-ranging judicial review of administrative acts and a significant role for courts in the pre-trial investigations, including an exclusive power to authorize pre-trial detention, involuntary searches, and wiretapping. Note that these enhancements of judicial power were to come at the expense of the procuracy, a powerful agency that during the Soviet period combined supervisory and prosecutorial powers.[20] To make the criminal process more fair and increase public respect for the courts, the reformers sought to reshape the Soviet version of the inquisitorial process, by making it more adversarial and removing some of its peculiar features. The desired transformation of criminal procedure included the revival of jury trials and justice of the peace courts, as well as the separation of the investigators conducting the pre-trial examination from the agencies of the police.

The Conception of Judicial Reform offered an ambitious blueprint for change, and its approval by the Russian Supreme Soviet did not guarantee fulfilment of any of its goals. In fact, political struggles were to ensue over many of the proposals contained in it, especially when they reached the stage of legislative proposals. During 1992–1993 progress was registered on many of the goals of the radical reformers, although their realization was not fully achieved.

The most striking achievements were made in the area of appointments and careers. The 1992 Law on the Status of Judges established the principle of life appointments for all judges (other than those on the top courts or the yet to be formed justice of the peace courts)—something that hardly any countries emerging from authoritarian rule have achieved. Moreover, the power to discipline and remove a judge was placed exclusively in the hands of the judiciary, through the Judicial Qualification Commissions (more in Chapter 4).[21] To be sure, there was some dilution of the principle—life appointments are made only after a probationary term, and, as we shall see, politicians at the level of the subjects of the Federation gained a role in screening appointments. We will discuss these issues in Chapter 2.

Another area of change was the expansion of the jurisdiction of regular courts. In 1992 they gained a virtually unlimited power to review complaints against actions of government officials and the right to hear appeals of decisions on pre-trial detention rendered by the procurators. The Constitution of 1993 promised even more; with the passage of a new Code of Criminal Procedure, judges would gain exclusive power to make initial rulings on detention and searches.[22] Most dramatically, following a directive from the Supreme Court (from October 1995), regular courts began considering the constitutionality of laws and regulations they encountered in hearing cases.[23]

A further achievement of the early 1990s was the development of corporate bodies of the judiciary, including the Council of Judges, the regional councils of judges, the Congresses of Judges, and the Judicial Qualification Commissions. In particular the various councils and the Congress have given judges opportunities to share common concerns and voice them to politicians.[24]

Finally, radical reformers were especially delighted to see the establishment of trial by jury as an option for cases serious enough to be tried at the regional court. The experiment started in five regions and was expanded to embrace nine subjects of the Federation (covering about 20 percent of the population)—all with considerable aid from Western countries. Jury trials did produce a more adversarial approach to trials, and by most accounts improved the standards of case preparation and the fairness of dispositions (with a much higher rate of acquittals). But they proved inordinately expensive, and with the financial crisis of the courts an unaffordable luxury. Expansion to other regions was put on hold, and opponents of the jury sought to further limit its jurisdiction. (The place of juries in the Constitution of 1993 made it hard to eliminate them entirely.[25])

Neither the radical agenda nor the Conception of Judicial Reform has become obsolete, if only because some of the unrealized items have constitutional support. But increasingly between 1994 and 1997 that agenda faced competition from what we call the moderate agenda of judicial reform. The moderate agenda, which is not written in one place, represents the aspirations of the people running the courts (as opposed to visionary scholars): we have discerned this agenda in various speeches and reports by leaders of the Supreme Court, the Ministry of Justice, the Supreme *Arbitrazh* Court, and the State Legal Administration. The moderate agenda focuses not upon the transformation of Russian justice through adversarial imports but on responding to pressing needs, such as underfinancing the courts and coping with case overload and backlogs. However, the projects of the moderate agenda do involve the creation of new institutions and have major budgetary implications.

One of the key planks in the moderate agenda is shifting the administrative servicing of the courts from the Ministry of Justice to a new Judicial Department attached to the Supreme Court. The goal was to gain power and prestige for the judicial branch by breaking its dependence upon the executive, giving it a separate budgetary line, and having judges (through the Supreme Court and the Council of Judges) supervise judicial administration.[26]

Another focus of the moderate agenda is the creation of a new service of armed bailiffs, designed both to improve security at courthouses and even more to strengthen the implementation of decisions in commercial cases. Supporters of this initiative believed that the bailiffs, as men with arms, would prove more effective than their predecessors, the judicial enforcers, who were unarmed women.[27]

Among the most important items on the moderate agenda were mechanisms for handling the rising caseloads of judges. These included: the development of various simplifications—from the broad use of single judges hearing cases alone to abbreviated trials following confessions —and, even more ambitious, the creation of a whole new layer of the court system, the Justices of the Peace. The radical reformers also supported the peace courts, as a way of bringing justice closer to the people. For the top justice officials their virtue lay mainly in relieving the regular district courts of much of their civil caseload (60 percent), minor criminal cases, and all cases of administrative violations.[28] And for politicians, as we shall see, the peace courts represented a way to respond to the demands of republican and regional governments to have courts of their own.

As of mid–1999, all of these initiatives had gained some approval. A law creating the service of bailiffs was passed in the summer of 1997, and gained funding in the fall; by spring 1999, as we shall see in Chapter 8, at least part of the service was functioning. A law creating the new

Judicial Department received approval of the legislature and president early in 1998, and both the Department itself and its regional units were created during 1998–1999. In December 1998 a revised draft law on the peace courts finally became law (its predecessors had suffered a presidential veto), and 1999 witnessed the first steps in the complicated task of actually establishing the new courts.[29]

Apart from the realization of these initiatives (the bailiffs, justice of the peace courts, and the Judicial Department), the politics of judicial reform in 1998–1999 revolved around three major questions whose resolution was vital for the reform of the courts—the adoption of a new Criminal Procedure Code; the determination of the court systems of the subjects of the Federation and their relationship to federal courts; and an adequate response to the financial crisis of the courts.

Only with the new Criminal Procedure Code will judges actually gain the exclusive power of decision over pre-trial detention, search and seizure, and eavesdropping, promised in the Constitution of the Russian Federation. The new Criminal Procedure Code must also serve as a vehicle for developing simplifications that will enable courts to handle caseloads more effectively—resolving *inter alia* whether to introduce abbreviated trials after an admission of guilt and for what cases single judge hearings are appropriate. In addition, the Code is to supply the rules of procedure for the justice of the peace courts (even though these courts are to be "local," that is belong to the governments of the subjects of the Federation). In late 1997–early 1998 there was serious controversy about the latest draft Criminal Procedure Code, as jurists close to the President opposed the draft that had passed first reading in the Duma for not advancing the cause of adversarialism to a sufficient degree. During 1998 a Duma drafting group composed of scholars and representatives of the judicial and law enforcement agencies, the Presidency, and the Duma itself studied the many suggestions for changes in the draft and worked on resolving many controversial points.[30]

A second major question in court reform discussions in 1998 was the determination of the nature of the courts of the subjects of the Federation (republics and regions) and their relationship to the federal courts. Ostensibly, the Law on the Court System of the Russian Federation, adopted at the end of 1996, had resolved this matter, by designating all existing courts (district, regional/republican supreme, and top courts) as federal and granting to the subjects control of the justice of the peace courts (though with federal funding) and the right to establish their own constitutional or charter courts. In designating all courts in the general court system as federal, the 1996 law confirmed the right of the President to appoint most judges and granted them the protections of the 1992 law on the status of judges (e.g., no firing except for cause as established by a judicial qualifications commission). The problem was that political leaders in some republics did not accept the provisions of the 1996 Law. On the one hand, this led to acts of disobedience. Thus, Bashkortostan adopted its own laws on courts and judges, which contradicted federal law on important particulars. Judges in that republic are selected not for life, but for ten-year terms and, according to Bashkir law, chosen by the republican legislature (upon nomination by the republican president). (A draft law on the court system of the republic of Tatarstan circulating in 1998 adopted the same model.) And for a time Bashkir officials refused to send the names of judges so chosen to the President of the Russian Federation, the only person with the legal right to appoint federal judges. In retaliation, the Supreme Court of the Russian Federation invalidated all cases from Bashkir judges appointed in the republic on the grounds that the judges were "illegitimate." For their part, leading Bashkir jurists, including the head of the republican constitutional court, defended Bashkir initiatives on courts as consistent with the bilateral treaty that the republic concluded with the Russian Federation in 1994.[31]

On the other hand—beyond acts of disobedience (and there is a long list), leaders of many of the subjects began pressing in Moscow for a reopening of the question of the distribution of courts between the Federal government and the governments of the subjects. Through parliamentary hearings (organized by the Federation Council), discussions with officials in the Presidency, and even an unsuccessful challenge to provisions of the 1996 Law on the Court System, regional leaders raised the question of whether the existing district courts should not be transferred to the subjects.[32] The question of the distribution of courts and structures of the court systems of the Federal government and the subjects became a crucial issue in discussions held in spring 1998 of the commission to draft a new law on courts of general jurisdiction, one of a number of laws needed to flesh out the 1996 Law on the Court System, which provided only the framework of the court system. At the first meetings of the drafting commission (under the lead of Ruslan Orekhov, head of the State Legal Administration of the Presidency), a range of options received airing. While the commission did not recommend transferring existing courts to the subjects (as Bashkortostan demanded), it seriously considered supporting the creation of new courts of the subjects to handle appeals from the justice of the peace courts, at least when local legislation was involved. (One version of the draft law went so far as to allow a person appealing a decision of the peace courts to choose between a federal district court and a local appellate-cassation court, a move that threatened the unity of federal jurisdiction in criminal law.[33]) After major objections from the judicial chiefs, articulated privately and reflected in a resolution of the Council of Judges of the Russian Federation objecting to any creation of independent court systems in the subjects of the Federation, the commission opted against including controversial changes in the court system, and sent to the Duma a tame version of the draft law.[34] But this was not the end of the story. Early in 1999 the President of Ingushetiia proposed to the Duma changes in the Law on the Status of Judges which would give subjects the right to determine, rather than merely vet, candidates for judgeships.[35] The larger implication of these political skirmishes lay in the fact that, despite the 1996 Law on the Court System, the basic shape of the courts of Russia was still unresolved.

Finally, a huge issue, intimately connected to most aspects of judicial reform, including its prehistory—the realization of steps already taken as well as new initiatives—was the massive underfinancing of the courts. In the late Soviet period, courts were underfinanced, and reformers began complaining about the consequences of poverty in the courts. The Russian government took seriously the need to raise the salaries of judges in relative terms to stop the flight of judges to more lucrative work that became available for lawyers in the 1990s. But these salary raises came by and large at the expense of the administrative budgets of courts. Moreover, when in 1995–1996 the Russian government failed to collect as tax revenue even the meager share of GDP (itself lower than ever) that it anticipated, it began holding back on the delivery of money already allocated to the courts in the state budget. In 1996 a significant share of budgeted funds (as much as 30 percent) never reached the courts.[36] After major protests from the judicial community, the government agreed that, from 1997, money allocated to the courts would join the priority category of "protected" expenditures that had to be covered even in the absence of revenue. At the time a leading justice official warned one of the authors of this study that the legal form of "protected status" had little meaning in practice.[37] He proved correct, for in April 1998 the government once again imposed a major cut (sequester) in the revenue it would supply to the courts, in this instance of 26 percent of the funds budgeted for 1998. This step led to an extraordinary outburst of protests from all levels of the court system, with the top judges complaining to the President about the government's violation of the provisions of the Law on the Court System forbidding any cuts in the budgets of the courts without the consent of the Congress or Council of Judges. As it happened, the 1998 budget law had provided the government with the power to cut all parts of the state budget proportionately to any shortfalls in revenue, in a blanket form that seemed to include the courts. Accordingly, the chiefs of the Supreme and Supreme *Arbitrazh* Courts brought a challenge to the constitutionality of this provision to the Constitutional Court of Russia, which at the end of July agreed with the petitioners, declaring that the provision in the law and the government's cuts to the court budget were unconstitutional.[38] Even before this legal victory, the President had supported the court leaders and instructed the government to reverse its decision and provide courts with the funding promised to them.[39]

Within days of the Constitutional Court's decision declaring unconstitutional any sequester of funds from the budget of the courts, Finance Minister Mikhail Zadornov asked the Council of Judges to consent to the cuts (an action that would remove one of the court's objections). But the Council of Judges naturally refused. Then the financial crisis of August 1998 hit Russia, leading to the devaluation of the ruble and making it more difficult for the government to restore the courts' budget. The judges, however, did not accede to the inevitable. Instead, after hearing nothing positive from Zadornov, the Presidium of the Council of Judges in early September instructed the head of the Court Department to sue the government for the illegally sequestered funds and asked the Procurator General of Russia to start criminal proceedings against the Minister of Finance Zadornov for failing to implement a court decision (article 315) and exceeding his authority (article 286).[40] Procurator General Skuratov did no such thing, but he did send an open letter to Prime Minister Primakov (in November 1999) adding his support to the need for better and more secure funding of the courts as necessary for minimum efficiency of the administration of criminal justice.[41]

The Russian government did respond to this pressure. Late in 1998 it handed over a "solid sum" to pay some of its overdue obligations to the courts; and early in 1999 it approved a law on court financing. The law did not provide new money to the courts, but it did reinforce earlier legal provisions limiting how much the government could cut the budget of the courts and requiring consent from an organ of the judicial community. More important, it supplied close to a guarantee that the courts would avoid the delays in payments that most government agencies had to endure. The courts' share was to be paid by the tenth of each month, and if this did not happen the judicial bodies could simply take the money directly from the government accounts without special authorization (*v bezaktseptnom poriadke*). Reportedly relations between the judicial agencies and the Ministry of Finance "normalized."[42]

Although the drama of 1998 over court financing ended, most courts remained in desperate straits, still lacking funds to cover basic needs. We will deal with the consequences of this situation later on, including renewed dependencies on local government. What is important here is to stress the difficulty of getting adopted and realized any reform initiative that costs money. As we shall see, the Russian government did come through with some funding for the bailiffs (though insufficient), perhaps in the anticipation that this institution would pay for itself in new money collected for the government. In the 1999 budget the government supplied funds to cover the operation of 5 to 6 percent of a full complement of justice of the peace courts. Clearly, the existing courts will not raise the standards of their operations with new infusion of money, nor will they succeed in recruiting high quality persons to work as judges.

Top legal officials in Moscow are well aware of the problem and have more than once asked their government to make courts more of a priority. In February 1998 the chairman of the Supreme Court of the Russian Federation, Viacheslav Lebedev, presented the Duma with a draft law on financing of the courts, setting norms well above current funding levels (the law passed in 1999 did not deal with the level of funding).[43] We, the authors of this report, strongly support this idea, not only because of the particular needs of the courts but also because well-operating courts will generate public respect and add to the legitimacy and support for government in Russia generally. Moreover, the absence of sufficient funding for the courts from the federal government threatens to make the courts supplicants of regional and local governments and de facto creatures of those governments (a problem dealt with in Chapter 2).

It should be clear from the discussion so far that the course of judicial reform in the Russian Federation is intimately connected with other political and economic developments. We have seen how the question of federalism intersects with the organization of courts and how the limited financial resources of the Russian government have affected its capacity to fund the courts and their improvement. There are two further aspects of the larger context that influence the progress of judicial reform.

One is the problem of crime and the way perceptions of the crime problem affect political decisions. The 1990s in Russia did observe a dramatic increase in property crimes, as might be expected in a society undergoing social disorganization and economic shock. But what mattered politically was the highly publicized activities of organized crime, including gangland murders. At least for a time, there was a crime scare, as the public reacted to the deluge of information provided by journalists and law enforcement officials. Public fears helped police agencies gain extra resources and, for a few years, special powers (e.g., the right to detain without charge for thirty days persons suspected of involvement with organized crime.)[44] The scope of the crime problem, and the difficulties law enforcement has in confronting it, may impede serious efforts to reduce pre-trial detention, and hinder as well the promotion of protections for the accused and the strengthening of adversarialism in Russian criminal justice.

Another matter constraining court reform is the system of taxation in the Russian Federation. We have already mentioned how the shortfall of revenue collected limits the funds available to support the courts, but there is another way in which taxes affect the role of courts. Many business firms (at least those that lack the connections to get dispensations) face excessively high tax burdens (when the demands of various levels of government and agencies are taken into account). The burden is so high as to threaten the survival, let alone profitability, of many firms, forcing their managers to evade taxes, often by maintaining a portion of the firm's activity off its official books. Firms in this position are typically loathe to bring disputes to the courts, for fear of exposing their illegal practices, and prefer to use various informal methods of dispute resolution, usually involving private enforcement.[45] All this suggests delay in the movement of courts into the resolution of commercial disputes, a new function that could raise their status.

In short, the future of the courts and judicial reform in Russia will be shaped to a considerable degree by the larger political context, and the progress of political and economic developments more generally.

Conclusion

This account of judicial reform in late Soviet and post-Soviet Russia has emphasized a number of themes:

1. the complexity and interconnectedness of the various judicial reform measures and ideas, which even in the moderate agenda involve fundamental issues such as the nature of institutions and procedures;

2. how much has been accomplished so far (especially relating to the appointments and careers of judges);

3. the presence of real threats to these achievements and further progress of judicial reform, including the financial crisis of the courts and the claims of republican leaders (the problem of federalism);

4. the crucial legislative agenda of 2000–2002, including new laws on institutions—such as courts of general jurisdiction; and on procedures—the Codes of Criminal and Civil Procedure;

5. the difficult political and economic context for the realization of judicial reform overall.

With these points in mind, we proceed in the chapters that follow to examine in more detail the problems of building judicial institutions and improving the performance of the administration of justice and to weigh the merits of alternative measures of reform.

Notes

1. Kathryn Hendley, "Legal Development in Post-Soviet Russia," *Post-Soviet Affairs*, Vol. 13, No. 3, July-Sept. 1997, pp. 228-51; Jeffrey Sachs and Katherina Pistor, eds., *The Rule of Law and Economic Reform in Russia* (Boulder, CO, 1997).

2. Stephen Holmes, "Cultural Legacies or State Collapse? Probing the Postcommunist Dilemma," in Michael Mandelbaum, ed., *Post-Communism: Four Perspectives* (New York, 1996), pp. 22-76.

3. Eugene Huskey, "Government Rulemaking as a Brake on Perestroika," *Law and Social Inquiry*, Vol. 15, 1990, pp. 419-432.

4. Robert Sharlet, "Bringing the Rule of Law to Russia and the Newly Independent States: The Role of the West in the Transformation of the Post-Soviet Legal Systems," in Karen Dawisha, ed., *The International Dimension of Post-Communist Transitions in Russia and the New States of Eurasia* (Armonk, NY and London, UK, 1997), pp. 322-49.

5. For discussion of the demand for law, see Hendley, "Legal Development."

6. Peter H. Solomon, Jr., "The USSR Supreme Court: History, Role and Future Prospects," *American Journal of Comparative Law*, Vol. 38, No. 1, Winter 1990, pp. 201-215; Gordon B. Smith, *The Soviet Procuracy and the Supervision of Administration* (Alphen aan den Rijn, 1978).

7. On the system of state *arbitrazh*, see Stanislaw Pomorski, "State Arbitrazh in the USSR: Development, Functions, Organization," *Rutgers-Camden Law Journal*, Vol. 9, No. 1, 1977, pp. 61-116, and Heidi Kroll, "The Role of Contracts in the Soviet Economy," *Soviet Studies*, Vol. 40, No. 3, 1988, pp. 349-66.

8. Peter H. Solomon, Jr., "The Case of the Vanishing Acquittal: Informal Norms and the Practice of Soviet Criminal Justice," *Soviet Studies*, Vol. 39, No. 4, Oct. 1987, pp. 531-55.

9. Peter H. Solomon, Jr., "Soviet Politicians and Criminal Justice: The Logic of Party Intervention," in James Millar, ed., *Cracks in the Monolith* (Armonk, NY, 1992), pp. 3-32; Yoram Gorlizki, "Political Reform and Local Party Interventions under Khrushchev," in Peter H. Solomon, Jr., ed., *Reforming Justice in Russia, 1864–1996: Power, Culture, and the Limits of Legal Order* (Armonk, NY, and London, UK, 1998), pp. 256-81.

10. Todd S. Foglesong, "The Politics of Judicial Independence and the Administration of Criminal Justice in Soviet Russia, 1982-1992," unpublished doctoral dissertation, University of Toronto, 1995, esp. Chapter 2; Todd S. Foglesong, "The Reform of Criminal Justice and the Evolution of Judicial Dependence in Late Soviet Russia," in Solomon, ed., *Reforming Justice in Russia*, pp. 282-324.

11. See George Ginsburgs, "The Soviet Judicial Elite: Is It?" *Review of Socialist Law*, Vol. 11, 1985, pp. 293-311; Foglesong, "The Politics of Judicial Independence," Chapter 5.

12. Peter H. Solomon, Jr., "Legality in Soviet Political Culture: A Perspective on Gorbachev's Reforms," in Nick Lampert and Gabor Rittersporn, eds., *Stalinism and its Aftermath* (London, 1991), pp. 260-87.

13. Peter H. Solomon, Jr., "Gorbachev's Legal Revolution," *Canadian Business Law Journal*, Vol. 17, No. 2 (Dec. 1990), pp. 184-94; Eugene Huskey, "The Administration of Justice: Courts, Procuracy and Ministry of Justice," in Huskey, ed., *Executive Power and Soviet Politics* (Armonk, NY, and London, UK, 1992), pp. 221-46.

14. Peter Maggs, "Enforcing the Bill of Rights in the Twilight of the Soviet Union," *University of Illinois Law Review*, 1991, pp. 1049-63; V. M. Pomazev, "Arbitrazhnyi sud Rossii: Opyt i problemy realizatsii novogo zakonodatelstva ('kruglyi stol zhurnal'), *Gosudarstvo i pravo*, 1995, No. 10, pp. 3-27 (esp.vystuplenie V. F. Iakovlev, pp. 4-10); Peter H. Solomon, Jr., "Reforming Criminal Justice under Gorbachev," in Donald Barry, ed., *Toward the 'Rule of Law' in Russia?* (Armonk, NY, and London, UK,1992), pp. 235-56; Todd S. Foglesong, "*Habeas Corpus* or 'Who Has the Body?' Judicial Review of Arrest and Pretrial Detention in Russia," *Wisconsin International Law Journal*, Vol. 14, No. 3, Summer 1996, pp. 541-78.

15. Solomon, "Gorbachev's Legal Revolution;" Foglesong, "The Politics of Judicial Independence," Chapter 5.

16. Solomon, "Reforming Criminal Justice under Gorbachev."

17. For a more detailed discussion of the two reform agendas see Peter H. Solomon, Jr., "The Persistence of Judicial Reform in Post-Soviet Russia," *East European Constitutional Review*, Vol. 6, No. 4, Fall 1997, pp. 50-56.

18. See Appendix A, "Key Laws in Russian Judicial Reform, 1991-1998."

19. *Kontseptsiia sudebnoi reformy v Rossiiskoi Federatsii* (Moscow, 1992). For an English translation see *Statutes and Decisions: The Laws of the USSR and Its Successor States*, Vol. 30, No. 2, March-April 1994.

20. The Conception of Judicial Reform included a root and branch attack on the supervisory role of the Procuracy, but that body successfully defended most of its prerogatives, and appropriately so. There remains in post-Soviet Russia a need for both the monitoring of the legality of subnational legislative enactments (and other normative acts) and for multiple forums for handling citizen complaints against illegal actions of public officials. The most objectionable features of prosecutorial supervision in the past—the right to pursue proactive fishing expeditions in search of illegalities without signals and the obligation of the procurator to supervise trial proceedings while also prosecuting—have been eliminated. For more on the procuracy's adjustment to the post-Soviet realities, see Gordon B. Smith, "The Struggle over the Procuracy," in Solomon, ed., *Reforming Justice in Russia*, pp. 348-73.

21. "O statuse sudei v Rossiiskoi Federatsii," Zakon ot 26 iiuniia 1992, with changes of 14 February 1993, 20 May 1993, 3 December 1994, and 21 July 1995, in *Delegatu IV (Chrezvychainnogo) Vserossiiskogo s'ezda sudei* (Moscow, 1996), pp. 11-23.

22. Peter H. Solomon, Jr., "The Limits of Legal Order in Post-Soviet Russia," *Post-Soviet Affairs*, Vol. 11, No. 2, 1995, pp. 89-115; "List of Key Laws."

23. See discussion in Chapter 4.

24. *Ibid.*

25. Solomon, "Limits of Legal Order," pp. 103-104; Peter H. Solomon, Jr., *Problemy razvitiia pravovogo stroia v postsovetskoi Rossii* (Moscow, 1997), pp. 14-15. See also Stephen Thaman, "The Resurrection of Trial by Jury in Russia," *Stanford Journal of International Law*, Vol. 31, No. 6, 1997, pp. 61-274; Sarah Reynolds, "Drawing upon the Past: Jury Trials in Modern Russia," in Solomon, ed., *Reforming Justice in Russia*, pp. 374-97.

26. "'O sudebnoi sisteme RF,' Federalnyi Konstitutsionyi Zakon ot 30 dekabria 1996," *Rossiiskaia gazeta*, 6 Jan. 1997, p. 3; "Proekt federalnyi zakon 'O sudebnom departamente pri Verkhovnom sude RF i vkhodiashchikh v ego sistemy organakh'" (versions of January 1997 and April 1997), and "Poiasnitelnaia zapiska k proektu." For discussion of the new Court Department see Chapter 3.

27. For the development of the bailiff service see Chapter 8.

28. "O mirovykh sudiakh v Rossiiskoi Federatsii," Federalnyi zakon RF ot 17 dekabria 1998 goda, *Rossiiskaia gazeta*, 22 Dec. 1998, p. 4; Sergei Ramazin, "Pravovoi status i kontseptsiia formirovaniia i funktsionirovaniia instituta

mirovykh sudei Rossiiskoi Federatsii," in *Sudebnaia sistema v Rossii* (kruglyi stol, 14 marta 1997) (Moscow, 1997). For discussion of the justice of the peace court initiative see Chapter 6.

29. "O sudebnom departament pri Verkhovnom Sude Rossiiskoi Federatsii," Zakon RF ot 8 ianvaria 1998, *Rossiiskaia gazeta*, 14 Jan. 1998, p. 5; "Komu podchiniaiutsia mirovye sudi?" Prezidentskoe veto, *ibid.*, 10 Feb. 1998, p. 5; V. Demidov, "Federalnyi zakon deistvuet—ochered za sub'ektamy Federatsii," *Rossiiskaia iustitsiia*, 1999, No. 5, pp. 2-4.

30. "Proekt Ugolovno-protsessualnogo Kodeksa Rossiiskoi Federatsii" (December 1996 version as submitted by Members of the Committee on Legal and Judicial Reform of the State Duma); *Stenogramma zasedanii Gosudarstvennoi Dumy*, Biulleten No.103 (245) ot 6 iiunia 1997, pp. 53-57; "Tablitsa popravok k proektu Ugolovno-protsessualnogo Kodeks RF (vnositsia deputatami Gosudarstvennoi Duma-chlenami Komitet Gosudarstvennoi Dumy po zakonodatelstvu i sudebno-pravovoi reforme).

31. "Stenogramma zasedaniia Soveta pri Prezidente Rossiiskoi federatsii po voprosam sovershenstvovania pravosudiia," 13 maia 1998, pp. 32-34; interviews; "O sudebnoi sisteme respubliki Tatarstana," zakonoproekt (1998); "Poiasnitelnaia zapiska k proektu zakona 'O sudebnoi sisteme respubliki Tatarstana'." The draft law on the court system of Tatarstan stipulated that judges were to be appointed by the State Council of Tatarstan upon nomination by the President of Tatarstan or one of the judicial qualification commissions. The Supreme Court of Tatarstan would serve as the highest court for cassation and appellate reviews, and the Supreme Court of the Russian Federation would be limited to reviews in supervision.

32. Konstantin Katanian, "Chto deliat Moskva i Kazan? Shaimiev predlozhil podelit sudebnuiu sitemuy mezhdu Federatsiei i Tatariei," *Nezavisimaia gazeta*, 12 Feb. 1998, p. 3; Pavel Mirzoev, interviews.

33. Pavel Mirzoev, "Sudebnuiu sistemu zhdut velikie potriaseniia: Regiony mogut poluchit bolshe, chem trebovali," *Russkii telegraf*, 14 May 1998, p. 2; *idem.*, "Strasti po sudebnoi sisteme prodolzhaiutsia: Regiony gotovy k pobede nad Konstitutsiei," *ibid.*, 19 June 1998; R. Orekhov, "Sudebnaia reforma trebuet radikalnogo podkhoda," *Rossiiskaia iustitsiia*, 1998, No. 8, pp. 2-4; "Sistema sudov obshchei iurisdiktsii: naostoiashchee i budushchee," *ibid.*, 1998, No. 10, pp. 5-7; "Stenogramma zasedaniia Soveta;" "Proekt Federalnyi konstitutsionnyi zakon 'O sudakh obshchei iurisdiktsii v RF'" (n.d., 1998).

34. "Postanovlenie Soveta sudei Rossiiskoi Federatsii ot 29 oktiabria 1998 goda;" "'O sudakh obshchei iurisdiktsii v Rossiiskoi Federatsii,' Proekt federalnyi konstitutsionnyi zakon ot 30 oktiabria 1998." For an articulation of the position of Orekhov and the State Legal Administration (GPPU) on federalism and the courts in Russia, see R. Orekhov, "Sudebnaia reforma trebuet radikalnogo podkhoda," *Rossiiskaia iustitsiia*, 1998, No. 8, pp. 2-4. For an articulate rebuttal by two judges from Rostov, see V. Tkachev and N. Chepurnova, "Edinstvo sudebnoi sistemy i printsipy federalizma," *ibid.*, No. 12, pp. 3-4.

35. "Vokrug statusa federalnykh sudei nachalis opasnye manevry," *Rossiiskaia iustitsiia*, 1999, No. 5, p. 1.

36. Iurii Feofanov, "Nishchii sud k pravosudiiu ne goden," *Izvestiia*, 9 July 1996, p. 5; "Sudebnaia vlast v finansovom tupike," *Rossiiskaia gazeta*, 14 Nov. 1996, p. 5; "Trevozhnoe soveshchanie k kontse goda (Iz stenoogramy zasedaniia Soveta po sudebnoi reforme pri Prezidenta RF)," *Rossiakai iustitsiia*, 1996 No. 12, pp. 2-8; S. Tropin, "Pismo delegatam IV Vserossiiskogo s'ezda sudei," ot 29 IX 1996, in *Delegatu IV*, pp. 77-82.

37. "O neotlozhnykh merakh po stabilizatsii polozheniia v sudebnoi sisteme Rossiiskoi Federatsii," Ukaz Prezidenta RF of 2 dekabria 1996, *Rossiiskaia gazeta*, 5 Dec. 1996, p. 6; "Rasshifrovka zapisi zasedanii Soveta po sudebvnoi reformy pri Prezidenta RF, 12 marta 1997," vystuplenie Kasmova, pp. 40-44; "Glavnoe kontrolnoe upravlenie Administratsii Prezidenta dokladyvaet: 'Provereno. Del net,'" *Iuridicheskii vestnik*, 1997, No. 6, p. 4; interview.

38. Igor Iurev, "Tikhii sekvestr pravosudiia. Minfin sdaet slug zakona v polzovanie regionalnym elitam," *Obshchaia gazeta*, 7-13 May 1998, p. 3; Mikhail Korolev, "Sudi na grani ostanovki" (Beseda s Venaiminom Iakovlevom), *Iuridicheskii vestnik*, 1998, No. 11, pp. 2-3; Vladimir Khitruk, "Nevozmozhno gosudarstvo bez pravosudiia" (Beseda s Viacheslavom Lebedevom), *ibid.*, No. 13, p. 9; Vladimir Galaiko, "Sudy podaiut...v sud," *Rossiiskie vesti*, 8 July 1998, p. 11; "Postanovlenie Konstitutsionnnogo Suda RF po delu o proverke konstitutsionnosti chasti 1 stati 102 Federalnogo zakona, 'O federalnom biudzhete na 1998 god,' ot 17 iiulia 1998 goda" *Rossiiskaia gazeta*, 30 July 1998, p. 5; V. Rudnev, "Deistviia Pravitelstva po sokrashcheniiu sudeiskogo biudzheta priznany nekonstitutsionnymi," *Rossiiskaia iustitsiia*, 1998, No. 9, p. 1.

39. "Ot Prezidenta RF Borisa Eltsina k S. V. Kirienko, M. M. Zadornovu," Pr-763 (1 iiuniia 1998).

40. V. Rudnev, "Slovo Konstitutsionnogo Suda i molchanie Pravitelstva," *Rossiiskaia iustitsiia*, 1998, No. 10, p. 1; "O vzyskanii zadolzhennosti na obespechenie sudebnoi deiatelnosti s federalnoi kazny Rossiiskoi Federatsii v sudebnom poriadke," Postanovlenie Prezidiuma Soveta sudei RF ot 2 sentiabria 1998 g.; "O vozbuzhdeniia ugolovnogo dela v otnoshenii Ministra finansov Rossiiskoi Federatsii M. M. Zadornova i drugikh dolzhnostnykh lits, vinovnykh v nezakonnom sokrashchenii biudzheta sudebnoi sistemy na 1998 god i neispolnenii Postanovleniia Konstitutsionnogo Suda RF ot 17 iiulia 1998 goda No.23n..." Postanovlenie Prezidiuma Soveta sudei RF ot 3 sentiabria 1998 g. Both of these resolutions can be found on the Web site of the Supreme Court of the Russian Federation (www.supcourt.ru).

41. "Generalnaia prokuratura RF: Bez privedeniia sudebnoi sistemy v nadlezhashhee sostoianie iskliuchena vozmozhnost deistvennogo nastupleniia na prestupnost," *Rossiiskaia iustitsiia*, 1999, No. 4, pp. 8-9.

42. "O finansirovanii sudov Rossiiskoi Federatsii," Zakon RF ot 10 fevralia 1999, *Rossiiskaia gazeta*, 18 Feb. 1999, p. 4; Vadim Mikhailov, "Rossiiskaia femedia bolshe ne zolushka," (Interviu s Iuriiu Sidorenko), *Iuridicheskii vestnik*, 1999, No. 5, pp. 6-7.

43. "Finansirovane sudov Rossiiskoi Federatsii," *Rossiiskaia iustitsiia*, 1998, No. 5, p. 1; "O finansirovanii sudov Rossiiskoi Federatsii," Proekt federalnyi zakon RF (n.d.:Verkhovnyi sud, 1998); "Poiasnitelnaia zapiska k proektu federalnomu zakona 'O finansirovanii sudov Rossiiskoi Federatsii;" "O finansirovanii sudov RF," proekt federalnyi zakon (n.d.: Vysshii arbirtrazhnyi sud, 1998).

44. Solomon, "Reforming Criminal Law under Gorbachev," esp. pp. 246-50; "Rasshifrovka zapisi," pp. 96-105 (vystuplenie Gilinskogo); "Materialy prilozheniia k informatsionnoi zapiske 'Nekotorye voprosy realizatsii ugolovnoi politiki v sovremennykh usloviiakh," (Moscow, 1997), pp. 28-35; "O neotlozhnykh merakh po zashchite naseleniia ot banditizma i inykh proiavlenii organizovannoi prestupnosti," Ukaz Presidenta RF ot 14 iiuniia 1994," *Rossiiskaia gazeta*, 17 June 1994, p. 1; Anna Feofilantov and Aleksei Grishin, "Prezident otmenil 'nekonstitutsionnye ukazy'," *Segodnia*, 18 June 1997, p. 1.

45. Alexander Morozov, "Tax Administration in Russia," *East European Constitutional Review*, Vol. 5, Nos. 2-3, 1996, pp. 39-47; "Moscow Tax Police head on Violations" (translated from *Nalogovaia politsiia*), FBIS=-SOV-96-209S; Barbara Zshoch, "Tax Fraud in Yaroslavl's Small Enterprises: Techniques, Causes, Cures" (unpublished; Kon, 1997); P. Skoblikov, "'Tenevaia iustitsiia' formy proiavleniia i realizatsii," *Rossiiskaia iustitsiia*, 1998, No. 10, pp. 21-23.

Building Judicial Institutions

In Part Two we examine the state and operation of courts and the judiciary in post-Soviet Russia. Our goals are to dissect their strengths and weaknesses, analyze the impact of judicial reform to date, and, above all, determine what needs to be done now and in the future to make courts in Russia independent, autonomous, powerful, respected, and well-run. Our perspective on these matters comes largely from an inside view of the courts, for we have benefited from unusually rich statistical data, helpful and candid informants, and extensive participant-observation.

In diagnosing and prescribing cures for problems in the courts of Russia, we have found the experience of the judiciary in North America to be of little help. The reason is that many aspects of Russia's political and economic development, not to speak of its legal traditions, make the process of building and improving judicial institutions in that country distinctive. For example, the bureaucratization of the career judiciary in Russia, however imperfect, generates powerful pressures on judges from their own court hierarchy to conform to the expectations of superiors, pressures that can be curbed only through improvements in judicial administration and career management. Other factors such as informal political relations, the bureaucratic economy, and enduring patrimonial patterns of authority at the level of local government also create special problems for judicial independence, which greater and more centralized funding alone may not resolve.[1]

In many aspects of judicial institution building, post-Soviet Russia has made great strides, and for this reason the recommendations we make tend to be modest in scope (though not necessarily in cost). By and large, the task now is not to create new institutions or write new laws, but to make existing ones work better. For example, over the past decade Russian courts acquired in law considerable new power, but there remains the challenge of realizing and consolidating it. This process will require advances in inter-institutional cooperation (between courts themselves and between courts and executive bodies), strengthening the organizations of judicial self-government, increasing rates of implementation of court decisions, and informing the public of the new remedies available to them. Likewise, improving the training of judges calls for not only curricular reform and new technologies but also less dramatic initiatives such as developing challenging judicial internships for law students and new opportunities for graduates to work as clerks in the courts. Finally, we see a great need for further analysis of the practice of courts and the judiciary in Russia, especially collaborative studies (evaluations) of the implementation of reform measures.

Notes

1. For an understanding of the evolution of the role of local government in Russian judicial politics, see Peter H. Solomon, "Local Political Power and Soviet Criminal Justice, 1921-1941," *Soviet Studies*, Vol. 31, No. 2, 1985, pp. 305-329, and Yoram Gorlizki, "De-Stalinization and the Politics of Criminal Justice in Russia, 1953-1964," unpublished doctoral dissertation, University of Oxford, 1992.

2

The Independence of
Courts and Judges

In the USSR a central shortcoming in the administration of justice was the absence of judicial independence. Courts in the Soviet Union were neither regarded nor treated as an institution separate from the political regime that they served. Accordingly, the Soviet state took few steps to buttress its constitutional proclamation of "the independence of judges."[1] Judges had no guarantees of professional security and private welfare, and the funding and servicing of the courts failed to shield judges from the outside world. In fact, in rendering decisions at trial, judges were exposed to, rather than insulated from, external pressures, some of them coming from political officials. To be sure, direct intervention in the resolution of cases was neither common nor officially condoned, but even this extreme violation of judicial independence was tolerated by the regime most of the time, as long as the interventions served the regime's purposes and were conducted discreetly.

The willingness of many judges to take occasional direction from politicians was based upon their dependence upon political bosses in their localities, dependence that was both personal and institutional in character. Judges themselves relied upon the goodwill of political bosses in their localities for tenure in office (both to gain renomination every five years and to avoid recall during the term) and for the provision of such important perks as apartments and vacations. To operate courts effectively the chief judges needed cooperation and supplementary funding from local leaders to get courthouses repaired and cars provided.[2]

Under the scrutiny of Gorbachev's glasnost the practice of political interventions in cases, now dubbed "telephone law," was condemned and measures adopted both to discourage it and to reduce dependency of judges upon politicians.[3] But the really bold measures to develop and enhance judicial independence in Russia were adopted in 1992–1993. As we shall see, the initial reforms in law were impressive; and the key to developing an independent judiciary now lies mainly in their implementation. We shall examine in turn the issues of security of tenure of judges and the judicial career; other aspects of personal independence (compensation, safety, and immunity from prosecution); and the problem of institutional autonomy (especially funding of the courts).

Judicial Careers

The 1992 Law on the Status of Judges established the principle of life appointments for judges on all existing courts (replacing the ten-year terms established in 1989) and even more important the rule that removal of a judge from office could come only for serious cause and only by decision of a judicial qualification commission, a body composed solely of judges. The Constitution of 1993 left both of these principles in place (though a 1994 law on the Constitutional Court limited the terms of its judges to twelve years).[4] It is worth noting that granting judges at all levels in the regular court system unlimited terms of office (until retirement) represents a major breakthrough, something achieved to our knowledge in no country of Latin America, not to speak of parts of the United States.

In practice, appointing judges for life is no simple matter. How does one assure that the appointments will be good ones? One means, used in Russia, is to institute careful review of all candidates for judgeships, including subjecting them to examinations. Another approach, adopted in Russia in 1993, is to compromise with the principle of life appointments and limit first appointments of judges to a fixed term, and appoint for life only after this period of probation (from April 1993 to July 1995 the probationary term stood at five years; thereafter at three).[5]

Another matter of controversy lay in the appointments process itself. The Russian Constitution of December 1993 established that the President would appoint judges on all "federal courts" (other than the three top courts whose members had to be approved by the Federation Council), and in 1994 the President acted as if all existing courts were "federal." But in deference to strong opposition to the concentration of the power of judicial appointment in the hands of the presidential bureaucracy, the President accepted a compromise. Starting in 1997 (when the 1996 Law on the Court System took effect) the actual system of appointing judges required candidates to be vetted by a number of institutions: those who passed screening by a judicial qualification commission had next to gain consent from the legislature of the region or republic in which their post was located before having their names forwarded to the Supreme or Supreme *Arbitrazh* Court.[6] Those bodies, after performing their own reviews, were obliged to present the nominations to the President, on whose behalf one or more further reviews were undertaken by his staff organizations. The compromise lay in the opportunity to vet judicial appointments provided (once again) to the legislatures of the subjects of the Federation.[7] From 1989 to mid–1992 these bodies had possessed a decisive voice in the selection of judges at lower levels, and some deputies had abused their privilege by dictating to judges in particular cases, much as Party bosses had done in previous times.[8]

Although the President has the right to make final decisions in judicial appointments (apart from those to the top courts), neither he nor his staff have thus far had much impact on actual choices. Acting on behalf of President Yeltsin, who reportedly has shown little interest in legal matters generally, are two staff bodies—a Commission of the Council on Cadres Policies of the President of the Russian Federation, and the Department (*otdel*) of Judges, Procuracy Workers, and Diplomatic Representatives within the Administration (*upravlenie*) for Cadres Policy. Each of these bodies in turn screens the nominations of judges passed on from the Chairmen of the Supreme Court and Supreme *Arbitrazh* Court. Data on the screening process for 1997 show a rejection rate of about 2 percent for new appointments to the courts. This low rate reflects the shortage of available candidates, the lack of useful information about them, and the likelihood that earlier review would have eliminated most of the inappropriate candidates (for example, those with records of corruption).[9]

One should not ignore the role of the Supreme Court and Supreme *Arbitrazh* Court in the screening process. The chiefs of these bodies can also reject nominations that come from the regional/republican legislatures, and in the case of appointments to the position of court chairman or to judgeships on higher courts, they are likely to have both an interest in and knowledge of the candidates in question.

What part regional and republican politicians now play in judicial selection is not clear. Certainly the door is wide open for them to refuse life appointments to judges whose records in the initial term they do not like, as well as to keep uncooperative judges out of positions of authority within the judiciary (more on this below). Initial reports suggest that the legislatures of at least some subjects—in regions and the city of Moscow, as well as in the republics—have exercised their right to refuse to endorse candidates for nomination.[10] And, as noted earlier, the governments of some republics (e.g., Bashkortostan) have even refused to send their judicial appointments for the approval of the office of the President, although such practice has not been the norm. While it is not unreasonable for elected politicians to play a role in this stage of judicial selection in Russia, secrecy about this process serves to undermine the integrity of the judiciary and the legitimacy of appointed judges.

The extent to which political criteria affect the appointment of judges, especially to posts of responsibility within the court system, may be uncertain, but what is clear is that the current system of judicial appointments suffers from excessive bureaucratization. It takes a long time for most nominations to make it through the various hoops. Study and discussion of the practice of judicial appointments in Russia could help to streamline judicial selection procedures and the resulting transparency improve public confidence in the quality, not to speak of the constitutionality, of judicial appointments.

What difference has the provision of life appointments for judges made so far? How many and which judges have attained these appointments, and how have life appointments affected their conduct and that of other judges? As the data on appointments show (see Tables 2.1–2.3), not all judges have equal amounts of professional security. For example, as of January 1998, only 23.6 percent of judges in Russia had achieved appointments for life; 43 percent were still completing terms of ten years (that had started between 1989 and 1993); 16.2 percent held five-year terms that had begun in 1993–1995; and 16.4 percent had three-year terms originating in or after 1995.[11] Moreover, the actual distribution of life appointments favors judges on the higher courts. As of January 1998, 77 of the 111 judges of the Supreme Court of the Russian Federation enjoyed life terms, and fully 74.6 percent of all judges on the regional and republican supreme courts had received appointments without limit. In contrast, only 12.3 percent of district court judges had life terms (including 14.9 percent of their chairmen).[12] Temporarily at least, judges of the two higher levels of the Russian court system had achieved de facto a strikingly better degree of security of tenure, and hence far greater protection from outside influences, than had their peers on the first level trial courts. The implications of this disparity in tenure for the autonomy of trial court judges is discussed in Chapter 3. Here we should emphasize that the real test of the new system of judicial appointments is going on right now. Up to 20 percent of judges were to face reappointment with tenure in 1998, and another 50 percent, including the present Chairman and First Deputy Chairman of the Supreme Court, between 1999 and 2001.[13]

TABLE 2.1   Security of Tenure of Judges, all courts, as of 1 January 1998

	All courts	Superior courts	District courts
No. of occupied posts	14457	2629	11828
No. / percentage appointed for life (*bez ogranichenii sroka*)	3,426 (23.6)	1,963 (74.6)	1,463 (12.3)
No. / percentage elected for 10 years	6,219 (43.0)	571 (21.7)	5,648 (47.8)
No. / percentage appointed for 5 years	2,350 (16.2)	11 (0.4)	2,339 (19.7)
No. / percentage appointed for 3 years	2,385 (16.4)	31 (1.2)	2,354 (19.9)

Appointments for life, however, do not resolve the question of professional security, for any judge aspiring to advancement in a judicial career—through appointment to a higher level court (such as a regional court) or to a position of authority within the court system (such as chairman of a district court)—must face a fresh review following similar procedures. The only difference between the procedure for these appointments and the original personal appointments lay in the level of the qualification commission reviewing the candidate's credentials.[14] Although the President had the final say in the actual appointments to the regional courts and of the chairmen of district and regional courts alike, he could consider only candidates who had received prior approval from the regional or republican legislature—which might well reject controversial candidates. In short, judges seeking promotion would face incentives to cooperate with and avoid offending political officials, both at the national and local level. Thus, particularly ambitious judges might come under legislative scrutiny many times—at the time of the initial probationary appointment; the appointment for life; appointment as a chairman of a district court; appointment to membership in a regional or republican supreme court; and, for a select few, appointment to the chairmanship of a regional or republican supreme court.

TABLE 2.2   Security of Tenure of Regional Court* Judges, by position

	Total	Chairmen	Deputy Chairmen	Judges
No. of occupied posts	2,629	83	204	2,342
No. / percentage appointed for life (*bez ogranichenii sroka*)	1,963 (74.6)	56 (67.5)	155 (75.9)	1,752 (74.8)
No. / percentage elected for 10 years	571 (21.7)	26 (31.3)	47 (23.0)	498 (21.2)
No. / percentage appointed for 5 years	11 (0.4)	0	0	11 (0.5)
No. / percentage appointed for 3 years	31 (1.2)	1	0	30 (1.3)

*In this table the heading "regional court" includes territorial and republican supreme courts, as well as the regional courts proper.

Since 1992, judges in Russia have been protected by and large against the threat of recall or dismissal from their positions (apart from reasons of gross incompetence or criminal activity). Some judges have been removed from office but only by their peers on the qualification commissions, which have as a rule insisted on hard evidence of wrongdoing. We have heard of one instance where a regional qualification commission removed a judge on charges concocted by regional politicians he had offended, but fortunately the Supreme Judicial Qualification Commission cancelled the decision; and of another drama, in which a bold regional court chief who repeatedly ruled against the interests of his governor had to face down a campaign of anonymous denunciations engineered by the governors' men.[15] Finally, there was the case of a well-known judge on the Moscow City Court, whose uncharacteristic liberalism had provoked his boss, the chairman of that court, to use a breech of procedural etiquette on the judge's part to press for his dismissal. Only a decision of the Supreme Court that overruled earlier resolutions of two judicial qualification commissions saved the job of this particular judge.[16] It is notable that these "renegade" judges did gain protection from the new system of removals, and that there have been complaints (from politicians and the public) about the obstacles to removing judges. In 1996 judges gained another protection, namely a prohibition on transfers from one court to another without their consent. In late Tsarist Russia (as in France through much of the twentieth century), nonconformist judges who offended politicians or their superiors in the judicial hierarchy (a matter for Chapter 3), faced the threat of transfer to an undesirable post.[17]

TABLE 2.3   Security of Tenure of District Court Judges, by position

	Total	Chairmen	Deputy Chairmen	Judges
No. of occupied posts	11,828	2,327	606	8,895
No. / percentage appointed for life (*bez ogranichenii sroka*)	1,463 (12.3)	347 (14.9)	101 (16.6)	1,015 (11.4)
No. / percentage elected for 10 years	5,648 (47.8)	1,716 (73.7)	432 (71.2)	3,500 (39.3)
No. / percentage appointed for 5 years	2,339 (19.7)	164 (7.0)	52 (8.6)	2,123 (23.9)
No. / percentage appointed for 3 years	2,354 (19.9)	93 (4.0)	18 (3.0)	2,243 (25.2)

Our 1997 survey of judges (mainly at the district level, where most judges had not yet attained life appointment) suggests that the new system was already making a difference. In our sample, 72.1 percent of our the respondents said that they considered themselves to be independent judges; and 51 percent claimed to be more independent in 1997 than in 1992 when the Law on the Status of Judges took effect! Most of the judges questioned had a positive view of the work of the judicial qualification commissions: 72.4 percent believed the commissions fair in decisions about dismissals and, in a separate question, in decisions about promotions. But nearly one-third declared that the mere existence of a power to dismiss a judge for cause infringed on judicial independence!

The critical point for most Russian judges is the achievement of the lifetime appointment, and we consider it important to protect judges at the probationary stage from pressures to take into account the interests of politicians or powerful private actors. We recommend that in any court that has more than one judge (80 percent of courts), judges who have not yet achieved life appointments should not be assigned the most serious or potentially controversial cases, criminal and civil alike.[18] A directive to this effect might be issued either by the Supreme Court or the new Judicial Department.

Other Sources of Dependence

Apart from security of tenure, the personal independence of judges in Russia could also be affected by the system of rewards, the degree of personal safety, and immunity from criminal prosecution. Good wages and other compensation stood to reduce the likelihood of judges' accepting bribes (not a major problem in Russian courts as of 1998), as well as making their jobs more attractive.[19] While judges in Russia in 1997 earned far less than jurists engaged in private practice, the compensation package for judges was competitive with those for other government employees, and better in relative terms than what judges received in the late Soviet period. The levels of pay (and of pensions) were pegged to those received by other government employees and there was a system of increases based upon years served and rank achieved. Judges had rights to such benefits as free transport, free state medical services, priority access to daycare, new telephone lines without a lengthy wait, and, most important, the right to receive from the state a private apartment of decent size (again without waiting in line), which would eventually become the judge's property. In the Soviet period, a key basis for dependence on local politicians was the anticipation of a benefit like an apartment; and in 1989 Soviet law required local governments to give new judges apartments. The problem, of course, lay in implementation, and many judges to this day are still waiting for apartments. According to data from early 1996, some 3,600 judges (more than a quarter) lived in dormitories, communal apartments, or with friends; and one-half of all judges lacked telephones at home. The long wait for benefits promised in law left some judges dependent upon local authorities and open to pressures.[20]

For judges to work free from external pressures, they need to be physically secure. Starting in 1990—as the political order was disintegrating and private economic interests gaining power—the USSR witnessed a wave of physical attacks on judges and fires and thefts at courthouses. The problem of physical security led in time to a 1995 law authorizing judges to carry handguns, and a 1997 law establishing a service of armed officers (bailiffs) to guard courthouses. But as of the start of 1999, most judges did not have guns, because local police departments lacked either the budget or the will to issue service revolvers to judges under threat. Resolving this dispute was for judges a matter of high priority, especially in the absence of real, or at least consistent, protection of courthouses.[21] As late as mid–1999 no bailiffs had been assigned to guard the courts for lack of budgetary support. Although there was a slight decline in 1997–1998 in the frequency of physical attacks on judges and arson attempts at courthouses, there was a remarkable increase in 1998 in incidents of theft of case files from the courts.[22]

Finally, the personal independence of judges was enhanced by a broad grant of immunity from prosecution—immunity that could be removed only by a judicial qualification commission and then only in the face of evidence of criminal wrongdoing sufficient to justify removal of the judge from his/her post.[23] As of 1997, the judicial qualification commissions were approving about half of all requests for criminal prosecutions against judges (usually after careful reviews), and the Supreme Judicial Qualification Commission supported most of these decisions. The immunity of judges from prosecution extends to administrative law violations as well, excluding them from responsibility for such infractions as driving offenses or public drunkenness and protecting them from arrest, even if caught at the scene of a crime. Procuracy officials have expressed frustration at these limitations, and gained the support of some Duma deputies (especially at the Committee on Security) for restrictions on judges' immunity from prosecution.[24] However, any such changes to the Law on the Status of Judges strike us as inadvisable. In the Soviet period, political authorities often sought to discredit judges by contriving charges of corruption and lesser offenses, and in the post-Soviet world, judges still need protection from any and all artificial charges.[25]

Funding the Courts

Not only judges personally but also the courts as institutions needed protection from external pressures, and in Russia as elsewhere this required above all adequate and stable financing. According to both the Constitution and the Law on the Court System, full financing of federal courts was to come from the federal government, thereby protecting courts and judges from any financial dependency upon regional and local governments, such as existed in the Soviet period. But the economic and political realities of the mid–1990s impeded delivery on this promise. The combination of a massive drop in the GDP of Russia (at least in the official sector) and the government's failure to collect taxes owed led to a serious shortfall in revenue, and, under pressure from international organizations, the Russian government decided not to spend much more than it received. Operating under tight budgetary constraints, the Russian government first of all failed to increase the official budget line for the courts to cover the various pay raises granted to judges; these came at the expense of money for operations. Second, as we saw in Chapter 1, in 1995 and 1996 the government reneged on its budgetary commitments (that had been reached after lengthy negotiations and parliamentary debates) and failed to deliver a sizeable part of the money allocated to the courts. The result was that in 1996 and 1997 most courts had funds to cover only wages and virtually nothing left to pay for paper, stamps, telephone, heat, and electricity, not to speak of repairs, cars, and gas.[26] The shortfall pushed some courts into crisis. Thus, three courts in Iaroslavl region lost their heat and light for failure to pay; a court in Murmansk was declared unsafe when repairs were not made and forced to close. In Adygee republic, the Supreme Court could not afford to stay in its quarters and was forced to rent space on the premises of a public bath. In a number of places the much needed construction of new courthouses has been stopped.[27]

Not surprisingly, judicial officials and the organizations of judges—the Congress and the Council of Judges—protested loudly about the "crisis in the courts," and the protests led to a government promise to "protect" all funds allocated to the courts in 1997 from sequestration, that is, guaranteed regardless of state income. However, the latest round(s) of pay raises ate up most of the added resources. Nor did the practice of sequestration end. At the beginning of April 1998 the government decided to reduce the 1998 budgetary allocation to the courts of general jurisdiction by 26 percent, and even the remaining funds were not delivered on time.[28] The spring 1998 sequester of funds promised to the courts provoked the heads of the Supreme Court and Supreme *Arbitrazh* Court to appeal not only to the President (who then directed the government to restore the funds) but also to the Constitutional Court of Russia. The top judges contended that the cut in funds for the courts violated the 1996 Law on the Court System (which disallowed such cuts without the consent of the Congress or Council of Judges); and that cut was based on unconstitutional language contained in the 1998 Law on the Budget. The Constitutional Court agreed, and in a decision of July 1998 declared that the provisions of the law used to justify the sequester were unconstitutional and insisted that the government meet its constitutional responsibilities to fund the courts. At the end of 1998, after further protests from the State Duma and the procuracy, some of the funds at issue were paid, and finally in 1999 a new law on court financing promised to prevent further sequesters by giving the courts authority to draw funds directly from treasury accounts should the money not be provided on time.[29]

As a consequence of the serious and persistent shortfall in funding from the federal government, local and regional governments in many places (but not all) stepped into the breach and provided, typically upon request from the chairmen of courts, small allocations for supplies, stamps, telephone, etc. According to our survey of more than three hundred district court judges, 58 percent of courts received some help from local governments in 1996 and 1997, and in most places this aid was something new. While according to our informants the norm was for local governments to make small emergency contributions, in some places the support was larger. This was the case in the cities of Moscow, where Mayor Luzhkov regularly contributed large sums (in 1998, 42 million rubles, and from 1999 he proposed tying the level of support to the number of cases heard by the city's courts), and of St. Petersburg, where Vladimir Iakovlev in 1997 dramatically increased funding of the courts, as well as in some regions. Thus, courts in Nizhegorod region received financing from local budgets for between 20 and 82 percent of their non-salary expenditures.[30] Sometimes, but less often, banks and commercial firms came to a court's rescue. In our survey 15.3 percent of judges reported receiving help from private sources, half for the usual paper/postage and supplies, the rest for other things. All the same, the relative poverty of the courts led to foolish economies. One example was the failure to use registered mail for delivering summonses to witnesses. The result was that when a witness failed to appear, a fine could not be applied because there was no record that the person had received the summons.[31]

The failure of the federal government to deliver adequate funding to its courts opened the door to a renewal of financial lines of dependency upon local and regional governments. Thus far, as of 1998, the threat was more potential than real. Although by 1997 the majority of courts were receiving some extra financing from local governments, the amounts of money were usually small. Moreover, the practice was in most places only of two years' standing; no quid pro quo had been exacted by the local governments; and most chiefs of the courts were proud and stubborn about their independence and unwilling even to admit the possibility of new pressures. On the other hand, fully half of the judges in our survey admitted that the contributions produced in them a sense of gratitude to local governments and that their sponsors seemed to have expectations from the courts. In fact, 7.2 percent of the judges surveyed reported that financial contributions of local governments had led to specific demands placed upon them; and of those judges who reported support from private firms, 22 percent admitted that this support had some influence on their handling of particular cases! Even those judges who did not experience specific demands or general pressure shared the bad feeling of being poor cousins, forced by circumstances to beg for help from their governmental counterparts, and this feeling did not breed the self-respect required for authoritative defenses of the law.

In the long run, a continued dependence of courts upon local sources of funding did represent a potential threat to judicial independence. After all, the local funding was unregulated and completely discretionary, opening the door for all kinds of expectations and tacit understandings. A further problem lay in the division of authority within local and regional governments. No longer was there one Party committee to please, but multiple executive and legislative authorities; and judges dependent upon local sources of financing could get caught in the middle of intra-governmental conflicts.[32] Then, too, the funding of courts by the local and regional governments at their levels of the political hierarchy seemed to feed aspirations of political leaders of the subjects of the Federation to assume greater control of their courts, including the right to appoint their judges.[33]

Without some decisive action by the federal government, it was likely that the emerging pattern of informal and unauthorized supplementary support of the courts by regional and local governments would continue.

After all, the governments of the subjects of the Federation had succeeded in keeping for themselves a larger share of tax revenue than in the past; in stark contrast to the Federal government, the consolidated tax revenues of the subjects did not decline between 1992 and 1997. Even if those governments were shouldering a larger share of budgetary responsibilities than in the past, at least some of them had more budgetary flexibility than did the federal government.[34]

To nourish judicial independence, maintain the morale of judges (to be discussed in Chapter 5), and improve the performance of the courts (Chapter 6), *stable funding at a decent level* is vital—a necessary, though perhaps not sufficient, condition for the achievement of those goals. The money should be delivered from the federal government, as constitutionally prescribed, and channelled through and divided by authorities not prone to using money as a means of imposing their own goals (as was sometimes the case with the Ministry of Justice). The new Judicial Department should in principle be able to perform this function, but efforts must be made to ensure that it does.

In 1998 the judicial chiefs of Russia were campaigning for major increases in financing. The heads of the Supreme *Arbitrazh* Court and of the Supreme Court each submitted to the Duma special draft laws on the financing of the courts. The Supreme Court's version was especially impressive, insisting that the "independent delivery of justice required providing courts with the full resources to cover" a whole list of significant expenses. The draft law goes on to specify that this will require observing an average norm for budgetary allocation of 5,410 minimal pay units per judge (this represents more than doubling of the current budget for general courts), and making the whole budget truly "protected" and not subject to sequesters regardless of the level of federal revenues. In addition, the draft calls for the creation of a federal fund for development of the court system, whose funds will be derived from a share of the tariffs imposed by courts and from the sale of confiscated property.[35]

We strongly support the funding initiative of the Supreme Court of the Russian Federation. There is no question that the development and preservation of a viable federal court system—the only way for Russia to achieve courts independent of local political power—requires a different order of funding from what is now available, and that that funding must be stable and separate from the levels of government revenue. In fact, we would urge the Russian government to privilege its courts and, for the time being while revenues remain low, to treat courts better than other government agencies by providing them with decent and reliable funding. The government should take these steps not only out of respect for courts and law, but also because they will in the long run actually improve economic performance. Only with sound and stable financing can the courts and the law gain in prestige and deliver the kind of regulation of the economy needed to enhance investment and economic performance and make possible improved tax collection.

We believe that there is room for foreign investment in the funding of regular courts. Western sponsors, governmental and non-governmental alike, should consider providing relatively inexpensive items like modern stenographic/taping machines, fax machines, and modems with Internet access to legislative data banks, as well as computers, to courts where they are not available (see Part I). Other special projects might include helping with the refurbishing of quarters, the development of court libraries and archives, and the provision of special facilities and conveniences for jurors and lay assessors.

Another question relating to the institutional independence of courts is the organization of their administrative servicing. In the Russian context, the reliance upon the services of the Ministry of Justice, a part of the executive branch, seemed to many judges and judicial reformers an obstacle to the achievement of the self-government needed by the judicial corps to gain self-respect and independence. The creation of a Judicial Department in Moscow and subordinate departments in the subjects of the Federation is well underway, and these departments will replace the corresponding units in the Ministry of Justice. We will discuss problems of the organization of the new departments in the Chapter 3.

Recommendations

2.1   That to the extent possible judges serving their first and probationary terms (before life appointment) be protected from external influences through the avoidance of assignments of difficult or controversial cases.

2.2   That stable and adequate financing of the courts from the federal budget be guaranteed through a law on court finances.

2.3   That foreign supporters of courts in Russia consider providing small material benefits to many or all courts, items such as recording devices, fax machines, modems, and computers.

Notes

1. For discussion of the struggle between judges and the regime over the meaning of the commitment to "judicial independence" introduced into the Constitution of 1936, see Peter H. Solomon, Jr., *Soviet Criminal Justice under Stalin* (Cambridge, UK, and New York, 1996), pp. 290-93.

2. Peter H. Solomon, Jr., "Soviet Politicians and Criminal Prosecutions: The Logic of Party Intervention," in James B. Millar, ed., *Cracks in the Monolith: Party Power in the Brezhnev Era* (New York and London, UK, 1992), pp. 3-32. On the financial problems of the courts in the late Soviet period see Aleksandr Borin, "Nishaia iustitsiia, ili Skolko stoit pravovoe gosudarstvo?" *Literaturnaia gazeta*, 22 Aug. 1989, p. 10.

3. Peter H. Solomon, Jr., "Gorbachev's Legal Revolution," *Canadian Business Law Journal*, Vol. 17, 1990, pp. 184-94; Todd S. Foglesong, "The Politics of Judicial Independence and the Administration of Criminal Justice in Soviet Russia, 1982-1992," unpublished doctoral dissertation, University of Toronto, 1995, Chapter 2.

4. "O statuse sudei v Rossiiskoi Federatsii," Zakon RF ot 26 iiuniia 1992, *Vedomosti S'ezda narodnykh deputatov i Verkhovnogo Soveta RSFSR*, 30 iiuliia 1992, No. 30, st. 1792; Peter H. Solomon, Jr, "The Limits to Legal Order in Post-Soviet Russia," *Post-Soviet Affairs*, Vol. 11, No. 2, April 1995, pp. 89-114.

5. "O vnesenii izmenenii i dopolnenii v Zakon RF 'O statuse sudei v RF'," Zakon RF ot 14 apreliia 1993, *Rossiiskaia gazeta*, 27 April 1993, p. 5.

6. See "O sudebnoi sisteme RF," Federalnyi konstitutsionnyi zakon ot 31 dekabria 1996, *Rossiiskaia gazeta*, 6 Jan. 1997, p. 3. Whereas the Law on the Court System specifically requires that the consent (*soglasie*) of regional legislatures be obtained before the President can consider as "nominees" candidates for judicial posts, the Law on the Status of Judges had merely required that the "opinion" (*mnenie*) of regional legislatures be taken into consideration when forwarding such nominees to the President for appointment.

7. For a discussion of the politics of compromise, see Peter H. Solomon, Jr., "The Persistence of Judicial Reform in Post-Soviet Russia," *East European Constitutional Review*, Vol. 6, No. 4, Fall 1997, pp. 50-56. In practice, according to Vladimir Radchenko, the First Deputy Chairman of the Supreme Court, even before the adoption of legislation requiring consideration of the "opinion" of regional legislatures in the selection and nomination process, the views of all local political figures—including Presidential envoys and Governors—were canvassed before the Supreme Court forwarded nominees to the President. See the discussion of cadres policy at the 10 October 1995 meeting of the President's Council of Judicial Reform.

8. On the new lines of dependence created by the reforms in the late Soviet period, see Foglesong, "The Politics of Judicial Independence," Chapter 5.

9. For more analysis (and data) on the role of presidential agencies in screening judicial appointments, see Todd S. Foglesong, "The Dynamics of Judicial (In)dependence in Russia," in Peter H. Russell and David O'Brien, eds., *Comparative Judicial Independence: Critical Assessments from Around the World* (forthcoming).

10. According to Aleksei Pakholkov, the Deputy Director of the Department of Cadres of the Supreme Court of the Russian Federation, statistics and information are kept on the number and character of judges refused endorsement by legislatures in the subjects of the federation. Unfortunately, we have been unable to examine these data.

11. The data in Tables 2.1 to 2.3 were provided by the Department of Cadres of the Supreme Court of the Russian Federation. See also Sergei Pashin, "Novye vozmozhnosti razvitiia sudebnoi sistemy Rossii," *Konstitutsionnoe pravo: vostochno-evropeiskoe obozrenie*, 1997, No. 2 (19), pp. 16-23.

12. Most of the judges on the Supreme Court of the Russian Federation were elected to life terms by the Federation Council in 1994. "O khode formirovaniia sudebnogo korpusa RF, po sostoianiiu n 16 oktiabria, 1995" otchet Ministerstva Iustitsii (n.d.); Pakholkov.

13. Both Lebedev, the Chairman of the Supreme Court, and Radchenko, his First Deputy, were elected for ten-year terms in 1989. Both received life appointments in 1999.

14. "Rasshifrovka zapisi zasedanii Soveta po sudebnoi reformy pri Prezidenta RF, 12 marta 1997," pp. 8-10.

15. Interview with S. Beliaev (from Ekaterinburg), 3 June 1997; Aleksandr Badanov, "Kak possorilsia gubernator s oblastnym sudei," *Nezavisimaia gazeta*, 13 Nov. 1997, p. 6.

16. "Belaia vorona pravosudiia: Sergei Pashin izgnan iz sudei za nedopustimyi gumanizm," *Obshchaia gazeta*, 4-10 June 1998, p. 4; "Tretii chelovek v stolitse: Shtrikhi k portretu predsedatelia Mosgorsdua Zoi Kornevoi," *ibid.*, 16-22 July 1998, p. 4; Igor Korlkov, "Lukavaia taina sudi," *Izvestiia*, 18 Aug. 1998, p. 5; Anna Politkovskaia, "Pokazaniia spiashchego prokurora," *Obshchaia gazeta*, 17-23 Sept. 1998, p. 2.

17. Citation on curtailing of transfers of judges. On the practice of transferring judges in late Tsarist Russia, see William Wagner, "Tsarist Legal Policies at the End of the Nineteenth Century: A Study in Inconsistence," *Slavonic and East European Review*, Vol. 14, No. 3, July 1976, pp. 371-94.

18. For cases of social significance in rural district courts with only one judge, a circuit session (*vyezdnoe zasedanie*) could be held by a regional court judge, or the regional court itself could assume jurisdiction over the case.

19. The conviction of judges on charges of bribery is not common in Russia. For the reports of two recent trials, see "Sud'iu, otpravivshego za reshetku mnogikh prestupnikh avtoritetov, smog soblaznit' tol'ko Iakubovskii," *Moskovskii komsomolets*, No. 56, 26 March 1997, p. 1, and the case of Viktor Zhidkykh, in *Kommersant*, No. 78, 4 May 1998, p. 7.

20. Citations on pay pegging and apartments; "Koe-chto o 'beloi kosti,'" *Trud*, 19 June 1997, p. 5.

21. "Postanovlenie Soveta Sudei RF ot 4 apreliia 1997," *Rossiiskaia iustitsiia*, 1997, No.7, pp. 9-10.

22. "Otchet o rezultatakh raboty Sudebnogo Departamenta pri Verkhovnom Sude Rossiiskoi Federatsii v 1998," p. 21.

23. On the handling of procuracy requests to remove judges, see A. Zherebtsov, "Povyshenie avtoriteta sudebnoi vlasi—glavnoe v rabote kvalifikatsionnykh kollegii sudei," *Rossiiskaia iustitsiia*, 1997, No. 8, pp. 6-8.

24. For an example of the procuracy position see Irina Aleshina, "Zakon o statuse sudei ne sootvetstvue vremeni," *Sudebnye novosti, obozrenie*, 1998, No. 3, p. 5.

25. V. D. Rozhkov, "Problemy sudebnoi reformy," in A. I. Dolgova, ed., *Prestupnost, statistika, zakon* (Moscow, 1997), pp. 51-59.

26. Iurii Feofanov, "Nishchii sud k pravosudiiu ne goden," *Izvestiia*, 9 July 1996, p. 5; "Sudebnaia vlast v finansovom tupike," *Rossiiskaia gazeta*, 14 Nov. 1996, p. 5; Pashin, "Razvitie sudebnoi sistemy," pp. 2-4. The judges surveyed by us confirmed the wholesale inadequacy of federal court funding.

27. Oleg Odnokolenno, "A sudi—eto voobshche kto? Sudebnaia vlast na izhdivenii mestnoi elity," *Kommersant-deili*, 29 April 1998, p. 3; Igor Iurev, "Tikhii sekvestr pravosudiia. Minfin sdaet slug zakona v polzovanie regionalnym elitam," *Obshchaia gazeta*, 7-13 May 1998, p. 3.

28. *Ibid.*

29. "Sudy na grani ostanovki" (Beseda s Veniaminom Iakovlevom), *Iuridischeskii vestnik*, 1998, No. 11, pp. 2-3; Vladimir Khitruk, "Nevozmozhno gosudarstvo bez pravosudiia" (Beseda so Viacheslavom Lebedevom), *ibid.*, No. 13, pp. 9-10; "Perepiska s B. Eltsinym po voprosu finansiroavniia sudov (April-June 1998); "Postanovlenie Konstitutsionnogo Suda RF po delu o proverke konstitutsionnosti chasti 1 stati 102 Federalnogo zakona 'O federalnom biudzhete na 1998 god' ot 17 iiulia 1998," *Rossiiskaia gazeta*, 30 July 1998, p. 5; Mikhailov,"Rossiiskaia femida bolshe ne zolushka;" "O finansirovanii sudov Rossiiskoi Federatsii."

30. "Protokol plenarnogo zasedaniia Soveta sudei Rossiiskoi Federatsii, 31 marta-3 aprelia 1998 goda," p. 4; Gennadii Titov, "Luzhkov zaplatil sudam 42 mln rublei," *Kommersant-deili*, 5 Feb. 1999, p. 2.

31. "Trevozhnoe soveshchanie k kontse goda (Iz stenogrammy zasedaniia Soveta po sudebnoi reforme pri Prezidenta RF)," *Rossiiskaia iustitsiia*, 1996, No. 12, pp. 2-8; S. Tropin, "Pismo delegatam IV Vserossiiskogo s'ezda sudei," ot 29

XI 1996, in *Delegatu IV (Chrezvychainnogo) Vserossiiskogo s'ezda sudei* (Moscow, 1996), pp. 77-82; Khitruk, "Sud i sut" (Beseda s S. Pashinym), *Iuridicheskii vestnik*, 1997, No. 20, pp. 9-10.

32. Interview with V. I. Radchenko, deputy chairman of the Supreme Court of the Russian Federation, 5 June 1997.

33. "Protokol plenarnogo zasedanii Sovet sudei," 26-29.

34. See Daniel Treisman, "Russia's Taxing Problem," *Foreign Policy*, Fall 1998, pp. 55-66.

35. "O finansirovanii sudov Rossiiskoi Federatsii," Zakonoproekt vnesen v Gosudarstvennuiu Dumu Verkhovnym Sudom 27 fevralia 1998; "Finansirovanie sudov Rossiiskoi Federatsii," *Rossiiskaia iustitsiia*, 1998, No. 5, p. 1.

3

The Autonomy and Accountability of Trial Court Judges

Some of the greatest threats to the autonomy of judges in Russia come from within the judiciary. Higher court judges, the chairmen of particular courts, and even the instruments of judicial self-governance like the judicial qualification commissions all influence the conduct of judges in trial courts. Without some such influence, there would be little consistency in judicial decisions or hierarchy of law, but there is a real danger that, as in the Soviet past, pressures for uniformity force judges to conform with regime policies, not to speak of the interests of bureaucratic superiors. The judicial system of post-Soviet Russia must not reproduce its traditional forms of judicial dependence.

Here we shall examine the pressures to conform faced by district court judges from four sources: their court chairmen; the regional or republican supreme court; the Supreme Court of Russia; and the judicial qualification commissions. We conclude with thoughts about how the new judicial departments may exacerbate or soften these pressures.

The Chairman

In Russia the chairmen of courts are powerful figures. At the district court, the chairman exercises control over many administrative functions that affect both the work lives and economic well-being of his judges. Typically, the chairman makes all decisions about the distribution of cases among the judges on his court and the choice of lay assessors. In the absence of rules governing the distribution of caseload, say, according to expertise or seniority—the chairman can determine the composition of the court in any trial. The fact that the chairman can assign cases to judges (and assessors) whose reliability and tendencies he knows well has led to suspicions and even allegations of a Russian form of "judge shopping."[1]

In itself, the power to determine who tries particular cases does not accord the chairman undue influence on individual judges or the outcomes of specific cases. The problem stems from the fact that the court chairman also has considerable control over both the welfare and the careers of his judges, and is in a position to penalize judges who fail to cooperate with his wishes. To begin, the chairman is usually responsible for obtaining benefits for judges. One such benefit is housing for new judges. Although local governments are obliged by the Law on the Status of Judges to furnish judges with apartments within six months of their appointment, this rarely happens (even well after the six months have passed) without the intervention or vigorous lobbying of the chairmen.[2] Furthermore, all judges, new and veteran alike, depend on their chairmen for the scheduling of vacations, help in obtaining holiday packages, arranging health- and child-care services, and gaining access to scarce consumer goods. Finally, judges need their chairmen's good will for the development of their careers. Whenever a judge is considered for permanent appointment or promotion to a higher court, the chairman writes an assessment (*kharakteristika*) for the qualification commission. Not surprisingly, judges describe their chairman as "employer" (*rabotodatel'*), "boss" (*shef*), "benefactor" (*dobytchik*), and "governor" (*khoziain*).

Reducing the chairman's potential to influence the decisions of judges is not easy. A revolutionary rise in judges' salaries might give them the wherewithal to use private rather than public sector housing, schools, and vacation spots, but no such change in the financial position of judges is in the offing. As long as judges depend upon public sector resources that are in scarce supply, they will need their chairman's help. And to obtain those resources the chairman must maintain good relations with local government officials as well. To be sure, the establishment of the new post of court administrator within each court (a post provided in the Law on the Judicial Department) should relieve the court chairman of a good part of his work as a provider. Still, political reality suggests that chairmen will still have to intervene directly to extract some favors from local governments and that the success of the court administrators will depend upon the quality of relations between court chairmen and outside officials. A more realistic approach is to introduce new and formal rules on case management. In the past there were no national regulations, and the departments of justice in most regions and republics left case management to the caprice of local custom.[3] Whether introduced at the level of the subject of the Federation or nationally, new guidelines on case management might remove some of the chairman's discretion and institute general principles of assignment that would please judges and reduce public suspicions of foul play. One key principle to include is that of "specialization"–dividing multi-judge courts into civil and criminal panels and enabling judges to develop expertise in particular kinds of cases or categories of law. Specialization is a subject that has received episodic discussion in the press, but is supported by a large number of judges.[4]

Developing guidelines on case flow management could be joined to the related question of refining and observing norms of the caseloads for individual judges, an urgent question since the sharp increases in cases of the early 1990s. The latter is listed among the responsibilities of the new judicial departments. There is room for Western specialists in court management to make a contribution to these subjects in Russia.

The Superior Court

The regional/territorial/republican supreme court (hereafter "superior court") is the guardian of the main indicator on which promotions within the judiciary and increases in "rank" (*klass*) are based: the rate of reversal —or what Russians call "stability of sentences." Judges with the fewest number of verdicts reversed or modified on appeal have the best chances of being promoted or advanced to a higher rank. While the salary raise occasioned by an increase in rank is not large, the prospect of being denied or overlooked for promotion for having made too many "judicial mistakes" does influence some individual judges' decisions. Certainly there is much incentive to render decisions and sentences that please the superior court in provincial Russia, where promotion from a rural district to the region's capital city can mean a huge increase in access to consumer goods and a significant improvement in the standard of living.

Until recently, this crucial statistical indicator—the rate of reversal —was even more important. A good deal more than a judge's promotion depended upon it. Monthly and quarterly bonuses—significant sums that were dispensed by the Department of Justice upon the recommendation of the regional court—and, more important, decisions about whether or not a judge would stand for re-election were also tied directly to this arbitrary numerical index.[5] Most judges, not surprisingly, worked hard to avoid being overruled, and develop good records. Some literally trembled before their superiors.[6] Since 1992, however, due to changes in judicial appointments (especially life terms), the weight of this indicator has decreased. Nevertheless, its continued prominence in performance evaluations fosters obsequiousness in the courtroom.[7] Some judges say they routinely "consult colleagues" when trying difficult or novel cases. Others admit that they "glance upward" or find other ways of ascertaining in advance the views of their superiors as to the proper resolution of a case *sub judice* in order not to be reversed on appeal. Such "consulting" and collaborative deliberation conspire to depress artificially the rate of reversal and give an exaggerated sense of uniformity and harmony in the administration of justice.

The peculiar character of appellate proceedings in Russia, and specifically the unusually broad scope of cassation review, extend these incentives to conform to findings of fact. Unlike "cassation" in its classical French conception, where on appeal the court evaluates only an alleged error of law in the trial court's decision, cassation proceedings in Russia are not limited to a review only of the legal questions raised by the appellant.[8] Russian courts follow a "principle of revision" according to which the reviewing court is entitled and even obligated to search the complete record of the proceedings in the trial court for errors of any kind. Accordingly, a cassation panel is authorized to change, even cancel, the verdict and/or sentence upon finding what amounts to errors of fact—the official grounds for reversal in such instances being "incompleteness or one-sidedness" of the judicial investigation of the evidence and "non-correspondence" of the trial courts' conclusions to the "factual circumstances of the case."[9] These criteria are so broad as to give superior courts arbitrary power.[10] Furthermore, upon finding errors of this kind, a cassation court can issue binding "instructions" (*ukazaniia*) about what needs to be rectified upon retrial. These powers enable superior courts directly to influence judges' deliberations and handling of new trials. This rule also compromises the appearance of fairness in administration of justice, since judges must hold a new trial subject to restrictions visible to all present.

The organizational and administrative structure of superior courts is designed to heighten their influence on lower court judges. Every judge and every district court has an appointed "supervisor" (*kurator*) in the superior court, who functions both as an informal "mentor" (*nastavnik*) and official judge of their decisions in cassation. In their roles as educators, superior courts periodically convene conferences to instruct judges about the law.[11] Quarterly summaries of the records of individual judges and courts are sometimes reviewed at such conferences, with superior court leaders registering their opprobrium for those with "bad numbers." Academic lawyers are invited to comment on recent case-law, and frequently single out for criticism courts with errant tendencies in sentencing or cases in which egregious "mistakes" were made by judges. Because of a fairly antiquated and heavy-handed pedagogical style, the "lessons" conducted in such schools are, on occasion, the cause of some humiliation.[12] Not surprisingly, of those judges in our survey who acknowledged being "dependent" in some way, 27.7 percent claimed to be most dependent on the "the higher court."

Eliminating the pressures to conform will not be easy. Certainly it is unlikely that Russian judicial authorities will renounce the rate of reversal as an indicator of judicial performance in the near future. Neither bureaucratic inertia nor the habit of using quantitative measures of performance in Russian public administration will be easily overcome. But given a growing objection to statistical measures of the quality of justice among rank and file judges, it is possible that the Council of Judges would issue an injunction against the use of rate of reversal as the *sole* or even *primary* indicator of judicial performance. A conference on alternative means of performance evaluation for lower court judges might help to get promulgated a norm prohibiting the use of the rate of reversal in certain situations. Such a ruling would be the first step toward the elaboration of measures for basing promotion and other decisions directly affecting judges' careers on factors such as seniority, education, courtroom comportment, and other factors more likely to improve the public estimation of justice. Of course, the experiences of countries such as Italy, Germany, and France will be especially useful in this respect, but procedures developed in the United States for the evaluation of the performance of state court judges may also be helpful.

A second way to curb excess pressure on judges to conform is to improve the administrative organization of superior courts. Superior court judges who sit in cassation and judge the work of their subordinates should not have any formal or informal administrative or teaching relationship with these same lower court judges. The prospect of collusion or coercion is too great in such layered relationships. A joint conference on judicial administration, sponsored by a Western organization like the National Center for State Courts, and conducted under the auspices of the new Judicial Department, might expose this problem and devise alternative ways of providing guidance to less experienced judges without the pressures implicit in the *kurator-nastavnik* system. The problem is that the decoupling of that relationship might lead to a decrease in the amount of professional retraining lower court judges receive, since many trial court judges get most of their retraining during "practicums" held in superior courts. Accordingly, improvements in judicial education, for example through a new Academy of Justice, should precede such organizational modifications.

The Supreme Court of Russia

Like the top courts of many countries, the Supreme Court of the Russian Federation is a powerful body, capable of shaping judicial practice at lower courts. The powers of the Supreme Court are not excessive, but they do, in our view, require some checking.

The Court has more than 115 judges, divided into four separate chambers or divisions (*kollegii*): criminal, civil, military, and the "cassation panel" (*kassatsionnaia palata*), a special board that handles only appeals of jury trial verdicts. Though the Court occasionally conducts trials—in cases deemed "of special social significance"—most of its work is appellate, generated either by cassational appeals or supervisory reviews. The majority of its judges work in cassational panels (of three persons each) reviewing cases from a particular geographical zone, and they are kept busy with a large appellate caseload. The flow of cases to the Supreme Court is guaranteed by its obligation to review in cassation on request the result of any trial that was heard at a regional court or republican supreme court, or at any military court. To be sure, this middle layer of the court system hears only a fraction of all trials (one percent of criminal cases and an even smaller percentage of civil cases), but these include the cases with the highest stakes, where the loser is most likely to take advantage of all his or her rights to appeal.

The Court also has a Presidium, consisting of the Chairman, the First Deputy Chairman, the six deputy chairmen, and five other judges. The Presidium is a unique and powerful body, itself a court of last resort. It hears appeals from contested rulings of Supreme Court cassation panels, and it can review in supervision any ruling, decision, or verdict made by any court in Russia.[13] Moreover, the seven ex-officio members of the Presidium (the chairman and deputy chairmen) are authorized to summon on their own initiative the files from any case in any court in Russia whose disposition is in doubt, and if necessary issue protests of all verdicts and rulings. The fact that, patience willing, any dissatisfied litigant can obtain an audience with one of these judges, and that protests can be submitted to and reviewed by the Presidium itself, gives a few Supreme Court judges enormous opportunities for shaping the administration of justice in Russia.[14]

Decisions of Supreme Court judges lack the power of precedent, but some of them influence the work of lower courts. The Court publishes in its monthly *Bulletin* a small selection of important decisions (a few dozen each year), and more decisions figure in the occasional surveys (*obzory*) of judicial practice circulated to judges but not easily available to the public. Both publications are circulated to judges for their "general guidance" in the administration of the laws.[15] While most of these decisions recite statutory provisions rather than offer legal reasoning and are not cited by other courts, the decisions do orient judges and alert them to the Supreme Court's preferences. For instance, when the *Bulletin* or a survey contains decisions reversing sentences in cases of "banditism" for "excessive leniency," judges reasonably conclude that the Court is encouraging and, if necessary, will enforce a stiffer standard of "proportionality" in punishment.[16] Lower court judges often phone the Court with questions or mail in "queries," some of which, along with the Court's responses, are later printed in the quarterly Reviews.

The main way that the Supreme Court shapes judicial behavior is through its issuance of "explanations" (*raz"iasneniia*) of the law. "Explanations" (formerly known as "guiding explanations") are issued after the conduct of a study of mistakes in judicial practice in a particular area of law and a discussion by a Plenum of the Supreme Court.[17] For example, one year after the initiation of jury trials in Russia, the Court commissioned a review of recent practice, discussed and censured what it considered "shortcomings" in the conduct of jury trials, and issued "explanations" as to how judges should apply the law.[18] While "explanations" are not in post-Soviet Russia "binding" upon lower courts, appellate courts routinely reverse lower court rulings that run afoul of the "explanations," and often cite specific points in the explanations which have been violated.

The Council of Europe has recommended that the Russian Supreme Court be stripped of its power to issue "explanations" of the law. It is unclear what specifically prompted this recommendation, but it may well be linked to a concern that the Court might abuse its power. This is a genuine concern, for not only in the Soviet period but also fairly recently the Court has abused its prerogative—for example in shaping the law on arrest and detention hearings and in regulating sentencing practices more generally.[19] But in our view it is necessary to preserve for the Court the power to issue "explanations." The Court's issuance of explanations serves a vital function—namely, the encouragement of uniformity in the administration of justice. Especially today, with the proliferation of new norms in hastily crafted legislation, and the increasing devolution of political authority to subjects of the Federation, some instruments for centralizing and stabilizing the administration of law in Russia must remain in the hands of the Supreme Court. District court judges surveyed by us agreed: 89.8 percent asserted that "explanations" from the Supreme Court improved judicial practice, while only 11 percent regarded them as an infringement on judicial independence.

There is, however, room for improvement in the process of publishing decisions of the Court and its promulgation of explanations and commentaries. First, the Supreme Court should publish a larger sample of its decisions—say, all rendered by the Presidium or a Plenum, and a representative sample from the various collegia. The longstanding pattern of publishing only dozens of decisions each year can lead to a misrepresentation of judicial practice, even unintentionally. Second, the process by which subjects are chosen for the issuing of explanations should be reviewed. At present, the Presidium alone decides what areas of law and judicial practice are to be reviewed and scrutinized at a Plenum. There is no formal procedure by which the public, elected representatives, or ordinary judges or other legal officials can influence the selection of issues.[20] This monopoly, and the potential for the agenda-setting power to be abused, is worrisome, especially since two key members of the Presidium (including the Chairman of the Supreme Court) faced reappointment in 1999. It is not inconceivable that the Presidium might use its ability to shape the law to curry political favor. Because the legitimacy of the Court's conduct could be tarnished by secrecy in such matters, we recommend that some means of introducing greater transparency into the agenda-setting process be adopted. Furthermore, the formalization of procedures for selecting subjects for the Plenum would be a salutary check on this important power.[21] Third, the Supreme Court must desist from circulating to lower courts post-plenary commentaries on recent judicial practice. In 1993, six months after a Plenum convened to discuss judicial practice in arrest and detention hearings, the

Court distributed to all courts a supplementary "survey" of mistakes in which it recommended that judges, in taking decisions to free illegally detained defendants, apply a higher burden of proof than was recognized in law and enunciated in its formal "explanations."[22] Even such ad hoc communications from the Supreme Court are received by judges as authoritative, notwithstanding their dubious procedural origins.

The Judicial Qualification Commissions

The establishment of the Judicial Qualification Commissions (JQCs) in 1989 is one of the great achievements of judicial reform in Russia. JQCs, which are made up solely of judges and elected at conferences that all judges in a region can attend, have a decisive voice in most decisions affecting the careers of judges. JQCs administer entrance exams for judicial candidates and must approve their credentials before review by political authorities. JQCs also give an "evaluation" (*zakliuchenie*) of all candidates for chairmen or deputy chairmen of federal courts. Without a commission's approval no judge can even be nominated for a leading post on a court.[23] The awarding of ranks (*klass*) and handling of complaints against judges is also the exclusive prerogative of the JQC. Most important, JQCs handle all requests for the initiation of criminal proceedings against judges and adjudicate all motions for dismissal. In sum, as institutions of self-government, the JQCs determine much of the meaning of judicial independence in Russia.

As we showed in Chapter 2, JQCs have made a substantial contribution to the independence of judges from the executive and legislature. The question, here, however, is whether JQCs enhance judicial independence at the expense of autonomy. Do JQCs, which typically are staffed by senior judges (primarily chairmen of district courts and judges from superior courts) and, as we have shown, exercise considerable influence on ordinary judges, jeopardize the latter's autonomy?

Despite occasional claims of nepotism and unionism, JQCs appear to perform the examining, ranking, and vetting functions well and without controversy. Few candidates for judgeships fail the qualifying exam or are not forwarded for nomination. Less than 5 percent of requests for an increase in rank are rejected. And only 10 percent of those judges aspiring to leadership positions on courts receive unfavorable reviews from the JQCs.[24]

It is less clear that the JQCs act impartially when handling complaints or adjudicating motions to dismiss judges, most of which are brought by the chairman of a superior court.[25] Since the Soviet period, there has been a steady rise in the number of judges dismissed for "negative" reasons. Whereas in the 1980s, on average between 5 and 10 judges were dismissed each year in the USSR, 54 judges were relieved of their duties in Russia in 1995, and in both 1996 and 1997, nearly 100 were dismissed. JQCs reportedly vote to dismiss judges in 56 percent of all such hearings.[26] The apparent increase in exactingness may be due in part to the absence of an intermediate sanction: whereas before 1989, judges against whom some charge of malfeasance had been made might receive one of three kinds of "disciplinary" punishment,[27] today, JQCs have only two options: leave the judge in the corps or dismiss him.[28] But it may also be due in part to the arbitrary handling of motions and a supercilious attitude toward lower level (and especially younger) judges.[29]

There are signs that JQCs have occasionally used the power of dismissal to get rid of unwanted but professionally competent and honest judges. For example, the Supreme Court of the Russian Federation recently reinstated a well-known judge whose notions of law and justice diverged radically from those of his superiors.[30] In another case, a judge was removed from office for having refused to return early from vacation and help clear his court's docket of delayed cases in advance of an "inspection" (*proverka*) by the superior court.[31] In fact, Anatolii Zherebtsov, the Chairman of the Supreme JQC, claims that it is not infrequent that judges get dismissed for "insignificant oversights" (*promakhi*).[32] In both 1996 and 1997, one-third of those judges appealing their dismissal by regional JQCs were reinstated by the SJQC.[33] Zherebtsov thus spends considerable time and energy trying to contain intrajudicial conflicts before they conflagrate, and organizes conferences to regularize and coordinate the practices of regional JQCs. But it seems that some regional JQCs have also indulged errant judges and adopted excessively corporatist practices. For example, in 1996 and 1997 there was a significant rise in the percentage of dismissal motions rejected by regional JQCs, often on the basis of such ostensibly mitigating factors as the age or inexperience of the judge under scrutiny. When the JQCs appear to protect judges who misbehave, they may be reviled by the press as "protectionist" organizations.[34] While the JQCs have a good reputation among judges (in our survey 90 percent regarded as fair the commissions' handling of disciplinary matters), there is much room for improvement and regularization in their performance.

As vital institutions of judicial self-governance, the JQCs deserve far more support and attention than they get. First of all, the commissions lack proper financing. Funding for the Supreme JQC comes as a favor from Supreme Court Chairman Lebedev, and its members, who must travel long distances, often work as volunteers.[35] Many regional JQCs are worse off. Lacking any financing, they can hire no regular staff, and as a result fail to keep minutes of their meetings and rely on officials from the justice administrations to conduct investigations. The lack of operational independence in these important bodies of self-government is dangerous. Consequently, stable and adequate funding for the JQCs should be included in the budget of the new Judicial Department, but the commissions could also benefit from the help of Western donors.

Second, the normative and procedural basis for the work of the JQCs should be improved. The grounds for dismissing judges are vague.[36] For one of these grounds—"creating red tape"—JQCs rely on an "explanation" of the Russian Supreme Court.[37] Also, the number of officials authorized to bring complaints and motions to the JQCs is unlimited; this threatens to bog down even further these overworked and underfinanced bodies. Finally, the standards of proof and rules of evidence in such hearings are fluid and informal, giving excessive discretion to adjudicators in fact-finding.[38] In our view, the judicialization of misconduct proceedings would help deter capricious handling of complaints and arbitrary decisions to remove judges.

Third, there is the controversial question of whether to empower JQCs to discipline judges, short of actual dismissal. The fact that the Supreme JQC has had to intervene and curb the tendency of some commissions to dismiss judges for "trivial infractions" argues in favor of allowing the commissions to impose lesser penalties—such as short suspensions or temporary demotions in rank. This position is shared by many chairs of courts and of qualification commissions, including the Chairman of the Supreme Qualification Commission, Zherebtsov, and by the leading Duma member working on judicial problems, V. A. Kaliagin. An irate lawyer, upset with the highhandedness of some judges in dealing with the public and their representatives before trial, recently proposed restoring to the remnants of the justice departments of the Ministry of Justice responsibility for disciplining judges.[39] At the same time, many judges, at all levels of the hierarchy, consider any formal discipline for judges to be inadvisable, on the grounds that informal warnings work well for minor infractions and that a formal system of discipline demeans the judicial role. Nearly two-thirds of the judges in our survey opposed any additional disciplinary measures. During 1998 and 1999 the issue of judicial discipline was discussed at two Russian-American seminars for the chairs of courts and qualification commissions, one in Belgorod (November 1998), the other in Kazan (March 1999), and a session of the Presidential Council on the Improvement of the Administration of Justice also discussed the issue.[40] But no resolution was reached. The authors of this report agree with ordinary Russian judges that informal warnings are better than a formal system of discipline for judges, but to stem attacks on judges (for example, from the procuracy) it might well be politically wise to institute some disciplinary measures. To ensure that any new system of discipline does not compromise the autonomy of judges, we would encourage the continuation of dialogue with Western judges on this issue. We would suggest the holding of another conference on problems of judicial misconduct and accountability—this time in cooperation with European judges as opposed to American ones.

A sure sign of the achievement of some judicial independence and power in Russia is the emergence of the issue of accountability. Critics, journalists, and procurators alike have charged the JQCs with bias in favor of protecting judges. One remedy supported by some observers is to add to panels that review cases of errant judges representatives of the public at large—not procurators or other government officials, but ordinary citizens.[41] This step might eliminate the appearance of corporatism and make judges subject to a broader kind of accountability without compromising the principle of corporate self-governance. As long as judges remained a strong majority on the panels, and the public were not members of the actual JQCs, the step might be a sensible one

The Judicial Department

Finally, it is worthwhile considering how the establishment of the new Judicial Department in the center and judicial departments in the subjects of the Federation might affect the autonomy of judges. The system of judicial departments gained legislative approval early in 1998 and the challenge of that year was bringing them into existence, even before full budgetary support had been authorized.[42] The departments were to replace the Ministry of Justice and its administrations in all matters of administrative support for the courts, and, at least in theory, would do a better job. The Department in Moscow would be a freestanding administrative agency subordinate to the Supreme Court and the Council of Judges; and the regional/republican- level departments occupy an analogous position.[43] The departments were to handle "all of the cares of the courts of general jurisdiction" including questions of cadres (determining norms for caseload, need for new positions, helping to recruit, developing training); organizational matters (including systems of court records, archives, statistics; organizing perks and benefits for judges and other court employees); and resource questions (support for not only the courts but also the agencies of the judicial corporation, such as the JQCs and the councils of judges). With a mission restricted only to judicial institutions and as a new organization with fresh staff, the court departments would, in the view of their supporters, work tirelessly for the courts, and not be tempted to divert funds to other matters, as the Ministry of Justice allegedly had.

Establishing any new agency, or set of agencies, is a huge task, especially in the Russian context, where the extent of bureaucratization assured the need for many authorizing documents from the President and Government. Further, resources had to be found, for the Ministry of Justice fought hard against automatic transfers of the funds and cadres it had used for administering the courts, on the grounds that its new responsibility for the prisons required those same resources.[44] New agencies also faced the challenge of establishing status and relations with other players, and some observers were concerned lest the court department chiefs lack the necessary access to top financial and government officials at both levels. However, the new chief of the Judicial Department, Valentin Cherniavskii, moved quickly to establish his authority and contacts; and the regional governments were given a voice in the approval of the chiefs of their judicial departments, thereby affording the latter legitimacy within the world of regional government.[45] Most of their predecessors, the heads of the judicial administrations of the Ministry of Justice, had operated in virtual dual subordination, serving regional governments as much as the Ministry of Justice in the center. As of March 1999, eighty-four regional/republican chiefs had been selected and the staffing of departments in the center and regions stood at more than 80 percent. Overall, 40 percent of the officials in the court departments had prior experience in the courts or their administration and another 26 percent in law enforcement. Ten of the chiefs of the regional departments had previously handled the administration of courts for the Ministry of Justice (one example was the chief of the court department of Moscow region).[46]

As of June 1999 the appointment of court administrators to serve at each court had not begun, in the main because the Federal Budget Law for 1999 did not allow any appointments that would involve increases in staff. Officials in the court departments were considering drawing on existing vacancies to provide openings for the appointment of court administrators, if necessary changing the name of their posts on the financial documents.[47]

The question was how well the new departments would function and whether they would help courts and judges, without infringing on their operations. There was room for improvement on this front, for the Justice Administrations had a reputation among some judges of imposing demands upon them in exchange for favors.[48] (In our survey, 13.7 percent of judges reported feeling most dependent on the justice administration.) One key factor in the success of the court departments will be the level of funds they obtain. Only with increased resources will the departments be able to help the courts, and with insufficient resources resentments will develop among the less favored judges. But how will the departments obtain resources? If the federal government comes through with major new funding for the courts, all well and good, but if court department chiefs must go hat in hand to regional and local governments, then the departments themselves may fall into new lines of dependency, with unfortunate consequences for the courts. Another factor is the performance of the new official, the court administrator, intended by reformers to serve as the right-hand person for the chief judge but carrying out tasks associated with the mandate of the judicial departments. It is important that the court administrators serve not as agents of the departments in the courts, but as representatives of the court chairmen in their relationships with all outside bodies, including the court departments.

The immediate danger is that the transition, organizational and financial, of court administration from the judicial administrations to the judicial departments will be a long and tortured one, leaving a period of weak servicing of the courts, a period in which they will have to fend for themselves and turn even more than now to local governments. This short-run threat, however, infringes more on judicial independence than on the autonomy of judges vis-à-vis the rest of the judicial hierarchy.

Recommendations

3.1   To reduce the power of court chairmen over other judges: (a) issues guidelines on case flow management; (b) establish the post of court administrator and empower him/her to handle to the

extent possible the obtaining of benefits for individual judges.

3.2   To reduce pressures on judges to conform: (a) discourage the reliance in evaluations of judges' work upon quantitative indicators of performance, especially "stability of sentences"; (b) reorganize the system of *kurators* so that the same superior court judge does not instruct and review cases from any particular judge.

3.3   To refine, but not eliminate, the guidance provided by the Supreme Court to judges on lower courts: (a) keep the "explanations" issued by the Supreme Court, but widening the process of selecting issues to be covered; and (b) increase the number of Supreme Court decisions that are published.

3.4   To improve the Judicial Qualification Commissions: (a) clarify legal procedures; and (b) increase funding.

3.5   Convene a conference on judicial misconduct and accountability, emphasizing European approaches to these issues.

3.6   In establishing the Judicial Departments: (a) ensure that the court administrators serve as the representatives of their court chairmen rather than of the departments; (b) make sure that the departments are well funded and not forced to seek resources below the federal level.

Notes

1. Memo to Rule of Law Consortium, reporting a judge's claim that chairmen give mafia cases to judges known to be lenient.

2. For the case of comrade Pichugin, a judge in Novosibirsk who joined the bench in 1990 solely in order to get an apartment but was forced to sue in order to obtain it, see Todd S.Foglesong, "The Politics of Judicial Independence and the Administration of Criminal Justice, 1982-1992," unpublished doctoral dissertation, University of Toronto, 1995, Chapter 5. More recently, the chairman of a district court in Ryazan was dismissed after it was discovered he used funds stipulated for judicial enforcers to obtain housing for three of the judges on his court, including himself.

3. Case management and distribution in the late Soviet period is discussed in Foglesong, "The Politics of Judicial Independence," Chapter 2.

4. Interviews.

5. On 26 June 1995, the Presidium of the Council of Judges overturned a regulation (*polozhenie*) of the Altai Territory Court which had authorized its chairman to deprive judges of their bonuses for reversals, delays, and even "poorly prepared procedural documents." For more observations on the subtle forms which higher court influence and directions take, see Sergei Pashin, "Razvitie

sudebnoi sisteme Rossiiskoi Federatsii," *Vostochno-evropeiskoe konstitutsionnoe obozrenie*, 1997, No. 2, pp. 16-23.

6. The Deputy Head of the Department of Justice in Omsk recalled one judge who fainted in the office of her *kurator* upon learning of a likely reversal. Foglesong, "The Politics of Judicial Independence," Chapter 5.

7. Although some Supreme and superior court judges claim in public that the rate of reversal is no longer linked to promotion and even that data on "stability of sentences" is no longer kept on individual judges, lower court judges insist that they are routinely apprised of their individual ratings. The judicial qualification commissions, whose work is discussed in this section, award increases in rank solely on the basis of rate of reversal. The fact that in at least one case a judge was removed from the bench for having been reversed shows the extent to which this indicator still dominates thought about judicial performance. See the 1997 Annual Report of the Supreme Judicial Qualification Commission.

8. O. P. Temushkin, *Organizatsionno-pravovye metodi proverki zakonnosti i obosnovannosti sudebnoi praktiki* (Moscow, 1978).

9. Code of Criminal Procedure of the RSFSR, articles 342-344.

10. See M. S. Strogovich, *Kurs sovetskogo ugolovnogo protsessa* (Moscow, 1970),Vol. 2, pp. 385-87, and *Kommentarii k ugolovno-protsessualnomu kodeksu RSFSR* (Moscow, 1976), pp. 480-84.

11. See, for example, the report of the educational work on the new criminal code conducted by the Komi Republic Supreme Court. Oleg Markov, "Novyi ugolovnyi kodeks Rossii i opyt primeneniia," *Rossiskaia iustitsiia*, 1997, No. 5, pp. 38-39.

12. For example, at the meeting of the Council of Judges, 29 October 1997, judges grumbled in dismay as Verin, a senior judge on the Supreme Court, attempted to deliver an impromptu "lesson" on the new Criminal Code.

13. For a disquisition on "supervision" in Russian procedural law, see A. W. Rudzinski, "Soviet Type Audit Proceedings and Their Western Counterparts," in Leon Boim, et al., *Legal Controls in the Soviet Union* (Leyden, 1966), pp. 287-331. For a recent explication of the law of supervisory review by a Russian scholar, see A. P. Ryzhakov, *Nadzornoe proizvodstvo* (Moscow, 1997).

14. The power of the Presidium and the character of its proceedings are poorly understood in both Russia and the West. For the most authoritative discussion of the internal organization of the Supreme Court, see Peter Krug, "Departure From the Centralized Model: The Russian Supreme Court and Constitutional Control of Legislation," *Virginia Journal of International Law*, Vol. 37, No. 3, Spring 1997, pp. 729-37.

15. For the Court's most recent defense of its prerogative to issue "explanations" and their meaning, see "O roli i znachenii postanovlenii plenuma Verkhovnogo Suda RF," *Biulleten' Verkhovnogo Suda RF*, 1998, No. 3, pp. 21-24.

16. For an account of the Court's role in shaping sentencing practices, see Todd S. Foglesong, "Senses of Justice versus Rules of Law: Introducing the New Criminal Code in Russia," paper presented to the annual meeting of the American Association for the Advancement of Slavic Studies, Seattle, WA, November 1997.

17. For much of the Soviet period (until the 1980s) "guiding explanations" were treated as policy statements subject to vetting by the Communist Party Central Committee. In the late Stalin and early post-Stalin years the Ministry of Justice initiated most of these resolutions. However, by the 1980s the USSR Supreme Court had become more autonomous and controlled the process of issuing the explanations. See Peter H. Solomon, Jr., *Soviet Criminal Justice under Stalin* (Cambridge, UK, and New York, 1996), pp. 416-18.

18. For a discussion of the Court's role in shaping jury trial practice, see Steven C. Thaman, "The Resurrection of Trial by Jury in Russia," *Stanford International Law Review*, Vol. 35, No.1, 1995, pp. 61-274.

19. Foglesong, "Senses of Justice versus Rules of Law."

20. The Procuracy, the MVD, and other institutions at various levels of government can and do submit to the Court requests that they re-examine practice in certain areas of law, but the Presidium is under no legal obligation to consider or respond to them.

21. For a study of how agenda-setting influences the development of case law in the United States, see H. W. Perry, Jr., *Deciding to Decide: Agenda-setting in the United States Supreme Court* (Cambridge, MA,1991).

22. Todd S. Foglesong, "*Habeas Corpus* or 'Who Has the Body?': Judicial Review of Arrest and Pre-Trial Detention in Russia," *Wisconsin International Law Journal*, Vol. 14, No. 3, Summer 1996, p. 570.

23. This is a fairly important function, since the authority to appoint chairmen of courts is not well regulated in Russian law and there has been substantial conflict over this prerogative. See, for example, the discussion of such appointments by Sidorenko, the Chairman of the Council of Judges, at the 12 March 1997 meeting of the President's Council on Judicial Reform, *Rashifrovka zasedaniia soveta po sudebnoi reforme pri Prezidente RF*, pp. 8-9.

24. See the "review" of judicial practice in judicial qualification commissions completed by the civil division of the Russian Supreme Court in October 1997. *Spravka po rezultatam obobshcheniiia praktiki rassmotreniia materialov kvalifikatsionnami kollegiiami sudei obshchikh sudov respublik v sostave RF, avtonomnykh oblastei, avtonomnykh okrugov, kraev, oblastei i gorodov Moskvy i Sankt Peterburga za 1996*. This review formed the basis for Zherebtsov's report at the Council of Judges on 28 October 1997.

25. Annual reports of regional judicial qualification commissions show that heads of Regional Departments of Justice do not frequently initiate investigations into judges, and when they do a motion is made only after prior consultation with the Chairmen of the Regional Court.

26. A. P. Zherebtsov, "Kodeksu chesti pridat' normativnyi kharakter," *Rossiiskaia iustitsiia*, 1997, No. 3, p. 2. In 1997 regional JQCs handled 146 motions for dismissal (91 from chairmen of regional courts and heads of regional justice departments; and 55 from citizen complaints), and removed 75 judges. In 1996, a year for which we lack data on the total number of motions for dismissal considered by the JQCs, they removed 96 judges.

27. All three punishments were mild: "notice" (*zamechanie*), "rebuke" (*vygovor*), and "stern rebuke" (*strogii vygovor*). In the mid-1980s, one out of every ten judges had received some form of disciplinary punishment. See Foglesong, "The Politics of Judicial Independence," Chapter 3.

28. Interviews with members of regional judicial qualification commissions indicate that some judges are merely reprimanded or warned in such hearings, in spite of the illegality of such sanctions.

29. In 1997, nearly 50 percent of the judges removed from the bench were junior judges, with fewer than five years of experience on the bench. See *Spravka o rabote Vysshei kvalifikatsionnoi kollegii sudei RF za period 1993–dekabr 1996 goda* and *Spravka o rabote Vysshei kvalifikatsionnoi kollegii sudei RF za 1997 god.*

30. For one newspaper's unusually detailed coverage of the dismissal and reinstatement of Sergei A. Pashin, see *Obshchaia gazeta*, 1998: articles by L. Sharov on 4-10 June, p. 4; 11-17 June, p. 1; 2-8 July, p. 4; and 9-15 July, p. 4; by Anna Politkovskaia, "Pokazaniia spiashchego prokurora," 17-23 Sept., p. 2; and "Sudia Fedin vyzval nedoumenie korporatsii potomu chto opravdal neugodnogo ei Sergeia Pashina," 8-14 Oct., p. 4; and by Igor Shevelev, "Delo sudi Pashina," 15-21 Oct., p. 8. See also Vladimir Khitruk, "Kvadratura kruga: anatomiia skandala v khrame femidy" (Beseda s Genri Reznikom), *Iuridicheskii vestnik*, 1998, No. 22, p. 8. The Supreme Court's decision to reinstate is on its Web site: www.supcourt.ru.

31. Personnel files of the Supreme Judicial Qualification Commission.

32. Zherebtsov, "Kodeksu chesti;" and *idem*, "Povyshenie avtoriteta sudebnoi vlasti—glavnoe v rabote kvalifikatsionnykh kollegii sudei," *Rossiiskaia iustitsiia*, 1997, No. 8, p. 7.

33. In both 1996 and 1997 approximately two-thirds of judges removed by regional JQCs appealed these decisions to the SJQC. One-third of these appeals was satistifed, according to the SJQC's Annual Reports, suggesting that as many as 20 percent of the regional JQC decisions to remove judges were made in error.

34. See Sergei Pozhivilko, "Spots on the Robe," in *Russian Politics and Law*, Vol. 35, No. 4, 1997, pp. 82-89, and Igor Korol'kov, "Osudit' sud'iu neprosto," *Izvestiia*, 15 March 1996, p. 3.

35. Interviews with staff members of the Supreme Judicial Qualification Commission, Moscow, 24-26 June 1998.

36. See paragraphs 7 and 9 of article 14 of the Law on the Status of Judges.

37. See "Postanovlenie Plenuma Verkovnogo Suda RF No.7 ot 24 avgusta 1993, 'O srokakh rassmotreniia ugolovnykh i grazhdansikh del sudami RF'," which stipulates that "premeditated, crude, or systematic violations of procedural legislation" can be considered an act "bringing into disrepute the honor and dignity of a judge and diminishing the authority of the judiciary."

38. In an August 1998 interview, Zherebtsov said he was opposed to the formalization of proceedings in JQCs, since their function is ensuring ethics, not legality, in the administration of justice.

39. Vladimir Filippov, "Pochemu my plachem ot nezavisimogo suda?" *Rossiiskaia gazeta*, 25 Aug. 1999, p. 2.

40. "Rossiisko-Amerikanskii seminar dlia predsedatelei sudov i predsedatelei kvalifikatsionnykh kollegii sudei subektov Rossiiskoi Federatsii: Otbor sudei, sudebnaia etika i distsiplina," g.Belgorod (15-19 noiabria 1998) i g.Kazan (22-25 marta 1999)." These meetings were conducted by the Supreme Judicial Qualification Commission and the Russian American Partnership, with funds from US AID.

41. Sergei Vitsin, the first Chairman of the President's Council on Judicial Reform, advocated at that body's meeting of 9 October 1996 installing a "public representative" on the JQCs.

42. "O Sudebnom Departamente pri Verkhvnom Sude Rossiiskoi Federatsii," Zakon RF ot 8 ianvaria 1998, *Rossiiskaia gazeta*, 14 Jan. 1998, p. 5.

43. At the March 1998 meeting of the Council of Judges, there was much discussion of the idea of having the Chairman of the Supreme Court assume, simultaneously, the position of Chairman of the Council of Judges. If approved, this would make the Head of the Judicial Department entirely and solely dependent on the Chairman of the Supreme Court. In our view, such a fusion of functions represents a danger; it vests much too administrative power in the hands of a judge who has considerable power to shape lower courts' application of the laws.

44. The transfer of the prisons from the Ministry of Internal Affairs to the Ministry of Justice took place officially on 1 September 1998, after lengthy negotiations between the ministries and between prison employees and the Ministry of Justice. "O peredache ugolovno-ispolnitelnoi sistemy Ministerstva vnutrennykh del Rossiiskoi Federatsii v vedenie Ministerstva iustitsii Rossiiskoi Federatsii," Ukaz Prezidenta RF ot 28 iiuliia 1998, *Rossiiskaia gazeta*, 16 Aug. 1998, p. 5; Andrei Kamakin, "GUIN—territoriia Miniusta," *Nezavisimaia gazeta*, 12 Aug. 1998, p. 1.

45. Aleksandr Linkov, "Sudebnyi departament nachinaet rabotu," *Rossiiskaia gazeta*, 3 Feb. 1998, p. 3; "Vystuplenie Generalnogo direktora Sudebnogo departamenta pri Verkhnom Sude RF, Cherniavskogo Valetina Semenovich," *Protokol plenarnogo zasedaniia Soveta sudei RF*, 31 marta-3 aprelia 1998 goda, pp. 1-8.

46. "Otchet o rezultatakh raboty Sudebnogo Departamenta pri Verkhovnom Sude Rossiiskoi Federatsii v 1998 godu" (Moscow, 1999); "Tezisy k vystupleniiu [Direktora Sudebnogo Departamenta] na Sovete Sudei RF, g. Suzdal

(29.03–02.04.99)."

47. "Tezisy k vystupleniiu," pp. 11-12; interviews.

48. Regional justice administrations routinely scolded judges for red tape and low quality decisions, and sometimes withheld bonuses in order to get judges to comply with their demands. See Foglesong, "The Politics of Judicial Independence," Chapters 4 and 5.

4

Jurisdiction, Power, and Prestige

To say that courts or judges in a country are powerful usually means three things: first, that courts have effective jurisdiction that reaches at least some politically sensitive matters or affects the working of the rest of government; second, that both the public and government respect the courts and their performance and readily turn to them for the resolution of problems; and third, that judges have institutions of their own through which they can influence public policy, especially in areas relating to their work. In none of these senses of "power" were courts or judges powerful in the Soviet period. For most of Soviet history courts had a highly restricted role in assessing the legality of administrative actions; they had no significant constitutional jurisdiction; and they played a limited role in commercial disputes and the management of criminal investigations. On the whole, the prestige of courts was low, among public and officialdom alike. Judges lacked any professional associations or bodies through which they could share concerns and express positions on policy matters.

In post-Soviet Russia, this portrait of weak courts and powerless judges has changed to a considerable degree. To begin, there has been a revolution in the jurisdiction of courts, such that courts of one kind or another now scrutinize the legality of officials' actions and the constitutionality of legislation, resolve commercial disputes, review decisions about pre-trial detention, and enforce a variety of citizens' rights. Furthermore, the community of judges has succeeded in forming a set of institutions—among them a congress of judges and councils of judges on the national and regional/republican levels—which, while lacking substantial and secure funding, have proved to be effective articulators of the interests of the judicial community. As we shall see, not all of this new authority means power: courts lack the ability to assure implementation of some of their decisions, and some of the new jurisdiction falls not to the regular courts but to various specialized bodies, stunting the growth in status and prestige of the judiciary as a whole. Also, it is not clear how much these gains have translated thus far into increased respect for the courts or a readiness to use the courts and abide by the decisions of judges—on the part of citizens, elites, and government officials alike. There is, no doubt, much room for improvement, but the great expansion in formal authority, and the nascent institutional identity and capacity of the courts, command our attention.

In this chapter we examine and assess a number of areas of new or widened jurisdiction of the courts in Russia; the quality and strength of the new institutions of the judicial community (*sudeiskoe soobshchestvo*); and, finally, the way that public and government officials alike regard and use the courts.

New Jurisdiction

In the past ten years Russian courts have expanded jurisdiction in at least five areas. Courts now review the legality of administrative acts; the legality and bases of procuratorial decisions regarding pre-trial detention; alleged infringements of a variety of citizens' rights (consumer rights, labor rights, right to reputation, etc.); commercial disputes, especially relating to non-payment of debts; and challenges to the constitutionality of laws and decrees of the subjects of the Federation and the national government alike.

Judicial Review of Administrative Acts

Since 1987 ordinary courts have begun playing an important role in the regulation of public life in Russia. Judges have been called on to review the legality of both administrative acts and inaction as well as local ordinances in a growing number of cases and broadening area of social regulation.[1] Between 1993 and 1997, the number of cases in which citizens sued the state rose from 9,701 to 53,659 (see Table 4.1). In 1998 it reached 91,300. Remarkably, by 1997 the courts supported more than four of every five requests for restitution and remedial action.[2]

In some cases citizens make modest claims against the state, by appealing decisions to rescind hunting licenses, curtail unemployment benefits, or withhold information about work records or illnesses. In other cases, the issues were more serious, involving refusals to register new places of residency (*propiska*) or to supply a passport for travel abroad. In a minority of cases judges made hard decisions in matters of public importance—such as the convening of elections,[3] the establishment of tariffs on interregional commerce,[4] and the privatization of state assets.[5] In several subjects of the Federation, local and regional courts have decided such matters against the wishes of political or legislative officials.[6] This information suggests that the ordinary courts in Russia now play an active, and apparently independent, role in safeguarding fundamental civil rights.

TABLE 4.1   Judicial Review of Administrative Acts

	No. of Complaints	Percentage satisfied
1988	2,869	38.0%
1989	2,646	59.8
1990	4,944	64.3
1993	9,701	73.5
1994	13,399	71.8
1995*	30,000	n/a
1996	43,600	74.4
1997	53,659	83.4

* estimate, based on report for first six months (~17,000)
NB: approximately one-fifth of the acts contested by citizens in both 1996 and 1997 were decisions made by "collegial organs." The success rate of such petitions was about the same (3,736 of 4,801 in 1997, and 1,805 of 2,668 in 1996).

Despite the apparent boom in judicial review of administrative action in Russia, the level of citizen-state litigation may still be low. Most Russian legal scholars think that such challenges could be many times higher, and we tend to agree. Given the vast size of the Russian state, the uncontrolled proliferation of sub-statutory regulations within state organizations, the poor training of its civil servants, the long history of arbitrary action by unaccountable officials, and the great number of services to which Russian citizens are legally and constitutionally entitled, there must be many disputes that could, but do not, reach court.

There are at least three reasons for the low level of administrative justice in Russia. One is the lack of unawareness on the part of many citizens of the opportunity to bring to court complaints against officials and of the likelihood of a favorable decision. Instead, many Russians have a stereotypical view of courts in Russia as: (1) costly—often requiring the assistance of lawyers who, in the absence of appropriate legal aid/consultation, participate only for a substantial fee; (2) slow (with backlogs and bureaucratic delays); and (3) lacking power to compel implementation of their decisions. A second deterrent to using courts to contest official action is the presence of a major alternative, namely, complaining to the procuracy. Through its general supervisory function, the procuracy has the right and duty to assess complaints against government officials and issue protests to the offending officials and agencies. And it does so faster and at much less cost than do the courts. Many citizens also continue the Russian habit of appealing to the highest authority (the President) and to the press.[7] Finally, there are complicated (and unresolved) technical questions in this area of law, including the absence in Russian law of specific provisions defining the accountability of civil servants, and clarity in the jurisdiction of *arbitrazh* as opposed to the courts of general jurisdiction.[8] These gaps in the law trouble some judges, and lead them to avoid taking risks by referring complainants to the procuracy or the offending agency.[9]

This brief analysis suggests a number of measures that might get citizens to turn more often to the courts. To begin, more and better publicity for the courts' activities in the administrative realm would help—whether through the popular press, television, or a new popular journal on courts (see the discussion later in this Chapter).[10] Further, some broadening of the possibilities for educating citizens about their legal rights and the relative merits of court vs. procuracy vs. other approaches would make a difference.[11] This could be accomplished either through formalizing the legal consultations provided by judges, and sometimes advocates, at court houses, sponsoring student-run legal clinics at law schools, or establishing "citizens advice bureaux" on the model used in England.[12] Apart from initiatives to help citizens learn how to use courts for their purposes, there is a clear need for the resolution of issues affecting the legal bases of the accountability of officials and the rules of procedure in administrative disputes.[13] Both of these would make worthwhile subjects for conferences and NGO projects involving international participation. Finally, we can see the utility of a study, by some kind of ad hoc commission that included representatives of all the agencies that handle such complaints, of the whole gamut of mechanisms used to respond to public complaints about illegality in government and administration. The purpose would be to determine how and why citizens choose particular approaches, which ones prove most effective, and then to rationalize the various approaches. We believe that there is room for both the courts and the procuracy in the handling of complaints, and that inter-institutional cooperation (as opposed to rivalry) would ensue from such a joint effort.

Arrest and Pre-trial Detention

In June 1992 the courts acquired authority to review the procedural legality and grounds for procuratorial decisions to detain the accused and order pre-trial detention. This meant that for the first time courts would be receiving from accused persons and their counsel complaints about the decisions to arrest and to extend the terms of detention, and that courts would be asked to ensure that police and procuracy officials did not overuse or abuse their legal right to hold accused persons. To be sure, reformers had asked for more. They wanted the initial power to approve pre-trial detention transferred from the procuracy to the exclusive domain of the courts, and for the courts to gain control over decisions regarding search and seizure and eavesdropping as well. As we noted in Chapter 1, the Constitution of the Russian Federation approved in 1993 in articles 23 and 25 calls for a complete transfer of these functions to the judiciary, but only as part of a new Criminal Procedure Code. In 1995, the adoption of a Law on Operational-Detective Activity effected part of this transfer, by requiring that police and procurators first obtain permission from courts before installing eavesdropping devices or interfering with personal correspondence. For several years now, judges in Russia have been reviewing both applications for eavesdropping permits as well as complaints about arrest and detention.

Between 1994 and 1997, Russian courts received approximately 70,000 complaints about detention—that is, from between 17 and 19 percent of those held in custody awaiting formal charges and trial. Each year, courts satisfied more than 20 percent of the claims (see Table 4.2). The result was that between 3.5 and 4 percent of accused persons whose detention procurators approved were released from prison by judges. A careful study of this process in one region revealed that the reviews usually did not happen within the tight five-day schedule stipulated in the law. At the same time, more than half of the accused waited a month before making their claims, and then seemed concerned mainly about their health and the need to look after dependants.[14]

TABLE 4.2   Judicial Review of Arrest and Detention

	1992	1993	1994	1995	1996	1997
Appeals of Detention	14,387	53,874	65,218	74,404	71,731	68,206
Percentage increase			21.0	14.1	-3.6	- 4.9
Percentage satisfied	14.1	17.3	20.0	20.4	20.8	19.3
Appeals of Extensions of Custody	752	5,412	7,237	7,919	8,130	5,234
Percentage satisfied	21.7	20.3	18.7	15.3	14.4	15.1

The issue of pre-trial detention itself is an important and controversial one, for the investigatory prisons display overcrowding and horrific conditions, and, arguably, pre-trial detention is overused. We analyze this issue in detail in Chapter 7. Here we draw attention to the fact that even this modest exercise of judicial power produced a backlash. The police and procuracy greeted the new power of the judiciary with dismay and disruption. Alleging "numerous" (*mnogochislennye*) arbitrary judicial decisions, and decrying the "disastrous" (*pagubnye*) consequences for the fight against crime of releasing defendants, police officials and procurators have on occasion deliberately sabotaged the courts' decisions in defense of constitutional rights, for example re-arresting detainees immediately after their court-ordered releases.[15] As if this were not enough, the Supreme Court cooperated with the needs of the procuracy by sponsoring a proposed restriction on the authority of lower level judges to release "unlawfully detained" defendants. The Court tabled draft legislation which would have delayed any release for at least another three days after the court's decision to enable the procurator to appeal that decision to a higher court. Such an appeal might delay actual release for another ten days. This legislative initiative came close to becoming law, dying only when the Council of the Federation (in September 1997) narrowly voted to reject the Duma's override of a Presidential veto.[16]

Incursions into the authority of the courts and attacks against judicial independence are common in most legal systems. In Russia, they are made more cogent by the state's monopoly of information and knowledge in court practice. Using in-house statistics and selective case reporting, the Supreme Court and Procurator General each distorted and misrepresented judicial practice in matters of arrest and detention, implying that aberrant court behavior (specifically, cavalier decisions to release detainees) was common.[17] The tight control of judicial statistics and incomplete record of case law published by the Supreme Court makes it difficult to fend off political criticism of court practice. In order to deprive foes of judicial power of this public relations armory, Russia must develop alternative and more independent sources of knowledge about the operation of the machinery of justice. The soon-to-be-established Academy of Justice is supposed to include a research center/institute on the administration of justice, with the capacity to study and report on judicial practice. We urge that this unit be developed into a full-fledged research institute and that it be given considerable operational autonomy, including the right to publish its findings without any clearance from any other agencies. The Institute must have the means of producing and disseminating knowledge about courts to thwart misrepresentations of the courts and judicial practice. It would be useful if the Council of Judges could serve as a founder or sponsor of the Institute, an initiative we discuss later in the Chapter.

Commercial and Civil Disputes

The economic transformation of Russia, including privatization and restructuring, was bound to lead to the emergence of many new kinds of disputes as well as the expansion of old types. Some of these new disputes centered around issues of great economic import, for example commercial matters involving large sums of money. The courts' new jurisdiction in the commercial and civil realms had considerable potential for raising the status of the courts and the attitudes of the public toward them. But in our view in the first eight years since the collapse of the USSR this potential was only partially realized, first because most business cases were handled by specialized courts wholly separate from the regular courts of general jurisdiction, known as *arbitrazh* courts, and second because of the reputation of the *arbitrazh* courts for low rates of implementation.

In some Western countries the handling of commercial disputes represents a source of the prestige of courts (even when these disputes are handled in special courts), and the lawyers and judges involved in these cases are the best paid. Under the Soviet regime, where firms were all state-owned, inter-enterprise disputes were handled either within the bureaucratic structures or by panels of the state *arbitrazh*, a set of quasi-judicial tribunals subordinate to the Council of Ministers. In late Soviet Russia, as the bulk of the economy moved into private hands, disputes among firms and between firms and the government took on new importance, and their resolution was entrusted to courts. Conflicts that reached the courts included such matters as pre-contract disputes, tax liability, bankruptcies, and challenges to refusals to register firms, not to speak of the even more common problems of failure to pay debts (to other firms and to banks). But responsibility for handling these cases was entrusted not to the regular courts but to the new *arbitrazh* courts, a set of courts with their own budget and system of administrative support, wholly separate from the regular courts. The judges on the *arbitrazh* courts, many of whom had previously worked for the state *arbitrazh*, were full-fledged members of the judicial community, and enjoyed all the same privileges as judges in the regular courts, including representation within the Council(s) of Judges. As of the start of 1999, 2,209 judges (68 percent of them women) worked at the 92 *arbitrazh* courts (81 in capital cities of regions or republics; 10 interregional courts; and the Supreme *Arbitrazh* Court). Of these, 1,717 (or 78 percent) received special training in handling business disputes sometime between 1993 and 1998, either at the Academy of State Service or the Academy of the National Economy.[18]

Even the basic level *arbitrazh* courts were situated only in the capital cities of the subjects of the Federation, and not in other and smaller cities, and it is unclear to what extent the prestige of regular courts benefited from the work of their cousins. Still, the concentration of business/commercial matters in specialized courts was common in West European countries, and if someday the *arbitrazh* courts gained a good reputation, it might help the prestige of the regular courts as well.[19]

The *arbitrazh* courts of Russia have proven thus far to work effectively in handling and deciding the cases brought before them, with reasonable dispatch. Only a tiny share of cases at the *arbitrazh* courts were concluded past the demanding statutory time limits (4.1 percent in 1997 and 3.3 percent in 1998 exceeded the usual norm of two months from filing); and this level of efficiency was achieved despite growing caseloads (from 20 cases a month per judge in 1996 to 24 cases in 1998) and difficulties recruiting new judges to fill vacant posts.[20] But the great problem for the *arbitrazh* courts lies in the low rate of the execution of their decisions, by most estimates standing at 40 to 50 percent![21] Arguably, one should not hold courts responsible for the afterlife of their decisions, and in the Russian case the fault does lie elsewhere, but the low rate of execution does affect the reputation of the *arbitrazh* courts, and possibly all courts. The reasons for the low rate of implementation of the *arbitrazh* court decisions will be discussed in Chapter 8.

Since 1990, other types of civil cases, those heard in the general court system, experienced a huge increase in quantity and an expansion in range as well. The bulk of the increased caseload came in traditional areas of law that had taken on new meaning. Thus, housing disputes which under the Soviets involved mainly questions of rights to particular apartments, now extended to the full range of conflicts over ownership and use of real estate.[22] Disputes over labor issues (wrongful dismissals, workers' compensation and employment injuries) and pensions assumed new importance in a time of growing unemployment (open and hidden). Other property issues—land ownership and intellectual property rights—also became more common subjects of suits.[23] In addition, there were a number of new areas of civil action whose presence gave courts new prominence. One was consumer protection suits, including such matters as investment fraud, product liability, transportation disputes (lost baggage, delayed flights), and medical malpractice. Often, the plaintiffs achieved some success.[24] Another new subject of suits was libel and slander (what the Russian law calls "defense of honor, worth, and business reputation").[25] In many of these areas, litigiousness is high, and judges are, incrementally, making new law.

In regular civil cases—as in commercial ones—good judicial decisions stood to help the reputation of courts only when they were implemented, and at least one common type of civil judgment was hard for judges to get realized—namely, awards to workers suing their employers for late or non-payment of wages. During the late 1990s a large number of workers turned to the courts to help them extract payments due from either state or private employers. From 122,000 suits in 1995, the number grew to 647,000 in 1996 and to 1,237,000 in 1997 (that is, from 4 percent to 31.6 percent of all civil cases). The official records of the Ministry of Justice show that the courts "satisfied" 99.1 percent of these claims—i.e., decided in favor of the claimants—but it is unlikely that most of these judgments were executed in practice.[26] In the long run, the low rate of implementation is likely to depress the demand for judicial remedies, and thereby sap the power of courts and undermine basic rights of citizens.

Constitutional Review

The quintessential mark of judicial power is usually taken to be the capacity of courts to review the constitutionality of the laws and actions of other branches and levels of government. In some Latin America countries the development of constitutionalism has formed the center-piece of judicial reform.[27] Russia, too, included in its judicial reform program the aim of creating constitutional order, and to do so adopted the European model of constitutional control, namely concentrating that power in a special body, the Constitutional Court. In Russia this body has no defined connection with the rest of the court system; and its relationship to the Supreme Court of Russia is ambiguous, the source of much conflict, and, most important, does little to promote the power of the courts of general jurisdiction.

Operating since early 1992, with an eighteen-month intermission due to the involvement of the Court's first chairman in the political struggles of 1992–1993, the Constitutional Court of the Russian Federation pro-duced an impressive record of hearing and resolving a variety of serious questions concerning the shape of political institutions and civil rights. It has done so in a highly professional and, most would say, fair way.[28] However, two fundamental problems have limited the gains that the power of constitutional review might confer upon the judicial branch—the diffusion of that power to other courts; and the difficulties in securing implementation of the Constitutional Court's decisions.

The diffusion of the power of constitutional review stemmed mainly from an "explanation" issued by the Russian Supreme Court in October 1995.[29] This resolution, through constitutional interpretation, instructed judges on all regular courts that they had the right and the duty to apply the Constitution directly in particular cases. Whenever a judge was *certain* that a law or regulation was unconstitutional, he/she was no longer expected to refer the matter to the Constitutional Court of the Russian Federation but rather to act as if the law (or part of the law) did not exist. The judge was to refer a matter to the Constitutional Court *only if unsure* about the meaning of the relevant constitutional provisions. From October 1995 some judges did apply the constitution directly (e.g., in cases of men who refused to serve in the army and claimed their constitutional right to alternative service, so far non-existent), but not necessarily with any consistency.[30] While it was not necessarily bad to have all judges thinking about constitutional issues, the absence of any obligation for judges to inform the Constitutional Court about applications of the Constitution could prevent the Constitutional Court from ever addressing important issues where violations of the Constitution were obvious and thereby imposing a common standard. This omission struck the authors of this report as anomalous, and we are pleased to report that after we wrote the first draft of this Chapter, the Constitutional Court of the Russian Federation took action to address it.

In its decision of 17 July 1998, dealing with appeals relating to the direct application of the Constitution by courts in the Komi republic and in Karelia, the Constitutional Court gave its reply to the Supreme Court's resolution of October 1995. Any and all courts, the Constitutional Court opinion stated, had an obligation to apply a higher law (including the Constitution) in a particular case whenever there was a conflict between two levels of legal norms. But no court other than the Constitutional Court had the right to declare null and void federal laws (or laws of the subjects on matters of joint jurisdiction or normative acts of the President or government). In fact, when a judge believed that any of these major normative acts contradicted the Constitution, he or she was obliged not only not to apply it but also to refer the matter to the Constitutional Court of the Russian Federation.[31]

The same opinion of the Constitutional Court went on to dissect the state of the law with regard to constitutional review of other normative acts, and in so doing created confusion and controversy. The Court decided (over the dissent of at least one member) that absent specific legislative provision (which the Constitution allowed for all norms not entrusted to review by the Constitutional Court), no court had a right to void either normative acts or agency regulations. This interpretation

—however well grounded[32]—opened up important gaps in the jurisdiction of the courts, and placed a variety of types of normative acts and regulations outside of judicial scrutiny. One example was the non-normative regulations issued by the President and the government; another was regulations issued by lower levels of government (although these might be subject to review by Charter or Constitutional Courts of the subjects—the only courts that could review the constitutionality of laws of the subjects in areas of their own jurisdiction).[33] In contrast, regulations issued by federal ministries could be reviewed and declared null and void by the Russian Supreme Court, but only because of stipulations in the Code of Civil Procedure (article 116).[34]

There is reason to believe that this checkered, complex, and incomplete set of jurisdictions for judicial review of laws, decrees, and regulations might discourage judges from applying the Constitution and citizens from taking their grievances to the courts. The silence or inaction of the regular courts on these issues would deprive many Russians of remedies for violations of basic constitutional rights.[35] The Supreme Court of the Russian Federation recognized this potential problem even before the decision of the Constitutional Court, in deciding in January 1998 to submit to the Duma a draft law amending the Code of Civil Procedure to establish for itself the power to review normative acts of the government.[36] We are also concerned that some courts, including the Supreme Court, will choose to ignore the ruling of the Constitutional Court and without a firm legal basis continue to void government resolutions.[37] The perpetuation of such unseemly jurisdictional competition between the two courts does damage to the legitimacy of the judiciary and jeopardizes the hierarchy of law. Therefore, we urge the Russian government to act as soon as possible on the invitation of the Constitutional Court in its opinion of 17 July 1998 to develop legislation granting particular courts the right to void normative acts and regulations not handled at present by the Constitutional and Supreme Courts.[38]

Note that in the past few years there has been another, less threatening, form of diffusion of constitutional review, namely the establishment of constitutional and charter courts in some of the subjects of the Federation. Although their mandate is to review the consistency of local legal norms with the fundamental law of the particular subject, they will likely encounter cases involving the Russian Constitution as well. Fortunately, thus far, most judges on these courts seem committed to the primacy of the Russian Constitution and to hierarchy in constitutional jurisprudence.[39]

Nevertheless, there is a plain need for organized efforts to coordinate the acts and communication of all constitutional courts in Russia.[40]

The other problem faced by the Russian Constitutional Court is one that other courts share, namely the incapacity to ensure implementation of its decisions. Neither officials of government, especially at the level of the subjects of the Federation, nor even other courts automatically observe and realize its decisions.[41] An early and telling example came in March 1992 when the government of Tatarstan proceeded to hold a referendum after the Constitutional Court in Moscow ruled that the Constitution forbade it. There followed a series of decisions by the Court denying governments of the subjects and cities the right to require residence permits (*propiska*) and use them as a way of excluding persons from their territories. Disobedience, direct and indirect, was rampant; even the mayor of Moscow, Iurii Luzhkov, has done everything possible to continue limiting the flow of population into the capital city. Finally, the most dramatic example of difficulty implementing decisions of the Constitutional Court is a series of cases relating to the election of mayors in cities. The chiefs of a number of subjects—the best known case involving the President of the Udmurt republic—have tried to acquire for their governments the right to appoint mayors. The Constitutional Court informed the Udmurt President in January 1997 that his government's new appointment procedure violated the Constitution, but initially he refused to comply. Only after President Yeltsin intervened behind the scenes, with whatever combination of threats and inducements, did the Udmurt president back down.[42]

The problem of non-implementation of decisions of the Constitutional Court of Russia lies less in contempt for the Court than in a lack of respect for the primacy of the Constitution itself. The regularity with which subjects of the Federation adopt constitutions, charters, and other laws containing clear and obvious violations of the Russian Constitution (sometimes justified with references to bilateral treaties) is a clear and dangerous sign of this disrespect. The attempt to create a constitutional order and invest courts with the task of maintaining it does not by itself make the judicial branch more powerful. Both the Constitution and the courts that apply it need to acquire the authority and respect that would make compliance with their decisions the norm.

To conclude, courts in post-Soviet Russia have entered center stage. They have acquired wide and important new jurisdiction, including, inter alia, review of administrative acts and of pre-trial detention decisions and the resolution of both business disputes and constitutional conflicts. But difficulties securing implementation of many of these decisions have thus far limited the gains that courts have made in status and respect. Remedying this shortcoming will require monumental measures, for the roots of the problem reside in both the weakness of state institutions and the uncertain place of law in contemporary Russian political culture.

The Judicial Community and its Institutions

It is difficult for courts anywhere to have power and prestige without also possessing institutional independence and a separate corporate identity. We have already discussed the important role assumed in Russia by the judicial qualification commissions (JQCs, made up only of judges), first in the selection of new judges, and then even more so in the disciplining and removal of their peers. But the JQCs were only one of a number of important new institutions created by judges in 1991 and 1992. The largest, and the parent body for some of the others, was the Congress of Judges. Directly representing the whole judicial community (its delegates are elected by the regional conferences of judges), the Congress of Judges must meet at least once every three years. As of 1998, it had met already four times. This large body elects (from candidates nominated at the regional judges' conferences) the members of the smaller Council of Judges (114 members, at present), a body that meets at least once a year (and so far more often). The regional/republican conferences of judges also elect regional councils of judges, which play important roles in regulating certain administrative and personnel matters in the judiciary.[43]

The meetings of the All-Russian Congress of Judges and of the Council of Judges of the Russian Federation have provided major fora of exchange on a wide range of issues that matter to judges, including the operations of the courts, their financing, and reform.[44] Thus, meetings of the Council have discussed a variety of draft laws relating to the courts—among them a Code of Judicial Ethics, a draft law on the financing of courts, and another on the Judicial community. A number of the Congresses have succeeded in calling public attention to judicial affairs and helped secure governmental actions to benefit the courts.[45]

Despite their importance to judges, the organs of the judicial community lacked financial security, and depended entirely on ad hoc government subventions, donations from private sponsors, and the support of the Supreme Court of the Russian Federation. Thus, the

Council of Judges of the Russian Federation and the Supreme Judicial Qualification Commission had to use space provided by the Supreme Court and rely on "sponsors" to cover the costs of travel, convening meetings, and publishing rulings. In addition, none of the bodies of the judicial community had adequate staff. This precarious situation must be corrected, if the judicial community is to develop institutions that are autonomous and strong. There is room for special contributions for projects from Western agencies and Russian funders alike. But to give the institutions of the judicial community financial security requires a steady and reliable source of income. We urge Russian legal officials to devise a means of supporting various bodies of the judicial community, especially the Council of Judges, for example through a small levy on judges' salaries, as well as a line in the budget of the Judicial Department(s).[46]

We would also welcome improvements in the work of these bodies. Although the Council discusses and assesses some pieces of draft legislation, the process is haphazard, such that only a portion of relevant drafts actually reaches its meetings. The omissions have had unfortunate consequences.[47] The Council should acquire greater access to the legislative process at many stages, so that it is able to give the Duma considered reviews of all draft laws relating to the courts.[48] In our view, these reviews should take place independently of discussions at the Presidential Council on the Improvement of the Administration of Justice, a useful body with interagency representation that does not necessarily voice the views and interests of judges.[49]

Finally, the Council would do a better job representing the interests of judges if it had fuller and better analyses of the work of courts. The answer, according to leaders of the Council itself, lies in the establishment of a Research Institute on the Administration of Justice, and the projected Academy of Justice approved by President Yeltsin in spring 1998 is supposed to include a research unit. We should note that a team of highly qualified scholars conducted empirical studies of courts and judicial practice in the late Soviet period, based in several departments within the All-Union Research Institute on Soviet Legislation (VNIISZ). The revival of this research capacity, preferably in a relatively autonomous research institute, would both inject realism into the process of drafting laws for judicial reform in Russia and dilute the Supreme Court's monopoly of knowledge about the functioning of the courts. Now that there is a real chance of establishing a research center on the courts, Western donors should consider sponsoring discrete programs of study, especially on the sociology of the courts. Sponsorship could include establishing awards for the best studies of judicial practice and problems and the creation of new venues for the dissemination of knowledge about the courts.

Public Respect for Courts

In the late Soviet period the citizens of Russia did not have a high regard for the courts nor did they seek judicial remedies for many infringements of their rights. Post-Soviet changes in the independence of judges and effective jurisdiction of the courts already discussed should eventually change that view, but it is unclear to what extent this has happened so far. Some recent survey data are positive. In a 1995 survey of mainly urban dwellers in 29 regions, 51.3 percent agreed that judges make just and fair decisions "sometimes" or "very often" (the rest said "rarely" or "never"). In a 1996 survey of 3,000 persons in 10 regions of Russia (70 percent urban), 41.3 percent said that they would turn to a court if any authority took a decision violating their rights; this contrasted with 21.8 percent preferring the media and 15.6 percent local administration.[50] Another 1996 study commissioned by the Presidential Administration found that only 11 percent of respondents were confident about obtaining justice in the courts.[51] This latter sample, however, apparently consisted mainly of businesspeople and may well reflect the difficulties in securing implementation of court decisions in commercial disputes. Public concern about implementation of decisions was reflected in letters sent to the President; in 1997, the President received some 4,900 letters about failures to carry out decisions of the courts.[52] It is worth noting that of the judges in our survey 73.3 percent believed that the public respected their courts; and 75.1 percent that the parties to cases did so. Finally, an indirect but telling indicator of improving public regard for courts is the large increase in the number of suits brought to the courts in the mid- and late-1990s, a fact already mentioned above.

The most authoritative study to date (based on a 1997 national survey conducted by the Foundation for Public Opinion) reveals once again a public divided in its attitudes toward the courts. Overall, one-third of the respondents gave a mainly positive evaluation of the courts ("serve the law and justice;" "protect citizens from arbitrary actions"), while two-thirds saw judges mainly as "heartless bureaucrats" or "servants of power." Interestingly, persons with recent experience in the courts were somewhat more likely to stress both negative features like red tape and positive ones like service to the law. It is also worth noting that the courts as institutions got much better ratings than either the government or the State Duma, and placed with the police and the presidency as agencies that did as much good as harm. The most telling finding concerned public impressions of the performance of the courts in handling complaints against public officials. In response to the questions "do you think that you would succeed if you complained to a court about the actions of a government agency?" only 20 percent answered "yes" or "likely yes," while 63 percent said "no" or "likely no." Yet, as we saw above, the actual success rate in 1996 for claimants who brought such suits to a court stood around 80 percent![53]

Any increase in public respect for courts and confidence in the courts' capacity to handle its problems can come only with changes in the work of the courts themselves, including the implementation of their decisions. But the public needs to know about those changes. After all, the stereotypes about courts inherited from the Soviet days were largely negative, and overcoming these stereotypes requires learning about the improvements to date. In our view, the public does not have sufficient opportunity to develop a new impression of the courts or to learn of their access to them. Coverage of trials and courts in the media stress mainly negative aspects of their work, as journalists write about injustices, corruption, or irregular decisions, not to speak of sensational crimes; and it is often biased and emotional, describing defendants in ways that undermine the presumption of innocence and the integrity of the judicial process.[54]

How can the public image of the courts be improved? Apart from measures to improve the work of the courts themselves, there is a need for advances in the marketing of the courts. To begin, top legal officials, with government support, should establish new journals—especially popular but also academic—relating to the administration of justice.[55] In the 1920s a popular journal called *Sud idet* brought to the public reports of important cases and much information about how to use the courts to pursue one's own rights. This journal deserves revival. Likewise, a new television program on courts and justice (as opposed to the law enforcement emphasis of *"Chelovek i zakon"*) could do much to educate the public. The program could include coverage of real trials (in the manner of the American cable channel "Court TV"), as well as interviews with judges and lawyers, and stories about the history of Russian and Soviet justice. Another approach is to introduce broadcasts relating to the courts and law into existing programs, as one thoughtful analysis has suggested.[56] These projects could be developed under the aegis of the

Council of Judges or the new Research Center on the Administration of Justice. It should also be possible to use the new Guild of Legal Journalists to try to promote stronger and less sensationalist coverage of legal matters in the media. The establishment (with the help of the Russian Foundation for Legal Reform), of a new journal aimed at legal reporters (*Sudebnye novosti*) should help.[57] Other activities of the recently announced program of the Foundation "Legal Awareness through the Mass Media" can also make a difference, but for the long term government support will also be needed.[58] There is also potential for extensive cooperation on such issues between NGOs and quasi-executive agencies such as the Judicial Department, which is to have a Department for Public Relations.[59] Support should be given for initiatives such as these, especially since they are linked with the emergence of civil-society-like organizations and thus will both help end the isolation of, and improve public access to, courts.

Finally, there needs to be much new research on public attitudes toward courts. Indeed, initiatives to enhance the esteem and legitimacy of courts, such as those outlined above, would have greater success if they were based on solid sociological ground. At present, knowledge about Russians' estimation of courts—especially among consumers of justice—is rudimentary. Hardly any of the surveys reporting public opinion about courts is tailored to the task of ascertaining whether or not people's impressions of courts are based on stereotypes and prejudices or contact with the machinery of justice.[60] Even the 1997 study described above only starts this inquiry. More specific research into the public's understanding of law and courts will improve efforts to change Russian perceptions of the usefulness of judicial remedies.

Recommendations

4.1   Publicize the work of the courts (especially such new areas of activity as judicial review of administrative acts, direct application of the Constitution, and consumer protection cases) through a new popular journal (perhaps a revived *Sud idet*), a television program, and work with the Guild of Court Journalists.

4.2   Enhance the role of courts in holding government accountable through (a) legislation clarifying the rules of procedure in the judicial review of administrative acts; (b) strengthening the system for legal aid, in particular free consultations; and (c) studies of the variety of institutions handling complaints against officials.

4.3   Develop and approve legislation to fill existing gaps in the jurisdiction of the courts to void certain kinds of normative acts and bureaucratic regulations and ensure that some court is empowered to deal with any and all legal norms that violate the Constitution of the Russian Federation.

4.4   Improve and regularize financial support for the institutions of the judicial community—the Congress of Judges, the Council of Judges, the Supreme Judicial Qualification Commission, and similar bodies in the subjects of the Federation.

4.5   Establish and support, probably within the new Academy of Justice, a research center on the judiciary and the administration of justice.

Notes

1. For a study of the development of the law and problems in its administration, see Todd S. Foglesong, "Judges versus Bureaucrats: Suing the State in Russia Under the Old and New Regimes," paper presented at the annual meeting of the American Association for the Advancement of Slavic Studies, Boston, MA, November 1996.

2. Data cited in the text and in Table 4.1 come from: "Rabota sudov RF po rassmotreniiu grazhdanskikh del (pervoe polugodie 1997 goda)," *Rossiiskaia iustitsiia*, 1998, No. 1, p. 51; "Rabota sudov Rossiiskoi Federatsii v 1997 godu," *Rossiiskaia iustitsiia*, 1998, No. 7, pp. 55-58; "Spravka o rabote sudov Rossiiskoi Federatsii za 1998 god." Also, between 1993 and 1997 there was a four-fold increase in the number of suits where a juridical entity contested state action in arbitration courts. Kathryn Hendley, "Commercial Litigation in Post-Soviet Russia: Temporal and Regional Patterns," *Post-Soviet Geography and Economics*, Vol. 39, No. 7, 1998, pp. 379-98.

3. For a discussion of problems of regulating the administration of electoral law in Russian regions, see S. Kniazev, "Primenenie zakonodatelstva o vyborakh v sub'ektakh RF," *Rossiiskaia iustitsiia*, 1997, No. 10, pp. 50-52, and L. Kiseleva, "Podvedomstvennost' del o zashchite izbiratel'nykh prav grazhdan," *Rossiiskaia iustitsiia*, 1998, No. 9, pp. 25-26. For the Supreme Court's explanation of the jurisdiction of courts in disputes about elections to the Federal Assembly, see "O nekotorykh voprosakh primeneniia sudami norm izbiratel'nogo prava pri razresheniia sporov, sviazannykh s provedeniem vyborov deputatov gosudarstvennoi dumy federal'nogo sobraniie RF," *Biulleten' Verkhovnogo Suda RF*, 1998, No. 1. For reports of Supreme Court rulings affecting the candidates and conduct of the Presidential elections of 1996 see *Izvestiia*, 13 April and 19 April 1996, p. 1.

4. For the report of the conflict between the Governor and Chief Judge of Ryazan, see "Kak possorilsia gubernator s oblastnym sudei," *Nezavisimaia gazeta*, 13 Nov. 1997, p. 6.

5. "Obzhalovaniiu podlezhit...", *Rossiiskie vesti*, 25 May 1993, p. 6.

6. For reports of important court rulings against local government interests in Vladivostok and Krasnodar, see *Izvestiia*, 20 Dec. 1996, p. 2, and *Izvestiia*, 24 Dec. 1996, p. 2. For a ruling in favor of the city government of Irkutsk in a dispute with both the regional legislature and executive, see "Sudebnaia vlast' v Rossii," in *Gosudarstvo i pravo*, 1996, No. 2, pp. 1-4.

7. For discussions of the Procuracy's and President's role in the resolution of such disputes, see A. Boikov, A. Skuratov, and A. Sukharev, "Prestuplenie i nakazanie," *Rossiiskaia gazeta*, 19 Jan.1994, p. 1; Iurii Skuratov, "Prokuratura zashchishaet prava i svobody grazhdan," *ibid.*, 18 Feb. 1997, p. 7; Foglesong, "Judges versus Bureaucrats."

8. For a discussion of the problem of determining jurisdiction in such cases, see E. Uksusova, "Osparivanie zakonnosti normativnykh aktov v sudakh obshchei iurisdiktsii," *Rossiiskaia iustitsiia*, 1998, No. 8, pp. 43-44, and L. Kiseleva, "Podvedomstvennost' del o zashchite izbiratel'nykh prav grazhdan," *Rossiiskaia iustitsiia*, 1998, No. 9, pp. 25-26.

9. O. Zhuravleva, "Obzhalovanie v sud nezakonnykh deistvii i reshenii: kak povysit ego effektivnost," *Rossiiskaia iustitsiia*, 1998, No. 1, pp. 25-27.

10. There has been an increase in the publication of major cases of citizens suing state institutions in *Rossiiskaia iustitsiia*, (see "Grazhdanin Minin protiv Pravitel'stva RF," 1998, No. 9, pp. 59-61, and "Grazhdanin Erokhin protiv Sberbanka," 1998, No. 8, pp. 59-61) and on the Russian Supreme Court's Web site. See the reports of decisions decided by the Court's Civil Division (under the rubric "Sud pervoi instantsii"), www.supcourt.ru.

11. Comparative experience suggests that members of the public turn to courts in new ways only when they receive help from public organizations that mobilize law. Charles Epp, *The Rights Revolution: Lawyers, Activists, and Supreme Courts in Comparative Perspective* (Chicago, 1998).

12. For a recent analysis of all forms of legal aid in England, see Jeremy Cooper, "English Legal Services: A Tale of Diminishing Marginal Returns," *Maryland Journal of Contemporary Legal Issues*, Vol. 5, No. 2, 1994, pp. 247-69.

13. For a recent call for such collective deliberation by a Russian scholar, see Iu. Tikhomirov, "Administrativnoe sudoproizvodstvo v Rossii: perspektivy razvitiia," *Rossiiskaia iustitsiia*, 1998, No. 8, pp. 35-37.

14. Todd Foglesong, "*Habeas Corpus* or 'Who Has the Body?' Judicial Review of Arrest and Detention in Russia," *Wisconsin International Law Journal*, Vol. 14, No. 3, April 1996, pp. 541-78. The data in Table 4.2 come from this article and from the Supreme Court's Department of Statistics.

15. *Ibid.* It should be noted that in no case did the federal government object to or attempt to curb or punish such efforts to undermine the law of *habeas corpus*.

16. A brief account of this development is given in Peter H. Solomon, Jr., "The Persistence of Judicial Reform in Russia," *East European Constitutional Review*, Vol. 6, No. 4, Fall 1997, pp. 51-52. See also A. Larin, "Nelzia ogranichivat pravo sud'i nemedlenno osvobodit' litso, lishennoe svobody nezakonno," *Rossiiskaia iustitsiia*, 1997, No. 1, pp. 15-16.

17. For details, see Foglesong, *"Habeas Corpus* or 'Who Has the Body?'"

18. V. F. Iakovlev, "Tendentsiia k povysheniiu roli arbitrazhnykh sudov sokhraniaetsia," *Vestnik Vysshego Arbitrazhnogo Suda RF*, 1999, No. 4, pp. 5-16.

19. Kathyrn Hendley, "Remaking an Institution: The Transition in Russia from State *Arbitrazh* to *Arbitrazh* Courts," *American Journal of Comparative Law*, Vol. 46, No. 1, Winter 1998, pp. 93-127.

20. "Osnovnye pokazateli raboty arbitrazhnykh sudov Rossiiskoi Federatsii v 1997-1998 godakh," *Vestnik Vysshego Arbitrazhnogo Suda RF*, 1999, No. 3, pp. 8-11; Iakovlev, "Tendentsiia k povysheniiu."

21. See, for example, Mikhail Nikolaev, "Sudebnyi pristav: On pristav k vazhnomu delu: okhaniat femidu i isponit ee reshenii" (Beseda s Valentinoi Martinovoi), *Iuridicheskii vestnik*, 1997, No. 22, p. 9; Iurii Senatorov, "Bronenostsy Stepanshina," *Kommersant-deili*, 19 Feb. 1998, p. 1. The data may well refer to the percentage of decisions referred to the judicial enforcers that the latter succeeded in implementing fully. The difficulties with implementing commercial decisions are dissected in Kathryn Hendley, "An Analysis of the Activities of Russian *Arbitrazh* Courts: 1992–1996" (A report submitted to the National Council on Soviet and East European Research, 1997), but Hendley does not trust any of the statistical estimates on rates of implementation because of the absence of record-keeping on this subject at the *arbitrazh* courts.

22. See Colin McC. Breeze, "Real Estate Transactions in Russia," *East European Constitutional Review*, Vol. 7, No. 1, Winter 1998, pp. 81-89.

23. "Spravka o rabote sudov...za 1998."

24. Pamela Jordan, "Russian Lawyers as Consumer Protection Advocates, 1992–1995," *The Parker School Journal of East European Law*, Vol. 3, Nos. 4-5, 1996, pp. 487-517. For the Supreme Court's most recent new rulings on court practice in this area of law, see "O vnesenii izmenenii i dopolnenii v postanovlenie plenuma verkhovnogo Suda RF ot 29 sentriabria 1994 g. N 7 'O praktike rassmotreniia sudami del o zashchite prav potrebitelei' (s izmeneniiami, vnesennymi postanovleniiami plenuma ot 25 aprelia 1995 g N 6 i ot 25 oktiabria 1996 g. N 10," *Biulleten' Verkhovnogo Suda RF*, 1997, No. 3. See also E. Kornilov, "Praktika primeneniia zakonodatelstva o pravakh potrebitelei," *Rossiiskaia iustitsiia*, 1998, No. 8, pp. 13-14.

25. In 1997, courts handled more than 8,500 libel suits. For a discussion of the Russian law of libel, see Peter Krug, "Civil Defamation Law and the Press in Russia: Private and Public Interests, The 1995 Civil Code, and the Constitution," *Cardozo Arts and Entertainment Law Journal*, Vol. 13, No. 3, 1995, pp. 847-79, and Vol. 14, No. 2, 1996, pp. 297-342. For a discussion of libel law from the perspective of Russian legal journalists, see "Kak slovo nashe otzovetsia," *Rossiiskaia iustitsiia*, 1998, No. 6, pp. 45-47.

26. "Spravka o rabote sudov...za 1998."

27. See, for example, Jodi Finkel, "The Politics of Mexico's 1994 Judicial Reform," paper presented at the annual meeting of the Latin American Studies Association, Guadalajara, Mexico, 16-19 April 1997.

28. Even in its most controversial decision supporting the legality of degrees associated with the war in Chechnya, the court acted according to legal procedures and rendered a legally sound judgment. See William E. Pomeranz, "Judicial Review and the Russian Constitutional Court: The Chechen Case," *Review of Central and East European Law*, Vol. 23, No. 1, 1997, pp. 9-48.

29. "O nekotorykh voprosakh primeneniia sudami Konstitutsii Rossiiskoi Federatsii pri osushchestvlenii pravosudiia," Postanovlenie No. 8 Plenuma Verkhovogo Suda RF, *Biulleten Verkhovnogo Suda RF*, 1996, No. 1, pp. 3-6. For a comprehensive treatment of the Supreme Court's intervention into constitutionalism, see Peter Krug, "Departure from the Centralized Model: The Russian Supreme Court and Constitutional Control of Legislation," *Virginia Journal of International Law*, Vol. 37, No. 3, Spring 1997, pp. 725-87.

30. For a recent study of this practice, see Peter Maggs, "The Russian Courts and the Constitution," *Indiana International and Comparative Law Journal*, Vol. 8, No. 1, 1997, pp. 99-117; Marina Latysheva, "Vybor bez vybora: Pravo na alternativnyiu sluzhbu prizyvniki ostaivaiut na skamke podsudimykh," *Segodnia*, 10 Oct. 1998, p. 6.

31. "Postanovlenie Konstitutsionnogo Suda RF po delu o tolkovanii otdelnykh polozhenii statei 125, 126 i 127 Konstitutsii RF ot 16 iiuniia 1998," *Rossiiskaia gazeta*, 30 June 1998, pp. 5-6; Konstantin Katanian, "Sam sebe sudia: Konstitutsionnyi sud RF utochnil sobstvennye polonomochiia," *Nezavisimaia gazeta*, 17 June 1998, p. 3.

32. For a recent criticism of the ruling by the President of the Russian Legal Academy, see V. Ershov, "Priamoe primenenie Konstitutsii RF," *Rossiiskaia iustitsiia*, 1998, in two parts: No. 9, pp. 2-4, and No. 10, pp. 2-4.

33. For a recent discussion of judicial review of normative acts of subjects of the Federation by a judge of the Russian Supreme Court, see G. Zhilin, "Priznanie normativnykh aktov nedeistvitel'nymi," *Rossiiskaia iustitsiia*, 1998, No. 7, pp. 40-42.

34. Dmitrii Zharkov, "Proizvol chinovnikov uzakonen Konstitutsionnym sudom Rossii," *Kommersant-deili*, 17 June 1998, p. 2; *idem*, "Mantiia velichiia," *Kommersant'-vlast'*, 30 June 1998, pp. 21-22; "KS razobralsia s kompetentsiei sudov" (Beseda Maksima Zhukova s Tamaroi Morshchakovoi), *ibid.*, 19 June 1998, p. 2; "Zaiavlenie press-sluzhby Konstitutsionnogo Suda RF," *Rossiiskaia gazeta*, 15 July 1998, p. 5.

35. In 1997, all courts of general jurisdiction tried more than 3,000 cases of complaints about legislative acts. One-fifth of these cases pertained to electoral rights. Before the 1999 parliamentary elections the courts heard many more disputes relating to the elections.

36. "O vnesenii v Gosudarstvennuiu Dumu Federalnogo Sobraniia RF proekt Federalnyi zakon 'O vnesenii izmenenii v statiiu 116 Grazhdansko-Protsessualnogo Kodeksa RSFSR'," Postanovlenie Plenuma Verkhovnogo Suda ot 15 ianvaria 1998 goda, No. 2. (On Web site of the Supreme Court: www. supcourt. ru.)

37. In September 1998, already two-and-a-half-months after the Constitutional Court's ruling, a panel of the Russian Supreme Court declared null and void a resolution of the government that introduced an extra tax to support the pension fund (a resolution from late July). Since the resolution was of a normative character, the Supreme Court appeared to be in direct violation of the ruling of its constitutional counterpart. Natalia Filippov, "Verkhovnyi sud otmenil novyi pensionnyi sbor," *Kommersant-deili,* 3 Sept. 1998, p. 2.

38. It now appears that a de facto division of authority has settled into place, with the Supreme Court policing constitutionality of legislation adopted by the subjects of the Federation, and the Constitutional Court maintaining its monopoly of constitutional control of the federal government. For an initial assessment of this implicit settlement between the two courts, see Peter Krug, "The Relationship Between the Russian Federation Supreme Court and the Lower Courts of General Jurisdiction," paper presented to the annual meeting of the American Association for the Advancement of Slavic Studies, St. Louis, Missouri, 19 Nov. 1999. For a Russian account of this conflict by a judge of the Karelian Constitutional Court, see A. Kinner, "Konstitutsionnoe sudoproizvodstvo nuzhdaetsia v unifikatsii," *Rossiiskaia iustitsiia,* 1999, No. 8, pp. 18-20.

39. In April 1998 one of the authors of this report attended a conference of judges from the constitutional/charter courts of the subjects.

40. See "Uchrezhden Sovet konstitutsionnykh (ustavnyk) sudov," *Rossiiskaia iustitsiia,* 1998, No. 7, p. 54.

41. Konstantin Katanian, "KS protiv vsekh ostalnykh sudov," *Nezavisimaia gazeta,* 13 Feb. 1996, p. 2.

42. "O merakh po realizatsii postanovleniia Konstitutsionnogo Suda RF ot 24 ianvaria 1997 g. No.1-P po delu o proverke konstitutsionnogo zakona Udmurtskoi Respubliki ot 17 apreliia 1996 g. 'O sisteme gosudarstvennoi vlasti v Udmurtskoi Respubliki'," *Rossiiskaia gazeta,* 12 March 1997, p. 1.

43. For example, a recent ruling of the Presidium of the Council of Judges affirmed the right of regional councils of judges to "draw the attention of" individual judges to "shortcomings" in their work and to convene meetings of the local judicial community to discuss such matters. See "O kompetentsii Soveta sudei sub"ekta Federatsii," 12 Feb. 1997.

44. The President of Russia also solicits nominations from the Congress before recommending to the Council of the Federation new members to the Constitutional Court.

45. Presidential decrees and government resolutions benefitting judges or courts are often issued shortly after (or occasionally before) a meeting of the Congress. For example, on the eve of the First Congress of Judges in October 1991, Yeltsin issued a decree ordering local governments to transfer buildings owned or occupied by district Party organizations to the courts. On 2 December 1996, one day before the convening of the "extraordinary" Fourth Congress, Yeltsin issued another decree ordering the payment of overdue court budget and other benefits for the courts. See "Ukaz Prezidenta Rossiiskoi Federatsii, no. 1612

ot 2 dekabria 1996 g. 'O nekotorykh merakh po stabilizatsii polozheniia v sudebnoi sistem Rossiskoi Federatsii', " *Sbornik normativnykh aktov o sude i status sudei Rossiiskoi Federatsii* (Moscow 1997), pp. 93-95.

46. A draft law on the bodies of the judicial community specifies the responsibility for financial and organizational support for each of them. It anticipates financial support from both the federal budget and other sources. "Ob organakh sudeiskogo soobshchestva v Rossiiskoi Federatsii," Proekt federalnyi zakon (n.d., 1997), article 44.

47. Some of the difficulties with the new, but impractical, Criminal Code of 1996 might have been avoided had the Council given that document more than a cursory review. See Todd S. Foglesong, "Introducing the New Criminal Code in Russia: Nations of Justice versus Rules of Law," paper presented at the annual meeting of the American Association for the Advancement of Slavic Studies, Seattle, WA, Nov. 1997.

48. Such access could be obtained, for example, by making public hearings on legislation mandatory, or by encouraging openness in the work of the Duma's Committee on legislation.

49. On the Presidential Council for the Improvement of the Adminstration of Justice (formerly the Council on Judicial Reform), see Vladimir Tumanov, "Ne za a rassudit'!" *Iuridicheskii vestnik*, 1998, No. 5, p. 8; "Plan raboty Soveta pri Prezidente Rossiiskoi Federatsii po voprosam sovershenstvovaniia pravosudiia na 1998 god," *Rossiiskaia iustitsiia*, 1998, No. 4, p. 52. Note that in 1997 the Presidential Council was provided with a staff of 14, after previously operating with none.

50. William M. Reisinger, et al., "Russians and the Legal System: Mass Views and Behaviour in the 1990s," *Journal of Communist Sudies and Transition Politics*, Vol. 13, No. 3, Sept.1997, esp. pp. 32-35; I. B. Mikhailovskaia, et al., *Prava cheloveka i sotsialno-politicheskie protsessy v postkommunistichestkoi Rossii* (Moscow: Proektnaia gruppa po pravam cheloveka, 1997), esp. pp. 58-60, 76-77.

51. "Burston-Marsteller Interim Report on Public Legal Awareness and Mass Legal Education to the World Bank and the Russian Federation Main State Administration" (4 Oct. 1996).

52. M. Mironov, "President's Mailbag," *Rossiiskaia gazeta*, 27 Jan. 1998, pp. 1-2, 7.

53. A. K. Simonov, ed., *Sredstva massovoi informatsii i sudebnaia vlast v Rossii (problemy vzaimodeistviia)* (Moscow: Fond zashchity glasnosti, 1998), part 4. The survey was conducted and analyzed by the experienced and skillful students of public opinion and the administration of justice, A. R. Ratinov and G. Kh. Efremova. Based at the Procuracy Institute, they have conducted surveys of this kind for more than twenty-five years, but as a rule the results were either confined to limited-access reports or published in small editions by the Institute.

54. F. Kravchenko, "Presumptsiia nevinovnosti v svete gazetnykh i zhurnalnykh publikatsii," *Rossiiskaia iustitsiia*, 1997, No. 10, pp. 26-27. Incautious reporting has also landed several journalists in court, as respondents in civil suits launched by offended judges. Some of these conflicts were discussed at the conference "Honor and Good Name: A Conflict Between Journalism and Juris-

prudence," organized by the Foundation for the Defense of Glasnost.

55. We are pleased to take note of plans for the publication and broad distribution by the publisher Spark of a new (or revived and improved) journal, *Biulleten Ministerstva iustitsii Rossiiskoi Federatsii.* See "O Biulletene Ministerstva iustitsii Rossiiskoi Federatsii," Prikaz Ministerstva iustitsii Rf ot 4 marta 1998, No. 25. As soon as the new research center/institute on the administration of justice becomes viable, it should establish its own periodical—say, quarterly collections of articles on courts and judicial practice.

56. "Otchet 'Analyz politiki televeshchaniia, perspektivy sotrudnichestva s televisionnymi i radioperedachami i perspektivy sozdaniia sobstvennoi televisionni produktsii v ramkakh proekta 'Pravovaia kultura',"(Moscow, Jan. 1998).

57. See *Sudebnye novosti: Obozrenie dlia SMI, vlasti i praktikuiushchikh iuristov,* 1998, No. 1 (June), edited by Valerii Rudnev, and founded by the Guild of Court Reporters and the information-publishing company "Moskovskie Novosti."

58. On the projects promoted by the Russian Foundation for Legal Reforms, see its information bulletin—Proekt Rossiiskogo fonda pravovykh reform, *Informatsionnyi biulleten* (Feb. 1998). The foundation follows the practice (perhaps copied from some Western foundations) of developing program guidelines and then soliciting applications from private actors and NGOs. The guidelines identify as targets for projects themes relating to legal education (textbooks, libraries, innovative teaching), legal culture (television, journals, information about law), court reform (studies of judicial practice, seminars for judges), alternative dispute resolution, and the improvement of the distribution of legal information.

59. See K. Katanian, "Sudebnaia reforma: ne vnutritsekhovoe delo," *Nezavisimaia gazeta,* 24 Feb. 1998, p. 3.

60. See, for example, the report "Sud v zhizni Rossiian," prepared by the Public Opinion Foundation, on its web site: www.fom.ru.

5

Staffing the Courts:
Recruitment and Training

The quality of justice, as well as its public reputation, depends on the character of the judges who administer it. This is especially so in countries (like Russia) where the contact between courts and the population, in both criminal and civil trials, is not mediated to any great extent by lawyers. In Russia, judges are often the first and sometimes only point of contact between individuals and the machinery of justice. "Cadres," one might say, therefore determine much if not most of the meaning of justice. Unfortunately for Russia, however, cadres are the Achilles heel of the judicial system. Especially in the post-Soviet period, Russia has had difficulty staffing its courts with a large and reliable corps of highly-qualified jurists.

The Russian Federation has approximately 15,000 posts for judges, most of whose occupants pursue careers in the judiciary. There are, however, some 1,500 vacant judicial posts; that is, one-tenth of the "personnel units" allotted the judiciary remain unfilled (Tables 5.1–5.3[1]). One reason is that since 1992 candidates for judgeships must have five years of prior legal experience, and it may be difficult for chairmen of courts to find persons with this credential.[2] Further, some cynics claim that the vacancies result from a purported "self-interest" of the judiciary in not filling the posts; with vacancies, it has been suggested, the wage bill apportioned by the Ministry of Justice can be divided up among the corps more favorably for stalwart judges.[3] But neither of these factors represents the underlying cause of the vacancies, for understaffing in the courts was a chronic problem in Soviet Russia. Not only does the problem predate the requirements of five years of legal experience, but it also has deeper roots than perverse provisions for paying salaries. The main reason for vacancies, rather, is that meting out justice in Russia was never and still is not a highly esteemed line of work. Working as a judge is neither a venerated form of public service nor a stepping stone to political power.

TABLE 5.1   Turnover of Judges and Vacancies, all courts, as of 1 January 1998

	Total*	District Courts	"Regional" Courts**
No. of Judicial Posts	15,521	12,700	2,821
No. of Positions Filled	14,352	11,749	2,603
No. of Vacancies	1,169	951	218
No. of New Hires	1,161	956	205
No. of Departures	1,047	876	171

* does not include 115 judges on Russian Supreme Court
** includes oblast, krai, and republican courts.

TABLE 5.2   Turnover and Vacancies in District Courts, by position (in 1997)

	Total	Chairmen	Deputy Chairmen	Judges
No. of Judicial Posts	12,000	2,440	698	9,562
No. of Positions Filled	11,749	2,363	592	8,794
No. of Vacancies	951	77	106	768
No. of New Hires	956	135	73	748
No. of Departures	876	186	66	624

TABLE 5.3   Turnover and Vacancies in Regional Courts, by position (in 1997)

	Total	Chairmen	Deputy Chairmen	Chairmen of Kollegii	Judges
No. of Judicial Posts	2,821	87	220	49	2,514
No. of Positions Filled	2,603	86	206	42	2,311
No. of Vacancies	218	1	14	7	203
No. of New Hires	205	1	10	2	194
No. of Departures	171	3	14	0	154

In addition, judges tend to be young (in their thirties or early forties) and relatively new to the job–especially those serving on the district courts.

TABLE 5.4   Age of Judges, all courts

	Total (No./ Percentage)	Regional Courts	District Courts
25 - 29 years	396 / 2.7%	n/a	396 / 3.3%
30 - 49 years	11,251 / 77.8	n/a	9,394 /79.4
50 - 64 years	2,350 / 15.8	n/a	1,644 /13.9
65 - 70 years	143 / 1.0	n/a	88 / 0.7
Pension Age	733 / 5.1	10/ 12.0	463 / 3.9

TABLE 5.5   Age of Judges, by position, District Courts

	Total No./ Percentage	Chairmen	Deputy Chairmen	Judges
25 - 29 years	396 / 3.3%	8 / 3.4%	2 / 0.3%	386 / 4.3%
30 - 49 years	9,394 /79.4	1,635 /70.3	485 /80.0	7,274 /81.8
50 - 64 years	1,644 /13.9	n/a	n/a	896 /10.1
65 - 70 years	88 / 0.7	n/a	n/a	32 / .35
Pension Age	463 / 3.9	192 / 8.3	39 / 6.4	233 / 2.6

TABLE 5.6   Experience (*stazh*) of Judges, all courts (in 1997)

	Total No. / Percentage	Regional Courts	District Courts
No. of Judges	14, 457	2,629	11,828
Less than 3 years	3,154 / 21.8%	134 / 5.1%	3,020 / 25.5%
Less than 10 years	5,760 / 39.8	650 / 24.7	5,110 / 43.2
Less than 20 years	4190 / 29.0	1,208 / 45.9	2,982 / 25.2
More than 20 years	1503 / 10.4	647 / 24.6	856 / 7.2

TABLE 5.7   Experience of Judges, by position, District Courts

	Total No. / Percentage	Chairmen	Deputy Chairmen	Judges
No. of judges	11,828	2,327	606	8,995
Less than 3 years	3,020 / 25.5%	135 / 5.8%	21 / 3.5%	2,864 / 32.2%
Less than 10 years	5,110 / 43.2	731 / 31.4	251 / 41.4	4,128 / 46.4
Less than 20 years	2,982 / 25.2	1,208 / 45.9	262 / 43.2	1,673 / 18.8
More than 20 years	856 / 7.2	425 / 18.3	75 / 12.4	356 / 4.0

TABLE 5.8   Experience of Judges, by position, Regional Courts

	Total No. / Percentage	Chairmen	Deputy Chairmen	Judges
No. of judges	2,629	83	204	2,342
Less than 3 years	134 / 5.1%	0	1 / .5%	133 / 5.7%
Less than 10 years	650 / 24.7	7 / 8.4	17 / 8.3	626 / 26.7
Less than 20 years	1,208 / 45.9	33 / 39.8	88 / 43.1	1,087 / 46.4
More than 20 years	647 / 24.6	41 / 49.3	96 / 47.1	510 / 21.7

The judiciary's lack of prestige means that the profile of jurists ready to become judges is less than ideal. Put simply, the Russian judiciary is still not an elite.[4] Indeed, there is a curious form of "natural selection" in staffing the courts. Because courts do not attract the best and brightest jurists from premier law faculties at leading universities, many "new" judges come from the ranks of former police officers, retired judges, and jurists unable to obtain work in the procuracy or bar (see Tables 5.9 and 5.10). Almost 60 percent of judges today are women, many of whom welcomed the secure jobs and benefits supplied to judges. The archetypical judge, according to a Supreme Court report, is now a middle-aged woman with a correspondence course or night-school law degree.[4] Especially in a country where the "feminization" of a profession connotes powerlessness, such a cadre of public officials will not inspire or increase respect for courts and justice.

TABLE 5.9   Professional Background of New District Court Judges (in 1997)

Prior Employment	No. and Percentage of Judges Appointed (total no. = 752)
Judges*	157 / 21.0
Court assistants / consultants	56 / 7.5
Secretaries**	11 / 1.5
Enforcers (*ispolniteli*)	9 / 1.2
Procurators***	128 / 17.3
MVD****	115 / 15.5
Bar	83 / 11.0
Notaries	5 / 1.0
Jurisconsults	80 / 11.0
Teachers and Jurists from State Organs	96 / 13.0

* some of these judges are being reappointed (that is, after the expiration of a probationary appointment), but most are judges moving laterally within the judiciary—that is, to a vacant post, usually within the same region.
** includes "trial secretaries" (*sekretari sudebnykh zasedanii*) and court clerical staff.
*** includes investigators, procurators, and their assistants.
**** mainly investigators
NB: approximately 90 percent of newly appointed regional court judges come from the ranks of district court judges.

TABLE 5.10 Professional Background of New District Court Judges, 1995–1997*

Prior Employment	1997 (%)	1996 (%)	1995 (%)	1994-1995 (combined %)
Judges	21.0	15.0	15.0	19.0
Court assistants / consultants	8.0	11.0	11.0	8.0
Secretaries and Enforcers (*ispolniteli*)	3.0	3.0	4.0	3.0
Procuracy Workers	17.0	20.0	14.0	14.0
MVD Employees	16.0	17.0	11.0	11.0
Advocates	11.0	9.0	12.0	11.0
Notaries	1.0	1.0	1.0	2.0
Jurisconsults	11.0	13.0	19.0	16.0
Teachers and Jurists from State Organs	13.0	12.0	10.0	6.0

* See notes to Table 5.9.

There are signs, however, that the attractiveness of judicial positions is improving. One can discern in reports from the Supreme Judicial Qualification Commission (discussed in Chapter 3) the emergence of competition for vacancies as well as an increase in the standards against which judicial candidates are evaluated. Whereas in 1996, only 9 percent of candidates who met the formal requirements for a judicial posting were nevertheless deemed unfit and rejected by a local qualification commission, in 1997, 13 percent of aspiring judges were refused.[5] Also encouraging is the fact that judges are now actively competing for promotion to the leading posts in the judiciary. In some cases, as many as fifteen judges have campaigned for the position of Chairman of a Regional Court.[6] This information suggests that, at least among its own members, the judiciary is becoming more important and the profession more appealing. Nonetheless, any major change in the attractiveness of judgeships and the quality of new judges will require special efforts.

In order to staff the courts with highly qualified and well-trained jurists, Russia must do three things: first, improve both the attractiveness of judicial careers and the mechanisms of recruiting judges; second, develop the legal education and special preparation of future judges; and third, enhance the access of new and veteran judges alike to legal materials and additional training.

One way to accomplish most of these tasks is through the establishment of a special school for the training and retraining of judges, something along the lines of the École Nationale de la Magistrature in Bordeaux, France, the model followed by many European countries.[7] In fact, top judges in Russia have sought the creation of a Russian school for judges since 1995, and in spring 1998 the chairman of the Supreme Court of the Russian Federation, Viacheslav Lebedev, believed that he had achieved success. Drafted in December 1997, the presidential edict establishing an Academy of Justice was signed on 11 May 1998.[8] The plans for the Academy are broad and ambitious. It is to include not only significant mandatory training for all new judges (approximately 750 per year), but also an expanded package of retraining programs for judges (until now handled by the Legal Academy of the Ministry of Justice) and a research institute on the administration of justice, complete with a data base on court decisions.[9] A separate line for the academy is to appear in the 1999 federal budget. It is important that the federal government not renege on the promises of the President.

The establishment of an Academy of Justice in Moscow would greatly help the development of a competent and respected corps of judges, and we shall offer suggestions for its various activities in this section. We now turn to the issues of judicial recruitment, training of new judges, and aids for judges already on the bench. Finally, we will say a few words about the recruitment and training of justices of the peace—a separate, but important topic.

Judicial Recruitment

Improving the recruitment of new judges can be accomplished by improving the package of compensation to judges and devising a variety of measures to encourage good law students to seek careers as judges. Even with recent pay raises judges in Russia are not paid well, and many jurists avoid judicial careers for financial reasons. The levels of remuneration for successful advocates and other jurists in private practice, by contrast, greatly exceed those of judges. On the other hand, the salaries of judges are now comparable to those of other state legal professions, like procurators, although fluctuations temporarily produce significant differences.

The compensation of judges, however, includes much more than basic salaries. It includes an assortment of supplementary payments, perks, and benefits, not to speak of security of tenure. The sum total of all of these items may well put judges ahead of their colleagues in the procuracy and police (though they, too, receive some extras) and may even prove attractive to many potential recruits. But the system of extra payments and benefits is so complicated that many potential recruits may not even be aware of all of them or their total impact. Thus, the Law on the Status of Judges conferred on judges provisions for "life-time support upon retirement" (i.e., more than an ordinary pension) and priority access to housing.[10] Judges also receive a slew of salary "supplements" (*doplaty*) and "additions" (*nadbavki*), as well as monthly and quarterly "bonuses" (*premii*), awards for "rank" and occasional "assistance," and even extra money for food purchases, which, in the aggregate, enhance their income consierably. In addition, a bewildering array of privileges has been tacked on to judicial service, including the right to a 50 percent cut in housing costs and an exemption from federal income tax.[11] Although similar benefits and privileges are accorded to all civil servants in Russia, and they do sometimes help to attract new judges, the procedure for paying judges has become ridiculously bureaucratic. Calculating the sum of money due an individual judge is now very time consuming, as well as the source of considerable legal dispute.[12] As in other countries, the sight of judges paying so much attention to themselves, and the public litigation of judicial salaries in particular, brings the courts into disrepute. More worrisome, the procedures for allocating bonuses leave room for adverse influence on judges' welfare on the part of judicial administrators.[13]

In our view, the system of remunerating judges should be simplified, and the number of incremental additions to their income sharply curtailed. Judges should simply receive an adequate salary, indexed to inflation, with modest annual increases, and one salary supplement for improvements in "rank." Such an arrangement would have the double benefit of cutting down the demeaning struggles of judges to obtain their due and of raising the visible salaries of judges to more attractive, and appropriate, levels.

Apart from raising the compensation of judges and making it simple and more transparent, the recruitment of future judges may be encouraged through a series of measures connected to basic legal education. One of these consists of encouraging law students to study subjects closely related to the work of judges. This represents a challenge. For while all students who graduate with a five-year degree in "jurisprudence" from state universities are exposed to such topics as forensic medicine, forensic psychiatry, and judicial statistics, and those who specialize in criminal or state law take courses such as "procuratorial supervision" and "court organization," no law schools have curricula specifically designed for future judges.[14] The plan to create an Academy of Justice, which will both educate jurists and train judges, is a salutary response to the problem. But the Academy's capacity to teach and train will be dependent on federal funding, and thus may fall well short of what is needed. It is therefore advisable for Russia to consider interim solutions and future supplements to the Academy's educational reach.

One possibility is for Russia to create special "judicial tracks" in law schools. Both the Procuracy and the Ministry of Internal Affairs (MVD) have secured agreements of this nature in order to help them overcome the dearth of jurists willing to make a career in the procuracy or police.[15] While judicial tracks cannot be established within law faculties at all universities, the Ministry of Justice or Judicial Department could sign special contracts with individual institutions of higher learning to establish feeder programs with highly practical curricula and thereby make more likely the selection of judicial career paths by some students.[16]

A second way is to create incentives for students to pursue the judicial track, or merely to specialize in such relevant subjects as criminal law and state law. This could be accomplished through the provision of "judiciary fellowships" or even "court loans for students." In Russia a number of corporations have established fellowships and special stipends for law school students who pledge to work for them upon completion of the degree. Were the judiciary to establish such systems of support, it would secure for itself more judges in the future. It would also improve the quality of these students' education. Even though most students do not pay tuition, the state's student stipends are ludicrously small, and almost all law school students are forced to work while they complete their education. Students receiving special aid from the judiciary would be free to spend more time studying the law in exchange for a promise of future service. Supported students who, upon completion of five years of work experience as a jurist, do not wish to work in the courts could repay the state for such fellowships.

A third way to attract jurists to a career in the courts before they complete law school is to establish higher paid and more interesting judicial internships. At present, each student who graduates with a five-year law degree must complete a short internship (*stazhirovka*) of one month in the Bar, Procuracy, MVD, and the courts (one per year during the last four years of education). In addition, each student must complete a three-month internship in the institution of his/her preference in the final year of education. It is important that students who select the courts for the three-month internship be paid well for their work and time. But it is even more important that they be treated well and with respect. They should, for example, be given audiences with leading judges and public officials during their internships, and become acquainted with the work of the judicial qualification commissions. Students who choose to intern with the courts should also be rewarded intellectually, for example, by having their honors theses published, and by being given non-monetary prizes and accolades (*zvaniia, pochety*, etc.)—which are highly valued in Russia—for exceptionally good work. Since internships constitute the first period of extensive contact with the courts for most jurists, it is imperative that they be a positive experience.

At present, the form and content of law school internships are not well regulated. All too often interns spend three months in the courts carrying out the judicial rubbish—such as typing decisions, filing papers, and taking down trial notes. This experience does not encourage students to pursue a judicial career. By contrast, students who experience the new power of the judiciary (discussed in Chapter 4) and witness the internal operation of higher level courts are more likely to seek a judicial post after gaining the requisite five years of experience. In short, while it is true that "money sings" in Russia—potential salaries play a large and often decisive role in career choices—it is also true that power pulls. It is thus imperative that the judiciary reorganize and revitalize the system of judicial interns. Since even law students in private universities must participate in internships, asserting control over the process could potentially increase the number of prospective judges.[17]

Training and Clerkships

The quality of new judges depends upon the panoply of their experiences before assuming office—their basic legal education, training for judgeships, and prior legal work.

Law school curricular reform in post-Soviet Russia has focused especially upon commercial law, but this is not the most important subject for the majority of aspiring judges. For them it is the teaching of criminal law, civil law (of which commercial is but one part), and public (especially administrative) law that matter most, and these fields have typically been construed in a narrow way, divorced from the social and political context. Law students in Russia need more exposure to the history and philosophy of law; comparative law (especially the background to procedural innovations being introduced into Russian practice, like jury trials and appeals); constitutionalism; and the sociology of legal institutions. The Russian legal curriculum would also benefit from more study of particular cases and issues in adjudication (as opposed to the formal law) and from the use of active and innovative teaching methods, including role playing, moot court, and the Socratic method. Clearly, there are opportunities for Western and Russian supporters of legal reform to help with the development of new teaching materials and the spread of new teaching methods, and the efforts in this direction of both the Central and East European Law Initiative (CEELI) and the Russian Foundation for Legal Reform deserve praise.[18]

As of the year 2000 new judges—that is, jurists who have passed the qualifying examinations and scrutiny of the judicial qualification commissions and then received approval of both the legislature of the subject of the Federation and the President of the Russian Federation—still receive little if any formal training. Preparation of newly appointed judges for the bench is organized chiefly by the chairmen of the district courts, and the nature of this preparation varies with local custom, the pending backlog of cases, and the style of the court chairs. Leading Russian judges have registered dissatisfaction with the inadequate and chaotic state of judicial preparation; and the idea of an Academy of Justice represents a direct response.[19] We strongly support the creation of the Academy, including a lengthy mandatory program of training for judges.

According to the current plans, the training for all new judges will take place in Moscow and last for an academic year. Certainly there are advantages to having all new judges prepared in the same place, and Moscow has the largest concentration of legal talent to take part in the process. A stint in Moscow might also familiarize new judges with the top courts and provide opportunities for exposing them to international dimensions of judicial work. But training all judges in Moscow might also prove expensive and hard to manage. It would be necessary to find accommodation for 300 judge-trainees at a time (if there were two six-month cycles per year); and also to pay expense allowances and travel costs, since local courts often lack the funds to support their judges' travel. The alternative of organizing the training of judges in a number of cities with strong law faculties, such as Ekaterinburg, Kazan, Saratov, and St. Petersburg, is available; but arguably those resources should be left available for use in a future training program for justices of the peace, when that institution is created. (As of the moment the branches of the Legal Academy of the Ministry of Justice train notaries, court secretaries, and judicial enforcers.) The judicial training program in Moscow should use as teachers not only academic jurists but also judges of long standing from the various capital city courts.

Designing the content of the training program for new judges at the Academy of Justice represents a special opportunity for innovation, in both the intellectual and practical aspects of the law. To begin, the program should contain exposure to the bases of higher law, including international pacts and covenants, rulings of the European Court, as well as theory of natural law and constitutional jurisprudence in Russia and other countries. Since these subjects do receive some coverage now in the three-week retraining courses offered to judges by the Legal Academy, they are likely to be part of the curriculum for new judges.[20] Another important subject is judicial ethics, a topic Supreme Court Chairman Lebedev considers obligatory for new judges. With the proposal of new legislation on ethics and judicial conduct and increased training for judges at the new Academy of Justice, there will be new opportunities for Western jurists to help their Russian colleagues develop the teaching of these subjects.[21]

There are as well many practical skills that could be taught, including the art of writing decisions. In this connection, new judges would benefit from studying controversial rulings that have received extensive treatment by higher judicial instances. They could follow the history of decisions modified or reversed on appeal, and compare them with decisions that were upheld, examining in detail so-called "judicial errors," thereby learning how to draft their own decisions to withstand later scrutiny by higher courts. Student judges might also be asked to conduct analyses of recent practice in a particular area of law for this purpose. Future judges will also benefit from learning about the local cultures associated with particular professional roles. In this regard, the Academy's program could contain a variety of internships, not only with judges but also with MVD investigators, district procurators, and advocates' consultation bureaux.[22]

A final way to help prepare jurists to serve as judges is to have them work as a clerk for a judge. Clerkships already exist in Russia on an experimental basis (the Ministry of Justice budget has provision for 250 such posts), but this is only a start.[23] Clerkships could be made available to two pools of persons—graduates of the new Academy of Justice who have not yet completed the mandatory five years of legal work and are therefore ineligible to work as judges, and other jurists interested eventually in becoming judges. It is important that clerkships be attractive posts, well-paid, and provide opportunities for some substantial and interesting legal work. One could envisage multi-year clerkships that would include not only rendering assistance to a judge but also stints working as legal defenders (staff counsel attached to the court, perhaps).

Informing and Retraining Judges

The Soviet Union lacked a decent system of disseminating legal information. Even codes and commentaries were printed in limited editions that were not available to judges working in remote locations. In post-Soviet Russia the need for all jurists, including judges, to have access to legal information has multiplied exponentially because of the high volume of new legislation and decrees and the revolutionary character of socio-economic change. Lawyers with financial means can take advantage both of the many new (but often expensive) legal publications from private publishing firms and of electronic databases of legislation and legal materials. But most judges, especially those far from Moscow, do not have access to these materials. They should. A particularly worthwhile investment, by Russian or foreign benefactors, might focus upon (1) the purchase and dispatching to every judge or every courthouse complete lists of new legal publications and materials, some prepared especially for judges (such mailings are common practice in the courts in Canada); and (2) providing each and every courthouse with access to the various Russian electronic databases of legal materials. This would entail supplying computers, modems, and probably funds to pay for services; and perhaps some training in computer skills for judges. Certainly all new judges should be taught how to use the electronic databases on Russian laws while at the Academy of Justice.[24] This training might then stimulate comprehensive publication of Supreme Court decisions on its Web site, which is becoming an important source of both information about and prestige for the Court.[25]

Improving access to legal information would make judges feel connected to the world of law in the capital and enhance the quality of their work. In addition, various kinds of refresher courses, special lectures, and conferences also can play a role in keeping judges informed and engaged. The Legal Academy of the Ministry of Justice continues to offer three-week seminars of high quality to judges from around the country, but its capacity is limited and the average judge gets to attend one of these seminars once every fifteen years. The new Academy of Justice will, according to its designers, improve on this record, and offer more seminars to more judges more frequently. But this will represent only a start. It is vital to encourage the organization of meetings of judges in regional and republican capitals, not only in connection with the councils of judges, but also for conferences and lectures. In the Soviet Union, Party committees convened gatherings of judges, sometimes with other law enforcement officials, but in post-Soviet Russia there is a shortage of funds to support such gatherings. It would be useful to send jurists, scholars and practitioners alike, from Moscow to the remote regional centers, not only so that they can lecture to their colleagues but also so that they can gain an understanding of the realities of the administration of justice outside of the capital.

All of these ventures—improving the access of judges to legal information, expanding opportunities for refresher courses, and mounting regional or interregional conferences—will improve the self-esteem and satisfaction of judges, as well as their performance. It is important that further benefits be provided to veteran judges who choose to pursue long careers on the bench. These could include educational rewards (books, even trips abroad to foreign legal centers), a program for publishing the memoirs of judges and collections of their decisions, and the establishment of special societies for long-serving judges. Veteran judges might also appreciate the opportunity to make short-term, and reversible, lateral career moves, especially into work in the procuracy. In the Tsarist period such mobility was available, and it tended to soften inter-institutional rivalries.

Training Other Legal Officials

The work of the court system depends not only upon the quality of the actual judges but also upon that of a variety of other legal officials. These include court secretaries, the judicial enforcers, or, as they are now called, the bailiff-enforcers, notaries, and the new "registrars" of real estate transactions, all of whom now receive training in the branch units of the Legal Academy of the Ministry of Justice. The training of most of these figures could use upgrading and further investment. In addition, members of the new service of bailiffs designated to work at the courthouses and the soon-to-be established justices of the peace will also require training programs.

The justices of the peace represent an especially important challenge. The designers of these new "judgeships" envisage a corps of some 10,000 justices across Russia, once the full complement of justices of the peace has been established. Although they will—according to the version of the Law on Justices of the Peace finally adopted—possess legal education and have the five years of experience in legal work required of any new judge, almost all of the justices (unlike their colleagues on the district courts) will be entry-level judges. Yet, they will handle the greater volume, and perhaps also variety, of cases than judges of the district courts once all administrative and much of civil and criminal caseload has been transferred to the peace courts. Moreover, responsibility for appointing and training the new justices of the peace falls into the hands of regional governments, with discrepant financial resources. As a result, without contributions from the outside (either the federal government or funders outside the Russian Federation), many justices of the peace may start the work of adjudication without adequate training. The experience of Western countries (such as Canada, where justices of the peace are lay judges) suggests that the training and long-term education support for justices of the peace are major undertakings.[26] The mounting of a well-organized and funded training program for justices of the peace in one region would be a highly beneficial demonstration project for an outside funder, be it domestic or foreign.

Recommendations

5.1   Improve the recruitment of judges by: (a) simplifying the current system of rewards and ensuring that judges' salaries exceed those of procurators and police officials; (b) creating special judicial tracks in some law schools and supplying special stipends to future judges; (c) enhancing the work and rewards for student interns at the courts.

5.2   Revise the content of law school education to promote understanding of the socio-political context of law.

5.3   Establish a major compulsory training program for all new judges (presumably at the new Academy of Justice) and design that program to include innovations in both intellectual content and practical training.

5.4   Develop and expand the institution of clerkships (*pomoshch-nik sudu*), especially to employ graduates of the new Academy of Justice not yet eligible to work as judges.

5.5   Improve judges' access to legal information by (a) sending to all judges on a regular basis a selection of newly published books (codes, commentaries, treatises); and (b) providing each courthouse with a computer, modem, and access fees for the major databases of Russian legislation.

5.6   Stimulate and improve the work of all judges by (a) upgrading and expanding the refresher courses; and (b) organizing local conferences, seminars, and other events.

5.7   Upgrade the training of other justice officials (court secretaries, bailiff-enforcers), paying special attention to the soon to be created justices of the peace.

Notes

1. The source of data for these Tables and the rest of the Tables in this Chapter is the Department of Cadres, Russian Supreme Court.

2. See, for example, the discussion in A. Dementev, "O preddolzhnostnoi podgotovke sudei," *Rossiiskaia iustitsiia*, 1994, No. 8, p. 10.

3. See I. L. Petrukhin, "A khramu nuzhen remont," *Iuridicheskii vestnik*, 1996, No. 2, p. 5.

4. George Ginsburgs, "The Soviet Judicial Elite: Is It?" *Review of Socialist Law*, Vol. 11, 1985, pp. 293-311. Many senior judges complained recently that few candidates are willing to serve as judges after acquiring five years of legal expertise. "Soveshchanie-seminar s predsedateliami kvalifikatsionnykh kollegii sudei Rossiiskoi Federatsii, 24-28 noiabria 1997 (v pansionate 'Lesnye dali'; stenograficheskii otchet" (unpublished document).

4. Women also hold positions of authority in the courts, in 1997 representing 42.2% of district court chairmen. Women made up 3.5% of regional court chairs and 24.0% of their deputy chairs. See "A sud'i kto?" in *Ogonek*, 1996, No. 6, pp. 44-45. See also the review of court-staffing practices discussed at the President's Council on Judicial Reform on 10 October 1995. Reported in *Rossiiskaia iustitsiia*, 1996, No. 2, p. 5.

5. See "Sud'i chistiat svoi riady," *Rossiiskaia iustitsiia*, 1998, No. 1, p. 1; and K. Katanian, "Komu podkontrol'ny sudy?" *Nezavisimaia gazeta*, 23 Dec. 1997, p. 3. There appears to be considerable regional variation, however, in the choosiness of judicial qualification commissions. For more on the politics of judicial selection in Russia, see Todd Foglesong, "The Dynamics of Judicial (In)dependence in Russia," in Peter H. Russell and David O'Brien, eds., *Comparative Judicial Independence: Critical Assessments from Around the World* (forthcoming).

6. A. Zherebtsov, "Kodeksu chesti pridat' normativnyi kharakter," *Rossiiskaia iustitsiia*, 1997, No. 3, pp. 2-3, and "Povyshenie avtoriteta sudebnoi vlasti—glavnoe v rabote kvalifikatsionnykh kollegii sudei," *Rossiiskaia iustitsiia*, 1997, No. 8, pp. 6-8.

7. See Jacqueline Lucienne Lafon, "The Judicial Career in France: Theory and Practice under the Fifth Republic," *Judicature*, Vol. 75, No. 2, Aug.-Sept. 1991, pp. 97-106.

8. See A. Kamakin, "V Rossii sozidaetsia akademiia pravosudiia," *Nezavisimaia gazeta*, 13 May 1998, p. 2.

9. Dmitrii Sokolov, "Novoe pokolenie rossian budut sudit professionaly. Ikh obuchat v Akademii pravosudiia," *Obshchaia gazeta*, 16-22 April 1998, p. 2.

10. Since 1990, there have been several cases of jurists joining the judiciary solely in order to obtain housing, whereupon they promptly leave the corps. For the most recent case of such deceit, see "Sudia lishen polnomochii za obman," *Rossiiskaia iustitsiia*, 1998, No. 5, p. 54.

11. For the list of privileges associated with judicial postings, see "Federalnyi zakon ot 10 ianvaria 1996 'O dopolnitelnykh garantiiakh sotsialnoi zashchity sudei i rabotnikov apparatov sudov Rossiiskoi Federatsii'," *Sbornik normativnykh aktov o sude i statuse sudei RF* (Moscow, 1997), pp. 39-42.

12. The Presidium of the Council of Judges, with the assistance of the Supreme Court, recently published fabulously complicated "explanations" of the laws and statutory acts relating to the compensation of judges. See "V Sovete Sudei RF," *Rossiiskaia iustitsiia*, 1997, No. 11, pp. 56-58.

13. Wherever regional judicial departments were not fully operational, the justice administrations of the Ministry of Justice remained responsible, as they had been in the past, for paying out the wages of judges and determining their bonuses. See the remarks of Cherniavsky, the Director of the Judicial Department, at the 31 March 1998 meeting of the Council of Judges. "Protokol plenarnogo zasedaniia Soveta sudei Rossiiskoi Federatsii," 31 marta-3 aprelia 1998 goda, p. 4.

14. For recent discussions of curricular reforms in higher legal education, see B. N. Topornin, "Pravovaia reforma i razvitie vyshego iuridicheskogo obrazovaniia v Rossii," *Gosudarstvo i pravo*, 1996, No. 7, pp. 34-52; and I. L. Petrukhin, "Problemy iuridicheskogo obrazovaniia v Rossii," *Gosudarstvo i pravo*, 1996, No. 9, pp. 3-20.

15. N. Zaikin, "MGIuA gotovit kadry dlia prokuratury," Interviu s Olegom Kutafinom, *Zakonnost*, 1997, No. 6, pp. 24-28; Petrukhin, "Problemy," p. 1.

16. Topornin, "Pravovaia reforma."

17. There are strong indications that students enrolled in law school at private universities experience difficulty finding a suitable organizational host for the internship. See, for example, M. Kaz'mina, "Chtoby stat' nastoiashchim iuristom," *Rossiiskaia iustitsiia*, 1997, No. 12, p. 50.

18. V. Mazaev, "Iuridicheskomu obrazovaniiu—finantsovuiu podderzhku," *Rossiiskaia iustitsiia*, 1997, No. 10, p. 1.

19. A key promoter of a program to prepare new judges was a leading official in the Ministry of Justice, Albert Dementev. See his "O preddolzhnostnoi podgotovke kandidatov v sudi," and "Podgotovka kadrov—vykhod est," *Rossiiskaia iustitsiia*, 1996, No. 2, p. 4.

20. See the series of "Uchebno-tematicheskie plany zaniatii s sudiami," prepared by the Russian Legal Academy of the Ministry of Justice. Interview with the Vice-Rector of the Academy, Lidiia Alekseevna, April 1998.

21. A draft law on the organs of the judicial community is at present in line for consideration by the Duma's Committee on Legislation. See "Ob organakh sudeiskogo soobshchestva v Rossiiskoi Federatsii," Proekt federalnyi zakon (n.d., 1997).

22. Dementev, in "O preddolzhnostnoi podgotovki," urged the creation of such internships.

23. In some courts, prospective judges work as lay assessors; some of the time spent as a lay assessor counts toward the requirement of five years' experience working in a legal capacity.

24. For a full listing of Russian electronic databases on laws and legislation, see *Dostup k pravovoi informatsii: Spravochnik* (Moscow, 1998), a compilation of information on access to legal information produced under the auspices of the Russian Fund of Legal Reform. See also "Informatsionnye pravovye resursy Rossii/Legal Information Resources of Russia," a CD-Rom published by the State Duma (Moscow, 1998).

25. V. Koiliak, the Deputy Head of the Court's Department for Informatization, suggested that plans for comprehensive publication had been discussed by the Presidium of the Court in early 1998. Interview, 28 June 1998. For the Court's Web site, go to: www.supcourt.ru.

26. See "Education Plan for Justices of the Peace," produced by the Ontario Court of Justice (Provincial Division), December 1997.

PART THREE

Improving Performance

In the following three chapters we analyze ways of improving the performance of the administration of justice in Russia through the reform of procedural law and institutions other than the courts (those involved in the pre-trial phase of criminal cases and the implementation of civil judgments). Throughout we pay close attention to the merits and feasibility of a wide variety of proposals offered by Russian jurists, and we adopt moderate positions on most issues. This moderation reflects both the lessons of the introduction of radical reforms in other countries and a holistic approach to the study of Russian justice.

First, recent attempts in other countries to resolve domestic judicial crises through procedural borrowings and other legal imports have had mixed results. In some cases, reforms have been hard to implement and led to distortions in practice.[1] In others, the introduction of legal "transplants" has triggered allergic reactions by the host organism, sometimes with lethal consequences for the reform initiative.[2] Though the sociology of comparative law and justice is in its infancy, the considered opinion of most scholars is that law is not infinitely fungible, and judicial procedure is not "separately portable."[3] This received wisdom alone should urge caution among reformists in Russia who seek salvation in the adoption of foreign legal instruments.[4]

Second, our analysis is informed by an appreciation of the institutional politics implied by procedural arrangments in the administration of justice. Western studies of justice reform have revealed that the practical meaning of any procedure or institution (in civil and criminal justice) reflects the interests and needs of the officials who implement it; and that, as a rule, reforms do not get implemented properly unless they take those interests into account.[5] At the same time, it is a truism in criminology and the sociology of law that changes in one part of the legal process produce compensatory changes in other parts. Restricting the sentencing discretion of judges (say, through determinate sentencing), for example, gives the decisions about charges (and as a result, police and prosecutors) greater influence on the choice of punishment.[6] Likewise, curbing the right to appeal, or limiting an appellate court's power, places a greater burden on earlier stages of the process and may require improved discovery in civil and greater openness in the criminal pre-trial process. Russian reformers, we believe, have not fully recognized this dimension of the "bureaucratization of justice." It is imperative that its lessons be considered in the evaluation of reform proposals.

The case for moderation is all the more compelling because would-be reformers of the Russian courts are not a cohesive group. As the now cool relations among the authors of the radical Conception of Judicial Reform indicate, there are sharp cleavages in the debates over reform even within like-minded groups. The lack of solidarity among reformers, and poor dialogue across institutions and within draft legislation "working groups," is destructive, diluting the constituency for judicial reform. In our view these divisions rest to some extent on stereotypes about "inquisitorial" vs. "adversarial" norms of law and systems of justice. Proponents and detractors of reform proposals often justify their claims and positions by reference to "anglo-saxon" or "continental" legal systems, with little understanding of the porousness of such categories or appreciation of the diversity within the traditions that gave rise to them. For most comparative legal scholars, these categories, and especially terms such as "inquisitorialism" (*inkvizitsionnost'*) and "adversarialism" (*sostiazatelnost'*), are not particularly useful; in general, they are considered both inaccurate and anachronistic.[7] In the current Russian environment, they are harmful sobriquets, which serve only to polarize legal scholars and officials into closed schools of thought. Especially since the Russian judicial system is itself a hybrid, or mixed system (even *sui generis* according to some scholars), it behooves reformers to abandon the stiff lexicon of legal casuistry and adopt a more pragmatic and flexible approach to reform initiatives.

Notes

1. See William T. Pizzi and Luca Marafiotti, "The New Italian Code of Criminal Procedure: The Difficulties of Building an Adversarial Trial on a Civil Law Foundation," *Yale Journal of International Law*, Vol. 17, No. 1, 1992, pp. 1-40; Marco Fabri, "Theory Versus Practice of the Italian Criminal Justice Reform,"

Judicature, Vol. 77, No. 4, 1994, pp. 211-16. Also, Carlo Guarnieri, "Justice and Politics: The Italian Case in Comparative Perspective," *International and Comparative Law Review*, Vol. 4, No. 2 (1994), pp. 241-57.

2. On the difficulty of implementing French pre-trial procedure reforms, see Helen Trouille, "A Look at French Criminal Procedure," *Criminal Law Review*, Oct. 1994, pp. 735-44. More generally, see Richard Frase, "Comparative Criminal Justice as a Guide to American Law Reform," *California Law Review*, Vol. 78, No. 3, May 1990, pp. 539-683.

3. See, for example, the symposium on civil procedure reform in the Fall 1997 issue of *American Journal of Comparative Law*, Vol. 45, No. 4, especially the essays by Andreas Lowenfeld, "The Elements of Procedure: Are They Separately Portable?" pp. 649-55, and Mirjan Damaska, "The Uncertain Fate of Evidentiary Transplants: Anglo-American and Continental Experiments," pp. 839-52.

4. Gianmaria Ajani, "By Chance and Prestige: Legal Transplants in Russia and Eastern Europe," *American Journal of Comparative Law*, Vol. 43, No. 1, Winter 1995, pp. 93-117.

5. David Rothman, *Conscience and Convenience* (Boston, 1986); Richard Ericson, "The State and Criminal Justice Reform," in R. S. Ratner and John L. Mcmullen, eds., *State Control: Criminal Justice Politics in Canada* (Vancouver, 1987), pp. 21-37.

6. Daniel J. Freed, "Federal Sentencing in the Wake of Guidelines: Unacceptable limits on the Discretion of Sentencers," *Yale Law Journal*, Vol. 101, No. 8, June 1992, pp. 1681-1754; Celesta A. Albonetti, "Sentencing under the Federal Sentencing Guidelines: Effects of Defendant Characteristics, Guilty Pleas, Departures on Sentence Outcomes for Drug Offenses, 1991-1992," *Law and Society Review*, Vol. 31, No. 4, 1997, pp. 789-822.

7. See, for example, the discussion by Damaska, Langbein, Lempert, Nijboer, and Twining in the symposium on "new trends in criminal investigations and evidence," special issue of *Cardozo Journal of International and Comparative Law*, Vol. 5, No. 1, Spring 1997.

6

The Administration of Justice:
Simplification and Efficiency

The widening jurisdiction of the courts, discussed in Chapter 5, was matched by a rapid growth in the demand for judicial remedies. Between 1987 and 1997, the number of civil, criminal, and administrative cases heard by courts in Russia more than doubled. The growth in civil litigation, especially since 1994, has been dramatic, and was, possibly, a hopeful sign of a growth of public confidence in the courts (see Table 6.1[1]). But the judiciary has been overwhelmed by the new demand for its services. Delays and backlogs are now commonplace—especially in criminal cases. The inability of courts to ensure a speedy trial has damaged their fragile reputation at a most inopportune time.

As we shall see, several measures were taken by government authorities to improve the capacity of the courts, including the creation of more judicial posts and the endorsement of procedural simplifications. But as a rule these measures represented too little too late. Throughout the 1990s judges in Russia worked under extreme pressure, struggling to find ways of coping with an excess of work and insufficient resources, exacerbated by rigidities in legal requirements and unrealistic demands. Every so often, as the pressure became too much for some judges, a significant number chose to leave judicial posts, and the leaders of the judicial community spoke of a "crisis." Such crises occurred in 1989, 1992, 1995, and again in 1996–1997, when some judges threatened to strike.[2] At each of these junctures, the government reacted by improving the salaries or benefits of judges themselves, but not, as we have seen, by augmenting the funding of the courts and their operations.[3]

TABLE 6.1   Trends in Caseload, all types, all courts (1987-1997)

	No. of criminal cases	No. of civil cases	No. of administrative cases
1987	558,720	1,839,000	n/a
1990	535,311	1,658,640	1,163,865
1993	794,965	1,839,290	1,473,507
1994	987,025	2,006,810	1,860,125
1995	1,143,485	2,938,719	1,927,339
1996	1,219,451	3,043,681	1,923,002
1997	1,057,761	3,916,839	1,879,541

Apart from pressing for new funds, the leaders of the judicial community have responded to the frustration of their members by promoting a variety of reform measures, including simplifications in civil and criminal procedure and the establishment of justice of the peace courts. In this Chapter we examine some sources of pressure upon Russian judges in the 1990s and then evaluate responses to them, including measures already introduced and others under discussion. The responses consist of changes in both procedural law and judicial institutions.

Sources of Pressure

The primary causes of the pressure under which judges in Russia work are: first, the mismatch between caseloads and the number of judges; second, the complexity of new laws and court jurisdiction; and third, the inadequacy of staff and administrative support. The strain these factors place on courts is aggravated by basic features of the judicial process inherited from the Soviet period, which make it difficult for judges to cope with their situation. We discuss these various problems and sources of pressure in turn.

First, the dramatic rise in caseload that has occurred from the late 1980s has doubled the number of cases handled by the general courts, but the increase in demand for justice has not been met by a commensurate expansion in the capacity of courts to supply it. Although the number of judges working at the district level grew markedly between 1987 and 1994, there has been very little growth since 1994, the year of the greatest increase in the volume of civil litigation.[4] Consequently, the ratio of judges to cases in Russia today is far in excess of the "caseload norm" (*normy nagruzki*) established by a joint study and decree of the Ministry of Labor and Ministry of Justice (see Table 6.2).[5] It appears that, in order to meet the caseload norms for individual judges, a doubling in the overall number of judges would be required.[6] A cheaper and more feasible alternative, already on the political agenda, is the creation of justice of the peace courts. We return to this idea later in this Chapter.

TABLE 6.2   Caseload per judge, district courts (1990-1997)

	Average Number of Cases		
	Criminal	Civil	Administrative
1990	5.9	9.1	16.5
1993	6.4	15.1	14.8
1994	7.4	15.2	17.0
1995	8.5	22.0	17.6
1996	9.0	22.0	17.5
1997	7.8	29.3	18.6

Second, not only the quantity but also the quality of cases handled by judges has changed in the past decade. To begin, traditional areas of jurisdiction have become more difficult and time-consuming, due to new legislation and new social conditions. Thus, privatization of businesses and housing and the wholesale revision of substantive civil law have changed the ground rules and added to the complexity of disputes over inheritance, wrongful dismissal suits, and even alimony claims. At the same time, there has also been an increase in the demand for adjudication in new and complicated areas of civil law—including defamation, intellectual property, and consumer rights—as well as administrative law, such as suits against government officials discussed in the previous Chapter.[7] Keeping up with, let alone understanding, changes in the law adds to the burden of judges and taxes the responsiveness of courts.

A third source of the pressure on judges is the underinvestment in the judicial infrastructure and the underdevelopment of judicial administration. There are far from enough courtrooms, secretaries, typewriters, computers, photocopiers, and other basic material to ensure the smooth administration of justice in Russia.[8] Many courts are housed in buildings not designed as court houses and thus have few rooms in which trials can be conducted. Unskilled secretaries first write out in hand and later type verdicts (sometimes on mimeographic or even onion-skin paper), and untrained archivists preserve case records on crumbling shelves in dank and unheated rooms. Judges spend a good deal of time resolving mundane administrative problems and performing routine clerical matters—such as rewriting decisions, locating lost files, and chasing down litigants. The problem with court records and the "account," or *protokol*, of the proceedings at trial is particularly acute.[9] The absence of a stenographic record often leads to disputes—even before appeal—about what was said by whom and when. The fact that there is often only one complete record of the case means that litigants have to wait in line, and take turns reading and then writing down by hand pertinent information from the files. Finally, as we saw in Chapter 2, judges are forced to find sponsors to cover the shortfall in office supplies and material. We must emphasize that it was the shortage of envelopes, paper, and stamps, more than anything else, that precipitated the work stoppages of 1996–1997.[10]

The exponential growth in caseloads, along with the collapse in financing, has generated a considerable problem with delays. Since the breakdown of the USSR, there have been marked increases in the time required for judges to dispose of criminal cases. For example, whereas in 1988 only 8.6 percent of all criminal trials were disposed of in excess of the trial time limits, in 1992 the number was 18.3 percent, in 1996— 23.1 percent, and in 1997—25.4 percent. There has also been a noticeable increase in the proportion of cases requiring very lengthy trials—that is, greater than 3 or 6 months (see Tables 6.3 and 6.4).[11] The Supreme Court reportedly now "assumes supervision" of any criminal trial that is not completed within 90 days—which, according to 1997 data, represented 16 percent of all criminal cases.[12]

TABLE 6.3   Delays in Criminal Trials, District Courts (1993-1997)

		Frequency and Duration of Delay*		
	Percentage tried in excess of norms	1.5–3 month delay	3–6 month delay	>6–month delay
1993	15.9	10.0	4.0	1.9
1994	16.4	10.1	4.8	2.3
1995	20.0	11.7	6.3	3.4
1996	23.1	12.0	7.3	5.4
1997	25.1	13.1	8.7	7.5

*"Delay" in criminal trials refers to the time between the decision to proceed to trial (taken by a judge within 14 days after receiving the case from a procurator) and the actual start of the trial.

TABLE 6.4   Delays in Criminal Trials, Regional Courts (1993-1997)

		Frequency and Duration of Delay		
	Percentage tried in excess of norms	1.5–3 month delay	3–6 month delay	>6–month delay
1993	28.5	18.4	8.2	3.7
1994	27.1	15.5	7.8	4.5
1995	28.3	17.5	9.1	6.3
1996	27.4	16.3	8.2	6.0
1997	26.0	17.9	9.8	8.1

TABLE 6.5   Delays in Civil Trials, All Courts (1992-1997)

		Frequency and Duration of Delay		
	Percentage tried in excess of statutory limits*	up to 3– month delay	3–12 month delay	>12–month delay
1992	12.9	10.2	4.9	0.8
1993	12.9	9.8	5.3	0.9
1994	13.0	10.1	4.9	0.8
1995	14.9	11.9	5.7	0.9
1996	15.7	10.1	6.5	1.2
1997	13.9	9.5	5.3	1.3

* For most kinds of civil proceedings, a "delay" means that the case is not disposed of within 10 days of beginning trial. See article 99 of the Code of Civil Procedure.

In comparison to the slow pace of the administration of criminal justice in other countries, of course, these rates of delay are modest. However, several factors conspire to make them appear grave to Russians. First, the pre-trial investigation often takes a long time (the average is ten months, and for complicated cases well over a year), and the conclusion of the investigatory stage thus brings with it an expectation of imminent resolution.[13] Trials, therefore, no matter how quickly concluded, inevitably appear to prolong the agony and uncertainty of defendants. Second, a large portion of defendants are remanded into custody; even minor delays thus make the administration of justice appear cruel and interminable. Third, the often mundane, and sometimes preposterous, reasons for the adjournments give justice an unseemly bureaucratic face. When judges cannot compel witnesses to appear, paper for decisions cannot be found, files and documents are misplaced, it is no wonder that courts appear to be mired in bureaucratic slovenliness. Finally, the law requires an unusually speedy handling of criminal trials—14 days to decide whether to commit the case to trial and another 14 within which the trial must begin. Criminal cases that do not start within a month of the conclusion of the preliminary investigation thus acquire an air of illegality and torpor. To some extent, then, the Code of Criminal Procedure fosters unrealistic expectations about when trials should start, especially for multi-volume cases with lengthy and complicated pre-trial investigations.

The problems with delays in civil trials appear less grave, especially in comparative perspective.[14] In Russia as a whole since 1993, the percentage of civil cases completed in excess of statutory limits has hovered around 14 to 15% (see Table 6.5).[15] In interpreting these data, one must take into consideration that, for most suits, judges have very little time first to prepare (7 days) and then to try (10 days) cases.[16] These rigid guidelines, and their fastidious policing by superior courts, prompt judges to speak of a "conveyor belt" of justice that both rushes them through decisions and fosters impatience in the public. Nevertheless, since such a large number of civil suits deal with matters requiring immediate resolution (e.g., unpaid salaries, alimony payments), any case not disposed of in a speedy manner frustrates litigants and tarnishes the reputation of the courts.

The ability of judges in Russia to react and deal with these difficult circumstances has been hampered by basic features of civil and criminal procedure. The still largely Soviet judicial process was designed for another era, in which uneducated claimants unrepresented by counsel needed the judge's help, in which it was easy to compel the participation of citizens in trials, and in which most disputes were straightforward. Procedures that worked decades ago now help to make red tape (*volokita*), in the words of one judge, "a characteristic feature, and perhaps even the most basic trait of Russian justice."[17] Thus, in criminal and civil trials alike judges have to establish "objective truth" and fulfil what an appellate court would consider to be "a thorough, comprehensive and objective judicial inquiry."[18] In criminal trials this included gathering evidence to fill lacunae in the pre-trial investigation. Generally, the fear of being reversed led judges to call more witnesses than necessary and engage in other procedures that prolong the course of justice with no purpose other than safeguarding against appellate reversal for lack of "objectivity." Another problem was the Soviet practice of requiring lay participation in most trials, in the form of a mixed bench that included two lay assessors, elected by the public and released from work by their employers. From the onset of economic reform in the late 1980s, employers became unwilling to release workers for service in the court. This led to frequent postponements—or worse, trials with unelected stand-ins[19]—as well as benches filled predominantly by retired women ("snoring grandnannies" [*khrapiashchie babul'ki*], as one judge put it), whose continuous service does not inspire respect for the administration of justice. Courts have had similar problems with witnesses and defendants. In many cases, judges have had to postpone trials because they cannot obtain the cooperation of the Ministry of Internal Affairs (MVD) in delivering to court remanded defendants or reluctant witnesses.[20] Finally, Russian judicial procedure is monolithic. Until 1992, virtually all trials were treated alike and governed by a uniform set of norms and rules. Since 1992, reformers have begun chipping away at the procedural monolith. But much remains to be done, and there are many ideas for procedural and institutional changes under consideration.

Civil Procedure

Several improvements in civil procedure have already been made, but they require consolidation as well as further development and research. First of all, the use of single-judge trials has expanded greatly. Whereas before 1992 most civil trials required the participation of lay assessors, since that time assessors may be used in only a small prescribed category of cases and then only if requested by one of the parties. As a result, in 1997 more than 80 percent of civil suits were heard in single-judge trials.[21] Since litigants and trial judges alike appear content to have most civil suits tried without assessors, this reform seems both rational and legitimate. But some legal scholars and higher court judges are concerned about the possibility of arbitrary and corrupt practices in single-judge trials, especially since so few are conducted in the presence of lawyers capable of scrutinizing judges' conduct and rulings. This legitimate concern suggests that it would be wise for Russia to retain its version of cassation (a review by a higher court on request of both procedure and substance of the case) for civil cases heard by single judges.

Two other innovations in civil procedure made in January 1996 have further expedited justice in civil trials. In a large number of proceedings, a judge can, upon the request of the claimant, issue mandamus-like judicial "orders" (*prikazy*), which oblige the respondent to comply with the wishes of the claimant if he or she cannot or does not register in writing an objection to the action or relief requested (whereupon a full trial is required). Judges also now have the right to make an "*in camera* decision" (*zaochnoe reshenie*) when the absence of one or even both of the parties is unexcused or unjustified.[22] Data on judicial practice show that judges have made extensive use of both of these new powers. In 1996, approximately one-sixth of all civil cases were disposed of by "orders" and *in camera* decisions. In 1997, approximately one out of every four civil suits was handled in these two ways.[23] These changes are in large part responsible for the recent reduction in the percentage of civil cases disposed of in excess of statutory time limits—from 17.4 in 1996 to 13.8 in 1997.[24] These innovations appear to command the support of the entire professional legal community in Russia, and it is important that they be incorporated into the forthcoming Code of Civil Procedure.[25]

Another proposal that would streamline civil trials and save judges' time merits further investigation. It has been suggested, primarily by practitioners, that judges should be relieved of the burden to write the explanatory portion (*motivirovochnaia chast'*) of their decisions in the absence of an expressed objection to the decision and intention to appeal made by one of the parties. More than two-thirds (70.2 percent) of the judges in our survey believed that the required writing of the explanatory portion should be dropped, mainly in order to economize. At present, judges spend considerable time writing out the entire decision—a laborious process that judges derisively called "scribbling"—mainly to facilitate appellate control over their work.[26] In our view, this proposal warrants serious consideration. Much valuable judge-time is indeed lost writing decisions directly deposited in the archive. Furthermore, the pressure to produce a complete decision before leaving the "deliberation room" generates distortions in judicial conduct: most judges prepare a "rough-draft" (*bolvanka*) of the verdict *before* trial so that, upon retiring, they may quickly complete the decision; others are forced to stay in their offices late into the night preparing the comprehensive decision in order to preserve secrecy in the deliberative process.[27] Clearly much time would be saved, and possibly greater impartiality and care in the preparation of decisions would be gained, if the requirement to produce a comprehensive decision before announcing the verdict was rescinded. However, in the absence of a complete stenographic record of events and rulings at trial, such an innovation might jeopardize the rights of dissatisfied litigants to appeal.[28] We believe that, at the very least, judges should have the right, and necessary support, to delegate the task of writing the descriptive and explanatory portions of their decisions to clerks (as this institution is expanded) or even court secretaries. We also believe that a pilot project designed to improve judicial administration through the provision of modern recording equipment could serve as a research laboratory for evaluation of this proposal.

Second, a law introduced in January 1996 narrowed the scope of civil cassation proceedings (limiting them to a review only of the errors alleged by the appellant) and enhanced the powers of cassation courts in civil appeals to issue new final decisions on the basis of different findings of fact. These changes save time not only for the cassational panel but also for the trial courts, which in the past had to retry cases whose judgments had been vacated in cassation. Lower court judges welcomed the decrease in the returning of cases (what they called "footballing"), and their position was endorsed by the Council of Judges.[29] However, the improvements in civil cassation procedures remain controversial among higher court judges and legislators, and might well be reversed when the new draft Code of Civil Procedure reaches the Duma.[30] Note that the jurists drafting the new Code of Criminal Procedure have discussed introducing as an alternative to cassation full appeals on the merits, in which the higher court would itself take decisions and stop "footballing" criminal cases. It would make sense to consider the transformation of civil and criminal appellate mechanisms together, and this proposal would make a good subject for a conference sponsored by Western organizations. Such a conference might defuse controversy about the provisions for appeal in both of the Codes of Procedure currently under consideration by the Duma.[31]

Finally, through minor adjustments to articles 14 and 50 of the Code of Civil Procedure, the same 1996 law reduced the burden placed on judges to collect evidence and play the role of grand inquisitor in civil trials. Instead of obliging them to compensate for shortcomings and defects in the evidence collected by the parties, judges now are responsible only for creating the "necessary conditions" for objective and impartial trials.[32] Once again, however, it is not certain that these improvements will be included without modification in the new Code. There is considerable variation in judicial practice—some judges gruffly ignore parties' requests; others slavishly indulge them—and opponents to these particular reforms have voiced concern lest changes that promote adversarialism place in jeopardy the constitutional norm of "equality of parties" in judicial proceedings.[33] An adjustment to these innovations may well be in order. Because of the underdevelopment of legal consciousness (or a lack of respect for courts) and the difficulty in obtaining qualified legal counsel, some parties do need the active assistance of the judge to obtain an equal and fair hearing.

Procedural reform in Russia has been dominated by a discourse of pragmatism, with justifications for proposals and changes rooted solely in claims about "effectiveness" and "rationality." Lamentably, there has been very little discussion or debate about the ends and purposes of these reforms and the values they are designed to support. In our view, this imbalance in the conduct of reform is unhealthy, for it is important that progressive pragmatic reforms not neglect or jeopardize substantive goals and objectives, such as broad and equal access to justice. Especially since "equality" is a subject on which there is considerable expertise in the West, in the fields of law, political science, and philosophy, it would be useful to organize both joint studies of these new areas of judicial practice as well as a conference on the meaning and various dimensions of equality in law. Encouragement of such debate prior to the adoption of the draft Code of Civil Procedure would add to its legitimacy and smooth its implementation.

Criminal Procedure

The drafters of a new Code of Criminal Procedure in Russia have debated a series of procedural simplifications that would save judges time and have strong support among judges. These include: first, eliminating obstacles to adjournments of trials; second, confirming and expanding the use of single-judge trials; and third, introducing shortened trials and a form of plea negotiation when the accused does not contest the charge.

First, Soviet criminal procedure, as represented by the much amended but still operating 1961 Code of Criminal Procedure, discouraged adjournments in trials by disallowing judges from hearing a second trial while another was suspended and forcing them to start all over again any trial adjourned for more than three days. The requirement of "continuousness" specified in article 240 meant that judges risked wasting time re-hearing the same testimony, re-examining the same evidence, and covering the same procedural grounds whenever they approved an interruption in proceedings. Naturally, the rule discouraged judges from approving adjournments, even when they were needed. In 1997 most judges supported the elimination of the requirement of "continuousness;" 88.5 percent of those queried in our survey took this position. Note that the draft Code of Criminal Procedure approved by the Duma in first reading in the fall of 1997 eliminated this requirement (see article 280), and to date the written comments on this draft reveal no opposition to this initiative.[34]

Second, since 1992, when the government first adopted legislation making it possible for persons charged with minor crimes to be tried by a judge without lay assessors, law-makers gradually expanded the scope of single-judge trials so that by 1996 any trial of a charge bringing a punishment of five years' imprisonment or less could be heard in that forum—with the exception of cases involving juveniles. As of 1995 one-third of criminal cases were heard by judges sitting alone; and this figure soon rose to more than 40 percent in some regions.[35] This innovation appears to have been justified on the grounds of both efficiency and quality. Various Russian studies report—though usually without controls for the types of crimes being studied—that fewer verdicts issued by judges sitting alone are appealed and overturned, and the rate of delays in such trials is significantly lower than for mixed panel trials.[36] At the same time, opponents of single-judge trials, especially from procuracy circles, have noted that these trials produced higher than usual rates of both quashed trials and acquittals overruled by higher courts, and they attribute this to judges' succumbing to corrupt practices.[37] Despite the controversy, there has been much discussion of expanding the use of single-judge trials even further beyond the current limit of crimes worth five years in prison.

Among the submissions after the first reading of the draft Code of Criminal Procedure Code, three (two from Duma deputies, one from the Komi legislature) proposed extending single-judge trials to crimes that can bring six or even seven years' imprisonment, and there is a good chance that the drafting committee will support this suggestion. One of the deputies identified a key reason for so doing, namely the need to accommodate "the large mass of cases of qualified theft," especially first-time breaking and entering cases, which according to the 1996 Criminal Code carry a maximum punishment of six years.[38] According to some of the judges in our survey, this category of cases (slightly more than 10 percent of all criminal cases) was not important enough to deserve a trial with assessors. We agree with this diagnosis, but would suggest as an alternative to the extension of single-judge trials beyond the five year limit a reduction in the maximum punishment for qualified theft to five years. Admittedly, this tactic would require changing the Criminal Code, a step that might prove difficult. But an analogous change in the criminal law will soon be needed to accommodate the simplest forms of theft (first-time offenders, charged with stealing items of moderate value, without a break-in), which now can bring up to three years' imprisonment. Such simple thefts belong in the jurisdiction of the new justice of the peace courts, but those courts will be limited to crimes bearing two-year maximums. It appears that a reduction of the maximum sentence for simple theft from three to two years is in order.

Any extension of single-judge trials to offenses worth six years should, however, be accompanied by the introduction of protections. There are dangers associated with single-judge trials, especially the possibility that the judge may act wilfully and without proper accountability. The issue of corrupt practices and special deals is real, but what is more disturbing is the possibility that an accused person might not get proper legal protection. A study of single-judge cases in parts of Moscow region (in 1996) revealed that 70 percent of the cases were heard without participation of defense counsel (or procurator).[39] This is not necessarily problematic for minor crimes, bringing up to two years in prison, but when a sentence of three, four, five (and even more) years is at stake, the situation changes. When threatened with lengthy imprisonment, no accused person should face trial by a single judge without the help of defense counsel. We recommend that single-judge hearings for crimes with a maximum term of three years or more require the participation of a lawyer serving as defender. We make this recommendation despite the possible shortage of both advocates and procurators to handle these trials. Another useful change would be the issuance by the new Judicial Department of a guideline specifying that in all multi-judge courts one judge perform pre-trial functions (e.g., set the trial date, rule on sufficiency of evidence and custody motions) and another try the case.

The third type of procedural simplification would involve shortening trials and introducing plea negotiation. In 1995, the Supreme Court tried unsuccessfully to get the Duma to adopt legislation making it possible in trials where the defendant pleaded guilty for judges to conduct an abbreviated judicial inquiry (*sokrashennoe sudebnoe sledstvie*), investigating only those circumstances or facts which were disputed by the parties to the case and might have relevance for sentencing. It is unclear why the Duma rejected this legislation, though it may relate to concerns about uncontrolled plea-bargaining.[40] As the experience of Germany makes clear, however, it is possible for countries with a system of preliminary investigation to establish adequate safeguards against forced confessions in such abbreviated proceedings (for example, through compulsory taping of police interrogations).[41] In Russia, where an estimated 50 percent of criminal defendants acknowledge guilt, shortened trials represented too useful a reform to be set aside. In its brief to the commission revising the draft Code of Criminal Procedure in 1997–1998, the Supreme Court of

Russia again proposed the introduction of abbreviated trials, for any crime worth up to five years. The conditions were to include an undisputed confession acceptable to the judge and the agreement of all parties to the case.[42] Reportedly, the drafting commission discussed this proposal at length, linking it explicitly to a form of plea negotiation, and, after strong support from a representative of the Supreme Court, decided to approve it. To overcome objections of jurists (like Valerii Savitskii) who insisted that the historical legacy of the Stalin era made an inducement to confess unimaginable, the committee decided not to require a confession, only an acceptance (or non-contestation) of the charge and evidence (that is, a plea of *nolo contendere*). Note that in exchange for confession (or non-contestation) the accused will get no guarantee about sentence, only the possibility that his or her "heartfelt admission" be treated as a mitigating circumstance (as the Criminal Code specifies) and will as a result soften the punishment assigned.

The absence of guidelines on reduction of punishment in exchange for guilty pleas could prove problematic, for in Soviet and post-Soviet practice confessions (especially of serious crimes) did not necessarily reduce sentences.[43] Once again, we support this measure of simplification, but only with the addition of protections. No shortened trial should be allowed for a charge that might bring three years' imprisonment without the participation of competent legal defense counsel. Wherever possible, the use of different judges at different stages of the judicial process would add another protection. For example, one judge could consider the plea and rule on sufficiency of evidence (for example, at the stage of setting a trial date), and another could conduct the abbreviated inquiry and set punishment. And, finally, to reduce police misconduct in inducing confessions from suspects and the accused, the taping of interrogations and preservation of the tapes should be made mandatory.[44] Another potentially effective way to curtail police-induced confessions would be to accept the recommendations of two Russian legal scholars and treat as valid only confessions made in the presence of defense counsel.[45] This idea, however, may not prove feasible, given the shortage of defense counsel outside the largest cities available to defend indigent accused, especially during the pre-trial phase.[46]

Institutional Change

Another way to relieve the pressure on judges and improve the performance of the courts is institutional reform. Here we examine and assess the most urgent measures—the expansion of the court system through the creation of a new type of court; the recasting of the system of lay assessors and expansion of juries; and the use of bailiffs to serve the courts.

Starting in 1994, top officials of the Ministry of Justice and the Supreme Court actively promoted the creation of justice of the peace (JP) courts, a new, lower-level court based on its Tsarist predecessor. The 1996 Law on the Court System promised that these courts would be created, and in fall 1997 a draft law on JPs received approval by the Parliament, only to be vetoed by the President on narrow technical grounds. In December 1998 a slightly revised version of the draft became law.[47]

For the jurists who first proposed reviving the justice of the peace (from Tsarist practice), including the authors of the Conception of Judicial Reform, this institution promised to make justice more accessible—by locating the JP courts in small cities and towns, where no district courts existed, and by establishing simple trial procedures. But to the leaders of the judicial community who pressed for the new courts, their main benefit lay in relieving the district courts of a significant part of their caseload and effectively expanding the court system. According to the new law, the JPs will eventually assume responsibility for all administrative offenses, a large part of civil suits, and all criminal cases with charges bringing a maximum of two years' imprisonment. To be sure, the district courts will have to handle appeals from decisions of the JP courts, but the designers of the new courts assumed that this new task would not prove onerous. In the original plan for justices of the peace (and all draft laws to 1995), the justices were to be non-jurists with higher education, but by 1996 the plan changed to require all justices of the peace to have higher legal education and meet all the other requirements for any new judge (five years of experience in legal work, recommendation of the qualification commission). In turn, the justices of the peace were to have all the benefits that other judges have, including immunity from prosecution, a variety of perks, and membership in the judicial community. Even the salaries of the justices were not to differ greatly from those of district court judges; the law specifies that the justices are to receive 60 percent of the salary of the Chairman of the Supreme Court of the Russian Federation, not much less than the 67 percent received by the average district court judge. In other words, justices of the peace were to be professional judges, differing in status from other judges only in the absence of lifetime appointments and a closer relationship to governments of the subjects.[48]

The design of the JP courts was complicated. The courts were to be "local" and belong to the subjects of the Federation, but at the same time represented a part of the unified federal system of justice. The justices were to be selected for initial terms of three to five years and subsequent terms of five years or more, with the choice of length of terms and means of selection left to the governments of the subjects. Responsibility for financing the JP courts was to be shared, with the federal government paying salaries (and presumably benefits) of the justices, and the republican and regional governments for staff and administrative support.

To get justice of the peace courts established anywhere required both more legislation and financial commitments from two levels of government. Federal law had to determine the number of JPs each subject would get; and the subjects had to adopt laws on the selection of their justices. Moreover, each government had to provide its share of the funding. In its budget for 1999 the federal government did allocate for JP courts 132 million rubles—enough to pay salaries and benefits for 443 positions (out of the more than 8,000 required eventually). This provided the opening for the subjects, starting with Rostov region in late January, to make proposals to the federal government for laws setting the numbers and districts of their justices. By June, 34 subjects had made these requests, even though there was funding available only for a handful. Moreover, most of them asked for the maximum number of places (based on the vague formula of one justice per 15,000–30,000 residents). As of the fall of 1999, 64 subjects had forwarded their requests for allocations of JPs, and a consolidated draft law had been introduced in the Duma, based on the principle of one justice per 22,500 residents. As a rule the subject governments had produced draft laws on the selection of their justices (none had opted for elections), but few had passed these laws or made firm budgetary commitments. Despite all these obstacles, top legal officials expected that the first JP courts would begin operation near the end of 1999, and were counting on new budget sufficient to start up 4,000 JP courts in 2000 and another 2,500 in 2001. Already local authorities in some places were trying to find premises for the new courts, which, according to the vision of legal officials in the center, would consist of a three-room apartment converted into a court. A staff of two would assist the justice, and the justice him/herself would live in the same or a neighboring building.[49]

Two major issues associated with this new court deserve special attention. The first of these, the system of appeals from the JP courts, is already a subject of controversy in Russia. The original scheme gave the losers of a JP decision the right to a full appellate hearing at the district court, which was authorized to issue a new ruling, but the review was to be conducted by a panel of three professional judges! Not only was it strange to assign three judges to review appeals from the simplest cases, but this plan could not be realized in the approximately 20 percent of district courts that employed only one judge.[50] A further problem was posed by the appeals from cases involving local law, that is, laws of the particular subject of the Federation. Authorities in some subjects insisted that as federal bodies the district courts could not perform this review; instead another local court (perhaps a local district court) belonging to the subjects should be created for this purpose. In our view, appeals from JP courts should be handled by single judges, at federal district courts, and at some new body to handle the local law cases.

In addition to providing a workable appellate process, the creators of the JP courts need to pay special attention to the recruitment, training, and support of the new justices. Finding candidates to serve as JPs will prove difficult wherever the alternative of a vacancy on the district court is available. But reportedly in some regions and larger cities there are backlogs of persons aspiring to judgeships (reserves), while in smaller cities with no district courts, the JP court would be the only option. To recruit and hold onto capable justices will require that they receive decent administrative support (including staff, buildings, operational budget), support that depends upon the largesse of the regional government. Moreover, justices of the peace will require training, and it is unclear which government, federal or regional, will organize and pay for it. In our view, when any subject of the Federation establishes JP courts, it should simultaneously establish a mandatory training program (of at least three months) for new justices, or assure that the new justices will receiving training at the new Academy of Justice or one of its branches. Furthermore, every new justice should be supplied with an appropriate library of legal materials, and be placed under the tutelage of a district court judge (or later on an experienced justice of the peace). The danger is that at least in some places JPs will begin administering justice without proper training and support, and perform their important tasks in a way that discredits the justice system. There is also a danger that, with each subject of the Federation responsible for its own justices of the peace, it will be hard to impose national standards. Training and support of the justices of the peace are an ideal focus for contributions from Western organizations (governmental and non-governmental alike). Working with Russian colleagues, Western jurists and officials experienced in managing and training justices of the peace (e.g., from Ontario, Canada) could establish pilot or demonstration projects in one or two regions/republics, to provide experience upon which other subjects could draw.[51]

Let us stress that, while we approve of the concept of justices of the peace, we regard the creation of this new institution as a huge undertaking. The establishment of more than 8,000 new judicial posts managed by regional/republican authorities, with partial funding from the center, will require years of administrative effort and creativity. It will also cost a great deal of money. Nonetheless, the investment is necessary if courts in Russia are to resume functioning in anything resembling a normal manner. The caseload pressure on the judges at the district courts is real, and simplified procedures alone will not prevent further deterioration in the performance of the courts. Policy-makers should take note: the number of judges in Russia must be greatly expanded, in one way or another—if not through the new justices of the peace then through new posts at the district courts. The option of standing still does not exist.

The district courts, regional courts, and republican supreme courts need resolution of another institutional problem—namely, the role of members of the public as lay assessors on mixed panels and as jurors. In the USSR verdicts and sentences in nearly all criminal trials were rendered by a mixed panel of one judge and two lay assessors. In some periods, the system worked efficiently. Assessors were elected to their posts from among politically active persons ready to fulfil their civic duties, and those chosen received releases from their jobs at full salary. (Whether they provided independent input into verdicts and made judges accountable is more doubtful.) In post-Soviet Russia, the recruitment of working-age persons to serve as assessors became impossible, as private employers would neither release nor pay their charges, and employees could not afford missing work. Nor was there any enforceable notion of civic duty. As we have seen, the difficulty in recruiting assessors led to the dramatic expansion of single-judge trials and the reliance on pensioners to serve at the mainly criminal trials where assessors were still needed. Often, pensioners serving as assessors continued well beyond the legally mandated two-week terms, sometimes serving for the whole year when the pay was worthwhile. This situation did not encourage their taking stands independent of the judge! Nor did the pensioner assessors fulfil their formal duties properly; they were famous for failing to pay attention at trial, even nodding off. It was also difficult to ensure their attendance during the summer months.[52]

What should be done about assessors? Many judges have concluded that there is no solution and that, even for serious cases, mixed panels are not worth the effort: 61.4 percent of the judges in our survey advocated eliminating the institution of lay assessors. Such a move strikes us as inadvisable. We agree with Russian colleagues who insist that the presence of lay judges in a mixed panel introduces an element of account-ability for the professional judge, accountability that should be retained in serious cases.[53] But if the lay assessors are to be retained, their status and organization require improvement. A version of the new draft law on lay assessors prepared by the State Legal Administration of the President should be approved. Such a law should simultaneously create a civic duty to serve as an assessor (which employers must respect by preserving the job of anyone serving) and provide from government coffers higher pay than the current modest sums now offered to the pensioners, perhaps the same as members of juries receive. (A draft law on peoples' assessors submitted to the Duma in September 1999 promised to accomplish all of these things, setting the daily salary of the assessor at one-quarter that of a judge, but tax-free, and a normal maximum period of service of fourteen days a year, with the continuation of regular employment and salary guaranteed by law. For each judge on a district court, 156 asses-sors, serving five-year terms, would be designated.[54])

A related problem is the future of jury trials. Trial by jury was introduced in nine subjects of the Federation during 1993–1995 as an alternative procedure available to any accused person facing trial in a regional/republican supreme court. Although the Constitution of 1993 makes trial by jury into a right (for crimes established in federal law), the high financial and organizational costs have stopped the diffusion of the jury to other parts of the Russian Federation.[55] Not only have no new subjects taken on the jury since 1996 but also at least two subjects have either stopped jury trials (Riazan) or indicated an intention of so doing (Altai territory). The objections to the jury involve not only its high costs but also the apparent liberalism of juries, which tend to acquit at a rate of 15 percent as opposed to the less than one percent found in non-jury trials of the same charges.[56]

But the current situation, where 20 percent of citizens have access to jury trials and the rest do not, is intolerable, violating both the spirit and the substance of equal protection of the law. In fact, the lack of access to jury trials for a large part of the population was one of the grounds cited by the Constitutional Court in its decision of February 1999 declaring the use of capital punishment unconstitutional.[57]

Because of the high costs associated with the jury (both one-time set up costs and pay for jurors), only a gradual expansion of the jury is feasible—say, at a rate of four subjects per year—but it should be pursued. It would be appropriate to select subjects in geographically dispersed parts of the country, and then to allow the accused in places that do not yet have jury trials to request trials in neighboring venues. (Even now the Moscow regional court hears jury trials that belong to the jurisdiction of the Moscow City Court, which thus far lacks juries.) It also makes sense to limit further the cases eligible for jury trial to those that bring sentences of fifteen years or higher. The experience of Moscow regional court suggests that this would reduce the incidence of jury trials in most places by 15 to 20 percent, eliminating the occasional instance of qualified theft and other less serious crimes and restricting the jury trial mainly to murders and rapes, real and attempted. The financial savings would be substantial. One could also envisage lowering the pay of jurors from the current level of half the daily pay of a judge to one-third of a judge's daily pay.

The main reason for expanding the jury throughout Russia, despite its cost and unpopularity with law enforcement officials, lies in its success in spreading adversarialism and sharpening the standards of the presentation of evidence and argument not only in jury but also in non-jury trials. Although the jury remains an "exotic growth" in the Russian judicial system, it has generated an important and vibrant debate about the informal laws of evidence and proof that operate in Russian courts, which is central to the survival of liberal changes to the system of administering criminal justice.[58]

Finally, there is another institutional reform of the courts, already underway, that has much potential for improving the efficiency of the administration of justice in Russia—namely the creation of a cadre of bailiffs attached to the courts. The law provides for two kinds of bailiff—"bailiff-enforcers" to handle implementation of civil/commercial decisions (to be discussed in Chapter 8) and regular bailiffs stationed at the courthouse. The latter will take over responsibility for maintaining order in the courts, the delivery of summons to witnesses, and the forced delivery to the courts of defendants and, where necessary, witnesses. Non-appearance of witnesses and other parties to cases has been a major cause of delay and interruptions of trials in recent years, and the availability of officers to overcome this problem should help greatly.

In our view, this is the right time to take further measures to ensure full cooperation and compliance with court orders. We support enhancing the power of judges to levy fines and hold in contempt of court any person who through non-cooperation displays "disrespect" for the judicial problem. At present those powers are severely proscribed and have negligible impact. Enhancing judges' power to fine and cite in contempt should have a double benefit.[59] Not only might it improve the conduct of trials but it stands to raise the public respect for courts and judges.

Recommendations

6.1   Modernize civil procedure by: (a) allowing judges to delegate the writing of the detailed reasons for a decision in routine cases to a clerk or court secretary; and (b) continue the recent expansion of the responsibilities of the sides.

6.2   Improve the efficiency of criminal trials by: (a) eliminating the requirement of continuous trials, and allowing judges to adjourn trials, hear other cases, and reopen the adjourned trials; (b) expanding—with the addition of suitable protections—the practice of single-judge hearings; and (c) developing shortened trial procedures—again with appropriate protections (including the taping of police interrogations)—for cases where the accused does not contest the charge.

6.3   In both criminal and civil cases heard at all levels of the court hierarchy, replace the Soviet version of cassation with a full appeal, in which the higher court reviews the substance of the case and affirms, changes, or cancels the decisions of lower courts.

6.4   In establishing the justice of the peace courts: (a) develop a workable appellate process, using single judges and special appellate bodies to handle appeals relating to legislation of the subjects of the Federation; (b) set up at the level of the subjects programs to educate and support new justices of the peace, starting with a pilot program in a few regions.

6.5   Retain lay assessors for the most serious non-jury offenses, and improve their work through a new law and increased financial support.

6.6   Resume the expansion of the jury to other subjects of the Federation, while limiting somewhat the scope of their jurisdiction.

6.7   Enhance the power and opportunities for judges to fine persons who fail to appear in court without excuse (witnesses, experts, and perhaps procurators and defense counsel).

Notes

1. Data for Tables 6.1 to 6.5 are from the Department of Statistics, Supreme Court.

2. The convocation of the 4th "Extraordinary" Congress of Judges in December 1996 was both preceded by and infused with predictions about the collapse of the courts and mass exodus of judges from the judiciary. Leading judicial figures flatly warned that "without decisive government action," the courts would "cease to operate." See, for example, the speech of Anatolyi Zherebtsov, Chairman of the Supreme Judicial Qualification Commission, at the Congress (on file with authors). See also the interview with V. M. Lebedev, "Nichto ne obkhoditsia strana tak dorogo kak deshevoe iustitsiia," *Iuridicheskii vestnik*, Oct. 1996, No. 21, p. 4. "Skol'ko mozhno nastupat' na grabli," *Iuridicheskii vestnik*, Dec.1996, No. 25, p. 4.

3. The USSR Law on the Status of Judges (1989) was enacted when many judges refused to stand for re-election; and a similar Russian law (1992) also reflected signs of a crisis. For details, see Todd S. Foglesong, "The Politics of Judicial Independence and the Administration of Criminal Justice in Soviet Russia, 1982-1992," unpublished doctoral dissertation, University of Toronto, 1995, Chapters 4 and 5. Between 1994 and 1997, at several crucial junctures in the protracted crisis of the courts, the Russian government has improved the pay and benefits of judges. See the series of Presidential edicts, laws, and government decrees affecting judicial salaries in *Sbornik normativnykh aktov o sude i statuse sudei RF* (Moscow, 1997).

4. At the 10 October 1995 meeting of the President's Council on Judicial Reform, Dementev, then Head of the Department of Cadres of the Ministry of Justice, claimed that only 198 new judicial posts had been created since 1993, and that most of these were designed to accommodate the need for more judges in regional courts arising from the introduction of jury trials. Vladimir Radchenko, the First Deputy Chairman of the Supreme Court, insisted at this meeting that another 4,302 judges were needed to cope with the growing caseload. He added that the Federal Program for Fighting Organized Crime in 1994 had envisioned increasing the size of the judiciary by 7,000 judges. "Rashifrovka zasedanii Soveta po sudebnoi reforme pri Prezidente RF ot 10 oktiabria 1995 goda," unpublished document, p. 44.

5. According to data obtained from the Ministry of Justice, the number of judicial posts in district level courts in Russia rose from 7,599 in 1987, to 12,526 in 1994. However, the number of judicial posts remained virtually unchanged since 1995. As of 1 January 1998, there were still only 12,740 judicial posts in district courts.

The caseload norms in Russia are based on a sophisticated formula that assigns average time lengths to particular kinds of cases. Thus, all administrative cases are counted at 1.2 hours per case. Civil cases average 5.5 hours and range from 2.5 hours for alimony cases to 6.5 hours for wage cases to 9 plus hours for most property disputes, including intellectual property. Criminal cases average 16 hours (for example, 12.8 hours for hooliganism; 16.3 for theft; 19.9 for robbery). In addition, separate periods of time are allocated to other case-related activity such as preliminary hearings and adjournments; and to other judicial duties (consultation with the public; reviewing petitions; writing analyses of judicial practice; and performing "assignments" from the chair of the court). The actual work load performed by a particular judge in a given month, or the average per judge on a given court, is calculated using this formula. The formula and its components (which runs to 25 pages) is based on joint decrees of the Ministry of Justice and Ministry of Labor issued on 27 June 1996. They are reproduced in *Normy nagruzki sudei, sudebnykh ispolnitelei i rabotnikov apparata raionnykh (gorodskikh) sudov* (Moscow, 1997).

6. See, for example, the remarks of Evgenii Sidorenko, the Deputy Minister of Justice, in "Rashifrovka," p. 12. See also the interview with Iuryi I. Sidorenko, the Chairman of the Council of Judges, in "Tret'iaia vlast'—ne tret'esortnaia," *Iuridicheskii vestnik*, 1996, No. 21, p. 7. See also "Normy nagruzki sudei," *Rossiiskaia iustitsiia*, 1997, No. 2, pp. 54-56.

7. In 1997, there was a 64 percent increase in the number of cases "arising from administrative-legal relations." Almost 2 percent of the civil caseload now consist of suits against government officials. For more details, see the report prepared by statisticians in the Ministry of Justice's Department of Legal Information, "Spravka o rabote sudov Rossiiskoi Federatsii za 1997 god." For a recent discussion of developments in administrative law by a Russian judge, see G. Zhilin, "Zashchita prav cheloveka v grazhdanskom pravosudii," *Rossiiskaia iustitsiia*, 1998, No. 1, p. 5.

8. At the 10 October 1995 meeting of the President's Council of Judicial Reform, Radchenko opined that another 10,000 support staff personnel, not just more judges, would be needed to ensure timeliness in the administration of justice. See "Rashifrovka."

9. For a recent discussion of the problem with court records, see V. Zubov, "Protokol kak zerkalo sudebnogo rassmotreniia," *Rossiiskaia iustitsiia*, 1998, No. 9, p. 14.

10. Some courts accepted suits only from litigants who supplied the courts with the requisite amount of paper, stamps, and envelopes.

11. See "Spravka o rabote sudov za 1997 god." The data from 1988 and 1992 come from the minutes of the discussion of problems with violations of trial time limits (*sroki*) at the Supreme Court's Plenum of 24 August 1993, p. 24.

12. See the report of Lebedev's remarks in "Sudebnaia reforma—ne vnutritse-khovoe delo," *Nezavisimaia gazeta*, 24 Feb. 1998, p. 3. See also the most recent Supreme Court review of the problem with sroki, "Obzor sudebnoi praktiki Verkhovnogo Suda RF o sobliudenii srokov rassmotreniia ugolovnykh del sudam RF," *Biulleten' Verkhovnogo Suda RF*, 1998, No. 2, pp. 18-24.

13. For a description of recent changes in legislation governing the length of pre-trial custody, and debates about how time in custody is counted, see V. Nalimov, "O predelnom sroke soderzhaniia pod strazhei," *Rossiiskaia iustitsiia*, 1998, No. 8, p. 41.

14. For example, Vincenzo Varano, in "Civil Procedure Reform in Italy," *American Journal of Comparative Law*, Vol. 45, No. 4, Fall 1997, pp. 657-74, reports that between one-and-a-half and two years are required to dispose of civil cases in the lower courts in Italy.

15. There appears to be considerable regional variation. For example, in Moscow in 1997, fully 30 percent of civil trials were concluded in excess of the statutory limits. See "Obzor statisticheskikh dannykh po grazhdanskim delam rassmotrennym sudami RF za shest mesiatsev 1997 goda," unpublished document.

16. While in complicated cases, judges can have more time, they must explain in writing the reason for such extensions. See article 99 of the Code of Civil Procedure.

17. "Protokol plenuma Verkhovnogo suda RF ot 25 aprelia 1995," p. 3.

18. A. M. Zhuikov, *O novellakh v grazhdanskom protessualnom prave* (Moscow, 1996), pp. 13-19. Foglesong, "The Politics of Judicial Independence," Chapter 3. "Objectivity" consistently received a strong defense from leading members of the Supreme Court in discussions of delays; see "Protokol plenuma Verkhovnogo Suda RF ot 24 avgusta 1993 goda"; and "Protokol plenuma Verkhovnogo Suda RF ot 14 maia 1996 goda."

19. A number of trial verdicts have been reversed and sent back for re-trial because of an "illegal composition of the court." The most famous instance of this was in the trial of the son of the mayor of Vladivostok. See the report of the appellate ruling in the case of Vladimir Cherepkov, "Cherepkov mladshii na svobode," *Izvestiia*, 17 Dec. 1996, p. 1.

20. The Russian Supreme Court estimated that 30 to 40 percent of all delays and postponements were due to difficulties with obtaining the participation of the parties to cases. See especially the speech of Verin at the 24 August 1993 Plenum of the Supreme Court; see "Protokol plenuma Verkhovnogo Suda RF ot 24 avgusta 1993 goda," esp. pp. 42-48.

21. See "Spravka o rabote sudov Rossiiskoi Federatsii za 1997 god."

22. Zhuikov, *O novellakh*, pp. 25-31.

23. "O rabote sudov Rossiiskoi Federatsii v 1-m polugodii 1996 goda," *Rossiiskaia iustitsiia*, 1997, No.1, p. 2, and "O rabote sudov Rossiiskoi Federatsii v 1-m polugodii 1997 goda," *Rossiiskaia iustitsiia*, 1998, No. 1, pp. 51-53. See also the "Obzor statisticheskihkh dannykh po grazhdanskim delam rassmotrennym sudami RF za 6 mesiatsev 1997 goda," prepared by N. Oleinik of the Department of Generalization of the Supreme Court.

24. See "Obzor statisticheskihkh dannykh po grazhdanskim delam rassmotrennym sudami RF za 6 mesiatsev 1997 goda," and "Rabota sudov RF v 1997 godu," *Rossiiskaia iustitsiia*, 1998, No. 6, pp. 55-58, and 1998, No. 7, pp. 55-58.

25. For discussions of the prospects of incorporating these innovations into the new Code of Civil Procedure, see I. Utkina, "Zaochnoe reshenie v grazhdanskom protsesse: voprosy i otvety," *Rossiiskaia iustitsiia*, 1997, No. 10, pp. 16-17, and L. Tumanova, "Proekt GPK i problemy zaochnogo proizvodstva," *Rossiiskaia iustitsiia*, 1998, No. 7, pp. 43-45.

26. See article 197 of the Code of Civil Procedure, and the discussion of its provisions in Zhuikov, *O novellakh*, p. 65.

27. Judges who fail to complete the written decision before the end of the working day or onset of the weekend are sometimes believed to have been exposed to undue influences in their rulings. See, for example, the discussion of this problem in V. Pastukhov, "Chto liudiam ne nravitsia v Rossiiskom pravosudie," *Rossiiskaia iustitsiia*, 1998, No. 8, pp. 22-23. See also the discussion of the case against judge Sergei Pashin, in Chapter 3 of this book.

28. It would, for example, be difficult for parties to make rational decisions about the appropriateness of appeal in the absence of an explanation of the legal reasoning behind the ruling. If this problem is not addressed, it is likely that appellate courts would receive more requests for review based on alleged errors of both fact and law.

29. See the 31 October 1997 decree of the Council of Judges, urging the legislature to call a spade a spade and rename cassation proceedings "appellate" trials, in *Rossiiskaia iustitsiia*, 1998, No. 1, p. 50.

30. See the debate between V. M. Zhuikov and T. K. Andreeva on this question, in *Rashifrovka*, 12 March 1997, pp. 62-69.

31. There is considerable confusion over the differences in appellate systems in continental and civil law systems in Russia. For example, V. I. Radchenko, the First Deputy Chairman of the Supreme Court, has repeatedly expressed the belief that cassation of the Soviet kind is analogous to appeal in North America, despite the fact that the latter is clearly limited to review of questions of errors of law, not fact.

32. See G. Osokina, "A prave sud'i vyiti za predely iskovykh trebovanii," *Rossiiskaia iustitsiia*, 1998, No. 6, pp. 40.

33. For example, at the Supreme Court Plenum of 26 December 1995, S. G. Kekhlerov, Deputy Procurator General, said that by introducing such elements of adversarialism "we move away from equality of parties, and put the burden of proof on one side." "Protokol plenuma Verkhovnogo Suda RF ot 26 dekabria 1995 goda," p. 17. See also the discussion in V. Anisimov, "Kak primeniaiutsia novye normy GPK," *Rossiiskaia iustitsiia*, 1998, No. 8, p. 21.

34. "Ugolovno-protsessualnyi kodeks Rossiiskoi Federatsii, proekt vnositsia deputatami-chlenami Komiteta Gosudarstvennoi Dumy po zakonodatelstvu i sudebno-pravovoi reforme" (May 1997).

35. The percentage of criminal trials heard by a judge sitting alone stood at: in 1993, 23.4 percent; in 1994, 36.5 percent; in 1995, 35.6 percent; in 1996 (first six months), 32.4 percent; in 1997 (first six months), 29.7 percent. T. Nichiporenko, "Effektivnost' edinolichnogo rassmotreniia ugolovnykh del," *Rossiiskaia iustitsiia*, 1997, No. 10, p. 37, and "Praktika realizatsii novykh form ugolovnogo sudoproizvodstva," Ministry of Justice memorandum, 1997.

36. *Ibid*; O. Damaskin, "Edinolichnoe rassmotrenie sudei ugolovnykh del," *Zakonnost*, 1996, No. 6, pp. 34-41; "Prokurorskii nadzor za zakonnostiu postanovlenii po ugolovnym delam, rassmotrennym sud'ei edinolichno," *Zakonnost*, 1996, No. 12, pp. 24-29; L. Antsiferova, "Narusheniia protsessualnykh srokov rassmotreniia del i nezavisimost sudei," *Zakonnost*, 1997, No. 9, pp. 31-32; Tatiana Nirchiporenko, "A vot chto nado by sokhranit," *Iuridicheskii vestnik*, 1997, No. 15, p. 5.

37. A. D. Boikov, *Tretia vlast v Rossii* (Moscow, 1997), pp. 155-56; E. N. Levakova, et al., "Garantii zakonnosti pri edinolichnom rassmotrenii ugolovnykh del v sudakh," in *Prokuratura i pravosudie v usloviiakh sudebno-pravovoi reformy* (Moscow, 1997), pp. 59-75.

38. "Tablitsa popravok k proektu Ugolovno-protsessualnogo kodeksa Rossiiskii Federatsii (vnositsia deputatami Gosudarstvennoi Dumy—chlenami Komiteta Gosudarstvennoi Dumy po zakonodatelstvu i sudebno-pravovoi reforme) (1998), pp. 3-18.

39. Levakova, "Garantii zakonnosti pri edinolichnom rassmotrenii," p. 67.

40. According to E. N. Sidorenko, the Deputy Minister of Justice, these proposals were received by Duma deputies "with bayonets" (*v shtyki*). " Protokol plenuma Verkhovnogo Suda ot 25 oktiabria 1995 goda." Many academics are worried about the prospect of abbreviated judicial inquiries and plea-bargaining. For the most recent, and reasoned, discussion of these problems by Russian scholars, see V. Mashkov and M. Peshkov, "Sdelka o priznanii viny," *Rossiiskaia iustitsiia*, 1998, No. 7, pp. 17-18.

41. Markus Dirk Dubber, "American Plea Bargains, German Lay Judges, and the Crisis of Criminal Procedure," *Stanford Law Review*, Vol. 49, Feb.1997, pp. 547-605.

42. "Predlozheniia Verkhovnogo Suda Rossiiskoi Federatsii k proektu Ugolovno-protsessualnogo kodeksa Rossiiskoi Federatsii," 11 Sept.1997, pp. 6-7.

43. Discussions with members of the drafting commission (spring 1998). Some scholars suggest that right now defendants who confess often receive *higher* punishments than those who contest their charges and leave doubt about their guilt in the minds of judges. See V. Makhov and M. Pershkov, "Sdelka o priznanii viny," *Rossiiskaia iustitsiia*, 1998, No. 7, esp. p. 18. For argument on the need for sentencing guidelines in cases featuring guilty pleas and shortened trials see Irina Ivanova, "Vozmozhna li sdelka?" *Militsiia*, 1998, No. 8, pp. 38-41.

44. For a report on research in England showing the effectiveness of tape recording of interrogations in reducing police misconduct, see Ian Bryan, "Shifting Images: Police-Suspect Encounters during Custodial Interrogations," *Legal Studies*, Vol.17, No. 2, July 1997, pp. 215-33.

45. Makhov and Pershkov, "Sdelka o priznanii," p. 18.

46. On the difficulties investigators already experience getting advocates to participate in the pre-trial phase where they are needed by law, see L. Tkachenkova, "Grustnye mysli o sledstvii," *Zakonnost*, 1998, No. 5, pp. 20-23.

47. B. Eltsin, "Komu podchiniaiutsia mirovye sudi: Prezidentskoe veto," *Rossiiskaia gazeta*, 10 Feb. 1998, p. 5. For an early version of the draft law see "Federalnyi konstitutsionnyi zakon 'O mirovykh sudiakh v Rossiiskoi Federatsii'," *Rossiiskaia iustitsiia*, 1997, No. 1, pp. 54-55. For the law itself see "O mirovykh sudiakh v RF."

48. *Ibid.*; S. Lonskaia, 'O statuse mirovykh sudei," *Rossiiskaia iustitsiia*, 1996, No. 1, pp. 45-46; S. Romazin, "Pravovoi status, kontseptsiia formirovaniia i funktsionirovaniia instituta mirovykh sudei RF," in "Kruglyi stol: Sudebnaia sistema v Rossiiskoi Federatsii, Moskva, 14 marta 1997" (Center for Constitutional Research, Moscow Public Science Foundation)); Vladimir Radchenko, "Dostupnoe pravosudie," *Chelovek i zakon*, 1999, No. 4, pp. 29-32.

49. V. Voronov, "Gde zh ty, mirovoi, sudia?" *Iuridicheskii vestnik*, 1999, No. 4, p. 3; N. Chepurnova, "Kak sformirovat korpus mirovykh sudei," *Rossiiskaia iustitsiia*, 1999, No. 4, pp. 2-3; V. Demidov, "Federalnyi zakon deistvuet—ochered za sub'ektami Federatsii," *Rossiiskaia iustitsiia*, 1999, No. 5, pp. 2-4; Radchenko, "Dostupnoe pravosudie;" "'Ob obshem chisle mirovykh sudei i kolichestve sudebnykh uchastkov v sub'ektakh Rossiiskoi Federatsii,' Proekt federalnyi zakon," n.d. (Oct. 1999); interviews.

50. Sergei Pashin, "Novye vozmozhnosti razvitiia sudebnoi sistemy Rossii," *Konstitutsionnoe pravo: vostochnoevropeiskoe obozrenie*, 1997, No. 2, p. 20. See also, S. Pashin, "Mirovoi sudia vozvrashchaetsia," *Chelovek i zakon*, 1999, No. 5, pp. 44-48, and No. 6, pp. 38-44.

51. Ontario Court of Justice (Provincial Division), *Education Plan for Justices of the Peace* (Dec. 1997). Note that Venezuela has recently introduced justices of the peace, passing a law in 1993, and starting to elect justices in 1995. Russians jurists should watch closely the experience of Venezuela in developing JPs. See Mark Ungar, "All Justice is Local: Judicial Access and Democracy in Latin

America," paper presented at the annual meeting of the Latin American Studies Association, Guadalajara, Mexico, 17-19 April 1997.

52. T. Nichiporenko, "Krizis instituta narodnykh zasedatelei?" *Rossiiskaia iustitsiia*, 1998, No. 2, pp. 5-6.

53. See the discussion of virtues and demerits of lay assessors in Nichiporenko, "Krizis instituta narodnykh zasedatelei," and N. Kolokolov, "Institut narodnykh zasedatelei: otvergnut' ili reformirovat'?" *Rossiiskaia iustitsiia*, 1998, No. 5, pp. 8-9.

54. "'O narodnykh zasedateliakh federalnykh sudov obshchei iurisdiktsii v Rossiiskoi Federatsii,' Proekt federalnyi zakon," 24 Sept. 1999.

55. Stephen C. Thaman, "The Resurrection of Trial by Jury in Russia," *Stanford Journal of International Law*, Vol. 31, No. 1, 1995, pp. 61-274, and "Questions of Fact and Law in Russian Jury Trials: The Practice of the Cassational Courts Under the Jury Laws of 1964 and 1993," paper delivered at the annual meeting of the American Association for the Advancement of Slavic Studies, Boca Raton, Florida, 25 Sept. 1998.

55. Documentary materials relating to the initiative of V. P. Liubimov, governor of Riazan region, to eliminate the jury in his region; correspondence between a procurator of Altai *krai* and a state Duma deputy—mainly in winter 1999.

57. In its decision of 2 February 1999, the Constitutional Court concluded that five years had been sufficient time for the authorities to create jury trials everywhere as required by the Constitution and that therefore the provision guaranteeing citizens a right to jury trial in capital cases (article 20) should come into effect. Since it would be unfair to subject only the accused in jury trial regions to the possibility of the death penalty (while their counterparts elsewhere faced no such possibility), the Court declared that there could be no capital punishment unless the jury trial existed everywhere. See Aleksandr Borin, "Ravnopravie pered 'vyshkoi'," *Literaturnaia gazeta*, 10 Feb. 1999, p. 7.

58. See, for example, I. Ovsiannikov, "Logika dokazyvaniia v ugolovnom protsesse," *Rossiiskaia iustitsiia*, 1998, No. 9, pp. 5-6, and V. Stepalin, "Pochemu otmeniaiutsia opravdatel'nye prigovory," *Rossiiskaia iustitsiia*, 1998, No. 8, pp. 7-8. See also Sergei Pashin, *Sudebnaia reforma* (Moscow, 1994).

59. L. Lobanova, "Ugolovnaia otvetstvennost za neuvazhenie k sudu," *Rossiiskaia iustitsiia*, 1998, No. 8, pp. 10-11.

7

Criminal Justice: The Pre-trial Phase

Two aspects of Russian criminal justice today give it a reputation, inside and outside the country, for being unfair and inhumane: the presence of bias against the accused; and the excessive use of pre-trial detention, in especially bad conditions and for unseemly lengths of time. The accusatorial bias represents an unfortunate legacy of the Soviet version of the Continental or neo-inquisitorial model of criminal procedure. The crisis in pre-trial detention, with persons charged with conventional offenses awaiting trial for prolonged periods in overcrowded, tuberculosis-infested prisons, is largely a post-Soviet product. To address either of these problems fully requires, in our view, confronting another, more basic issue, namely the situation of the "investigator" (*sledovatel*)—the definition of his or her role, his/her place in the institutions of justice, his/her training and support, and the incentives shaping his/her performance.

Investigators and Investigations

From the Judicial Reforms of 1864, criminal justice in Russia has been based upon the Continental (or neo-inquisitorial) model, in which trials that featured such adversarial elements as open, oral review of the evidence were still based upon a written case file representing pre-trial gathering and evaluation of the evidence. The preliminary investigation in late Tsarist Russia, as well as the USSR in its first years, was conducted by a legal official known as the "judicial investigator," a figure modelled after the *juge d'instruction* in France. Since the conclusions of the judicial investigator were introduced directly into a trial whose purpose lay in confirming them and sentencing, it was vital that the investigator be in fact as well as law a *neutral* figure, committed to finding exculpatory as much as incriminating evidence. Observers from Anglo-American adversarial legal tradition have often found this very structure of criminal procedure to be fundamentally flawed. Arguably, particular versions of the Continental model of criminal justice can meet our own standards of fundamental fairness, if they are designed carefully, with due attention to the rights of the accused and inclusion of some adversarial elements.[1] However, the Soviet version of the neo-inquisitorial model not only failed to include these elements, but it also modified the basic elements of the model to the point of distortion. This was especially so, we shall see, with the investigator and his/her role.

To begin, in Soviet criminal justice the investigator, whose neutrality in both theory and practice was so crucial, became an official of the law enforcement agencies rather than of the courts. Shortly after the Revolution of 1917 Soviet investigators had been placed in an uneasy dual subordination to the procuracy and the courts, but in 1928 the tie to the courts was severed. From that point until 1956 most investigators were simply officials of the procuracy, the agency responsible for the conduct of prosecutions. To be sure, the procuracy also had the job of monitoring the legality of public administration, but its functions outside of criminal justice did not protect its investigators from their agency's interest in achieving successful prosecutions.[2] As if this were not enough, from 1956 the position of investigator was also established within police departments (in part to handle cases that the procuracy had simply ignored and left to less qualified police officials to process through simpler procedures). It was not long before the majority of investigators were located within city, district, and regional police departments and most cases that received a preliminary investigation were handled by them. The police investigator was still a legal official, and in the 1970s and 1980s most investigators in the police possessed higher legal education. But, as employees of police departments, investigators became vitally concerned with their goals, such as rates of "solutions" to crimes, deemed "solved" as soon as an investigator sent the case file to court. Instead of providing a fresh assessment, based upon careful screening and review of the evidence, investigators often did little more that give legal form to the inclinations of the detectives.[3]

In addition to transforming investigators from supposedly neutral officers of the court to members of the police/prosecution team, Soviet criminal procedure developed an armory of rules favoring the prosecution or disadvantaging the defense. For most of the Soviet period, defense counsel had little or no involvement in the pre-trial investigation in most cases; no access to the file of the case until the conclusion of the preliminary; and no right to conduct parallel inquiries on their own. (Note that in France defense counsel was admitted to the preliminary examination in 1897.[4]) Moreover, Soviet procedural rules assured that when investigators had not delivered sufficient evidence to convict, they could be afforded a second (or third) chance, through the uniquely Soviet institution of "return to supplementary investigation." In Tsarist law, such returns were allowed from the trial, but only in the rare situation of the appearance of new evidence about a more serious crime. Already in 1923 the new Soviet procedural law opened the door for much broader use of supplementary investigations by empowering judges of the provincial courts (which heard the more serious cases requiring preliminary investigations) to order supplementary investigation "only when the court establishes gaps in the evidence that could in no way be filled during the trial." This cautious expansion in the legal grounds for return to supplementary investigation led from the 1930s to a situation not anticipated by any code of criminal procedure. Returns to supplementary investigation became a commonplace outcome at trials at any court (people's as well as regional) and of cassation and supervisory reviews, often substituting for acquittals. This broad use of "returns" gained full legal authorization only in 1961.[5] Finally, in Soviet law the procuracy rather than the court was charged with making the key pre-trial decisions—for example, about detention and search and seizure—and with reviewing the work of the investigators. Partly for this reason, the legal restrictions on the length of pre-trial detention came to have no meaning, as investigators' requests for extensions were routinely accepted.[6]

Between 1989 and 1997 two measures of reform addressed some of these manifestations of accusatorial bias. First, the establishment in 1990 of a right to counsel to begin within 24 hours of arrest was an achievement, though its realization was limited by the shortage of available lawyers and later the breakdown of the system of state-supported legal services. Nor were counsel given access to the case files or a broad right to conduct inquiries. Second, from mid-1992 accused gained the right to appeal procuratorial decisions on pre-trial detention to the courts, and did so nearly 20 percent of the time (with a success rate of about 20 percent). Furthermore, in 1991–1993, judicial reformers actively sought the creation of a separate agency for investigators (a draft law got first reading in the Supreme Soviet), but the effort was stillborn.[7]

Meanwhile, the 1990s witnessed a marked deterioration in the qualifications and performance of investigators. Increasing crime rates prompted the Ministry of Internal Affairs to expand the number of investigators, but at the same time the opportunities for jurists to earn serious money in the private sector led to an exodus from the pool of police investigators. As a result, the police found it necessary to hire many new recruits who lacked legal training. By 1998 just over 43 percent of the investigators of the police had higher legal education compared with 80 percent in 1988.[8] The lower level of training had grave consequences—the average number of cases handled annually per investigator fell, while the shares both of cases completed on time and of cases "returned" by the courts for supplementary investigation increased![9] The new recruits who lacked legal education were all the more likely than their predecessors to become captives of the police, its culture, and its needs. The less competent investigators relied, even more than before, on the habit of "locking up" the accused simply to build cases against them. Investigators found it convenient to have the accused ready and available for questioning at a moment's notice, with the helpful bonus that some of the accused suffering in the "investigatory isolators" (SIZO) were more likely to confess. The circumstances were such that investigators in police and procuracy alike could plausibly claim to be incapable of processing cases absent the current rates of pre-trial detention—overcrowding and appalling conditions notwithstanding.

What is the best way to respond to the accusatorial bias in the criminal process and the over-reliance on pre-trial detention? One approach, favored by some of the radical reformers in Russia, is the wholesale abandonment of the neo-inquisitorial procedural framework in favor of creating an adversarial system.[10] In our view, this approach is neither feasible nor realistic, since it involves rejecting not only Russian traditions but also the European legal heritage to which Russian law is intimately connected. A better strategy, we believe, is to make the existing Continental system of criminal justice in Russia as fair and workable as possible, through desovietization and the addition of adversarial elements. Even taking this approach leads us to recommend a package of reforms that is far-reaching and radical. It is, however, one that even conservative jurists in Russia can understand and that does not fully reject Russian legal traditions.

The starting point in any plan for transforming Russian criminal justice must be a redefinition of its core goal. Russian justice should seek not the maximization of repression for all offenders and offenses (a goal implicit in current procedures), but rather proportionality in the use of coercive means to achieve ends—which might be called an "economy of repression." This goal implies distinguishing serious law-breakers from the ordinary and trivial offenders, and targeting resources of law enforcement agencies and courts mainly on the former. Such a differentiated approach will promote fairness and at the same time help the Russian government defend its society from criminal actions.

The key to achieving a differentiated approach within the neo-inquisitorial framework lies in restoring the investigators to their normal role and status as neutral legal officers who review and assess the evidence in a case. In Russia this requires first of all the removal of investigators from the police and the procuracy and their concentration, as some reformers have sought, in a separate agency. At a minimum, such a step would remove the investigators from the direct influence of police chiefs who are preoccupied with rates of uncovering crime.[11] A partial step in this direction was taken with the creation in the subjects of Main Administrations for Criminal Investigations (GSU), which, although housed within regional Police Departments, answer directly to the national-level Ministry of Internal Affairs (MVD). These GSUs thus enjoy some independence from the regional Chiefs of Police, but their autonomy remains incomplete, by virtue of a defacto dual subordination.[12] Along with the creation of a fully autonomous agency, it is also necessary to upgrade the status and qualifications of investigators and to redefine their mission. The investigators working in the new agency should be provided an opportunity to obtain legal education and receive salaries at the same level as judges and procurators. They should be assessed and rewarded for making independent judgments about the evidence, the nature of the offenses committed, and even the question of pre-trial detention. To enable investigators to pursue cases without the accused close at hand in a detention cell (in a prison known as "investigatory isolator"), investigators should be provided with staff (akin to the bailiffs) to execute summonses and bring the accused in for interviews.

Making the investigator once again a quasi-judicial, neutral figure, engaged in reassessing the work of police and screening cases, would substantially reduce the accusatorial bias that developed in the Soviet period, and would improve the situation of all accused persons. However desirable, the establishment of a separate investigatory agency was not as of late–1998 a priority measure supported by most legal officials in Moscow. Both the financial costs and political opposition of various agencies to losing their investigators deprived this potential reform of political feasibility. It remains possible to move in the direction of neutral investigators by reorganizing the investigators within the MVD into a separate, self-contained administrative hierarchy. This would involve ending the traditional dual subordination of investigators to district police chiefs as well as the investigatory departments of the regional and republican police, and cutting off the subordination of those departments to the police chiefs at that level. Breaking the administrative ties to the police chiefs, particularly if such a move were accompanied by separate budgets for investigators at all levels and requirements that local governments provide appropriate quarters for the investigatory units, could remove the investigators of the MVD from dependence on the police and its culture, and provide a starting point for the development of a neutral posture.

Another way to combat bias in favour of the prosecution is to strengthen the hands of the defense. To be sure, as we have seen, from 1990 defense counsel in Russia had the right to participate in the major events of the pre-trial investigation and to meet frequently with their clients. But in some inquisitorial systems of Western Europe the defenders had other rights, including the right to conduct parallel investigations (e.g., Denmark) and the right to early disclosure of evidence collected during the investigation (e.g., France).[13] The drafters of the new Code of Criminal Procedure in Russia were well aware of this omission and they chose to include in the version submitted to the Duma for first reading a new section (article 82.3) giving the defender of the accused the right to collect evidence, including interviewing private persons, requesting documents from organizations (in turn obliged to provide copies), and making inquiries from specialists.[14] As might be expected, this new package of rights provoked opposition from the law enforcement agencies, which objected to "surrogate investigations" by persons not obliged by law to be "objective," but the drafting committee chose to keep these provisions in the version to be submitted in the second reading.[15] We agree with the drafters of the new code that defense counsel in Russia should have the right to make inquiries, especially when investigators lack the organizational prerequisites for neutrality, but we do not expect that this step will help most accused persons. As of

2000, there is little money to pay defense counsel to conduct inquiries during the preliminary phase, and advocates providing low-cost services through the colleges (the Russian version of legal aid) lack time and incentives to engage in investigative activity. This situation raises the question of the need for restructuring of the delivery legal services, and of incorporating rules about discovery.[16]

The old Soviet system of organizing defense counsel through regional colleges and local consultation bureaus, which obliged nearly all of them to perform legal work for the indigent in return for guaranteed salaries, no longer meets the demand for advocates in criminal cases, even where involvement is obligatory. For one thing, the regional colleges have lost their monopoly and face competition from a variety of parallel bar associations, which do not as a rule require their members to perform legal aid. For another, the opportunities for all lawyers to do well-compensated commercial work have reduced the time that they are willing to allocate to criminal work. The problems are especially acute outside the largest cities, in places where the number of lawyers was always small. Thus, in Altai territory investigators report difficulty moving through the pre-trial phase in cases were defense involvement is needed because the local defense counsel refuse to participate, not least because of the low rates of compensation offered by the state legal consultation bureaus for representation during investigations.[17]

It is difficult to imagine serious progress in overcoming the accusatorial bias in Russian criminal process without improvements in the representation of the accused. Above all, advocates are needed to help and protect their clients during the pre-trial phase—to challenge inappropriate detentions and monitor the conduct of the official investigation, not to speak of conducting parallel ones. Yet, it is precisely in the pre-trial phase that many, if not most, accused do not now receive adequate representation. As things stand, only two types of accused have a good chance of obtaining real defense before trial—those with means and those whose cases are tried in Moscow and a few other large cities.

For at least four years lawyers and politicians in Moscow have struggled over the writing of a new law on the defense bar; and by all accounts the sharp divisions of opinion—for example, over the desirability of providing permanent legal status to the parallel bars associations—have led to paralysis. In spring 1999 a compromise version of the draft law on the bar was prepared for second reading in the Duma, with support from the Federal Union of Advocates of Russia, but in the opinion of the leaders of the parallel bars this version was not only mistaken but unconstitutional.[18] In our view, the development of a new system to guarantee legal services to non-paying clients, especially in criminal cases, represents a priority for criminal justice reform. And we agree with Russian colleagues that the new system should include some kind of duty counsel (public defenders attached to the courts), funded directly from the state budget, not through a special scheme (such as the deductions from pension fund contributions recently declared unconstitutional by the Constitutional Court). Without a cadre of adequately compensated, full-time advocates focused on providing service to the non-wealthy accused, it will prove hard to make meaningful participation of defense counsel in pre-trial investigations a reality.[19]

Supplementary Investigations

Another important measure for reducing the accusatorial bias in Russian justice is the elimination of the practice of returns of cases from trials or appellate reviews for supplementary investigations. The idea of giving a second chance to the representatives of the state when they fail to prepare a case adequately offends our sense of fair play, and it has opponents within Russia.[20] Nor is the practice of supplementary investigations necessary. It does not exist in most countries within the inquisitorial tradition. Through much of the post-Stalin period (until the 1980s), one-third to one-half of returns to supplementary investigations constituted surrogates for acquittals, with cases eventually closed by the investigators. From the 1980s, however, there was a substantial rise in returns (from 4.2 percent of cases with supplementary investigations in 1979 to 9 percent in the early 1990s, reaching 10 percent in 1997), and some of them were the result of failures by investigators to provide judges with information needed for sentencing, such as valuations of stolen goods or losses, or assessments of the character of the accused.[21] Of course, the very existence of "returns" enabled investigators and procurators to pass on to the courts cases that had not been fully prepared, and the removal of this possibility would induce them to do their work more thoroughly the first time round.

As of spring 1998 even the chiefs of the MVD had turned against the continuation of the broad use of supplementary investigations.[22] Joining some of the more radical academic proceduralists, the MVD submitted suggestions for a revised version of the articles on supplementary investigation in the draft Code of Criminal Procedure (articles 272 and

296), which would curtail the grounds for its use. Supplementary investigations would no longer be allowed on the grounds that the evidence was incomplete, but would be allowed primarily to correct violations of procedural law that occurred during the original investigation—such as one lawyer representing two accused with conflicting interests, or the failure to provide a translator during interrogations. Not content to wait for the adoption of a new Code of Criminal Procedure, in April 1999 the Constitutional Court of the Russian Federation declared unconstitutional the provisions of the existing Code of Criminal Procedure that obliged judges to return for supplementary investigation cases where the evidence was incomplete or there was a need to change the charge.[23] As judges start to follow this decision, there should be a substantial reduction in the use of returns, but the procedural law itself still requires change.

In our view, it would be better if the practice of supplementary investigations were eliminated entirely, but any steps to reduce its use are to be welcomed. Apart from narrowing the grounds for its use, we urge that law-makers and legal officials alike make every effort to use alternative approaches to handling omissions and anomalies. For example, if judges need further information for sentencing, they should be encouraged to suspend trial for a few days while the procurator and/or defense provide it. This option will be possible with the elimination of the requirement of "continuousness" in the draft Code of Criminal Procedure. It would also be useful to grant procurators the right, in special circumstances, to introduce at trial newly found evidence not included in the dossier from the preliminary investigation, and defense the right to a short break to confront it; and to give judges the right to change a charge where appropriate. Such steps address situations where judges typically send cases back to the investigator.

Eliminating returns to supplementary investigation would likely lead to a rise in the rate of acquittals, but in serious cases this rate would still not exceed one-and-a-half percent of dispositions.[24] Some judges worry that an increase in acquittals would lead to overruling of their decisions in cassation with calls for new trials. It might well be appropriate to narrow the grounds for reviewing acquittals to genuine procedural errors—perhaps using the same criteria now used in jury trials. Note that the jury trial procedure now used in Russia does not allow supplementary investigations, and as a result, the preparation for trials tends to be more thorough than usual.

Not only would the elimination of supplementary investigations make the criminal process more fair, but it would also reduce the length of time some accused spend in detention, with resulting savings for the Russian state. Most often, cases undergoing supplementary investigation do not come back to the courts for months, and usually the accused continue to sit in the investigatory prisons.

Pre-trial Detention

Finally, the burning issue of pre-trial detention—its overuse, excessive duration, and subhuman, tortuous conditions—deserves to be addressed directly. The conditions in pre-trial detention centers, called "investigatory isolators" or SIZO, are far worse than in prisons and labor colonies. The overcrowding problem is acute and, according to many politicians, now constitutes a "crisis of national security."[25] Each year, nearly 300,000 persons enter a SIZO, while the legal limit is less than half that number.[26] The Ministry of Justice, which acquired responsibility for the entire prison system from the MVD on 1 September 1998, estimates that 30,000 persons infected with tuberculosis enter the prison system each year. At least 92,000 persons in detention or prison at present are infected with TB, and the incidence of TB in the SIZOs now exceeds that in the general population by a factor of twenty.[27] Because the system lacks the capacity to house sick prisoners separately from healthy ones, the combination of overcrowding and disease is lethal. In 1996 and 1997, more than 16,000 persons died in jails and prisons from various illnesses and disease. In 1996, alone, at least 1,500 detainees died in the SIZOs, primarily from tuberculosis. In some regions, jail wardens and public health officials now claim to have stopped the growth in mortality and infection rates among detainees, but the incidence of death in SIZOs has grown substantially in the last two years and remains intolerably high.[28]

The new managers of Russian prisons are fully aware of the desperate situation in the investigatory prisons, and have pressed for (and in some cases received) extra funding to support renovation of some old prisons and the building of new ones. They have also improvised by using free space in neighboring labor colonies (meant only for convicted offenders) to house accused persons awaiting trial.[29] Such steps are useful as short-term palliatives, but they do not address the fundamental issues. Overcrowding is not primarily a housing problem, as some Russian politicians maintain.[30] Although funding for the penal system for the past few years has been half of what both the Ministry of Justice and MVD deemed "essential minimum levels," and construction of new facilities as well as repairs of old institutions has been negligible, the roots of the problem are much deeper.[31]

Simply put, Russia places in preventive detention too many persons accused of crimes. Although procurators decline a substantial number of police requests for pre-trial detention, and order detention for slightly more than one-third of all persons facing trial, a large number of accused are nevertheless imprisoned unnecessarily.[32] Data compiled by the Main Penal Board of the Ministry of Justice for 1998 show that approximately 125,000 persons were released from detention centres. Although very few of these (perhaps 3 percent) were not subject to any penalties (i.e., the charges were dismissed or they were acquitted), more than half of these were released upon being sentenced to time served, conditional conviction (i.e., probation), or received a non-custodial punishment—all signs that they did not present a substantial danger to the community. Another 20 to 30 percent had their measure of restraint changed, pending the conclusion of the investigation or outcome of trial.[33] Furthermore, the incidence of flight for persons released on their own recognizance or on a "signed promise to appear"—the two main non-custodial measures of restraint—is very low.[34] These data strongly suggest that many orders of detention, while plainly legal, are excessive, and that there is room for a reduction in the use of detention.

In 1997–1998 leading officials from the Procuracy, Ministry of Justice, and MVD publicly criticized the use of pre-trial detention for crimes of small or average seriousness, a practice made possible by loopholes in the law.[35] This criticism was on the mark, for overcrowding results from the excesses of criminal law and procedure, and underdeveloped institutions of criminal justice, not a shortage of jail space. A more commodious prison system might alleviate some of the present symptoms of the crisis, but long-term solutions lie in fundamental reforms to the administration of criminal justice. Put simply, the problems of pre-trial detention in Russia cannot be solved in a supply-side manner.

In our view, Russian authorities should undertake a package of reforms designed to reduce both the use and the duration of pre-trial detention. Some serious legislative proposals, which we examine below, are already under consideration. But we must emphasize at the outset that the available pool of remedies is not limited to law. Changes in the regulatory and supervisory regime of policing and investigating crimes represent an equally if not more important source of reform. For the excessive use of detention is in part the product of the habits and incentive structures surrounding police investigators and procurators.

First, to reduce the use of pre-trial detention in Russia to acceptable levels and to limit detention to cases where it is absolutely necessary calls for a revamping of the criteria for the selection of detention as a measure of restraint. Here what matters is not only the Code of Criminal Procedure, but also the operating instructions of procuracy and police. Thus, while the current Code of Criminal Procedure (article 96) provides a list of crimes for which detention may be ordered by the procurator "solely on the basis of their gravity," a 1995 joint directive of the Procurator-General and the Minister of Internal Affairs "suggests" that for these charges detention "maximally" be used for any crime classified as "serious."[36] Because the law does not encourage thrift in the use of detention as a measure of restraint for this category of cases, and investigators' political superiors actively encourage profligate practices, most thefts (even a first offense) that involve a trespass or break-in, even for items of little value, now lead to detention before trial.[37] And since theft constitutes a very large percentage of all criminal activity in Russia, the indiscriminate use of detention for such cases is a serious factor in the problem of overcrowding.

Two legislative proposals—one a bill proposed by the Ministry of Justice, the other a new draft Code of Criminal Procedure—have targeted these problems. The Ministry of Justice bill, submitted to the Duma in spring 1999, recommends converting second-degree theft into a crime of the "moderately grave" category (by dropping the maximum penalty from six to five years), thereby eliminating it from the ranks of offenses for which there is, in effect, a rebuttable presumption of detention. The same bill also proposes an amendment to article 96 of the Code of Criminal Procedure, which would prohibit detention (barring "exceptional circumstances") for offenses carrying less than three years' imprisonment.[38] The Main Penal Board (GUIN) of the Ministry of Justice projects that these measures alone will substantially reduce the population in Russian prisons.

The draft Code of Criminal Procedure, which is currently under consideration in the Duma, surpasses these recommendations and makes a genuine advance over the existing Code. It stipulates that detention is not to be applied (except when there is a demonstrable likelihood of flight) to persons accused of offenses bringing less than two years' imprisonment (the current minimum is one year). Moreover, the list of offenses whose gravity alone justifies detention is eliminated. Institutional changes required by the draft Code should also diminish the use of detention. Since, after the Code's adoption, courts will assume responsibility for initial decisions to impose pre-trial detention, in most situations in the future procurators will have to convince a judge that the accused might hide from or hinder the investigation, commit new crimes, or disappear before or after the trial. Presumably, this will mean that in the main detainees will consist of recidivists and persons without fixed addresses (of whom there are many among criminals in Russia today). However, much will depend upon how these criteria are interpreted and used in practice, by judges as well as procurators.[39]

New regulations from the procuracy and guiding directives from the Supreme Court must convert these criteria into tough standards designed to keep people out of detention rather than put them into custody. Here what is required is a change in the rationale for detention, and an explicit demand for proportionality in the use of coercion. At present, detention is construed principally as a deterrent to anti-social behavior and a form of preliminary punishment. In the future, detention must be deemed the least preferable of a host of means for facilitating the appearance of defendants in court. To accomplish this shift, new regulations and guidance might include the following provisions: (1) no detention at all for persons charged with offenses below the legal category "serious" (i.e., with terms under five years), or for breaking and entering under article 158.2, Criminal Code of 1996, except when the accused is likely to flee (e.g., lacks a fixed address); (2) that the imposition of detention in cases of "serious crime"—including article 158.3—take into account the likelihood of the commission not of any new crime but only a violent crime; and (3) that pre-trial detention of juveniles be limited to persons accused of violent crimes and specifically exclude underaged persons charged with any and all forms of theft.[40] Only in cases involving "especially serious crimes" (threatening more than ten years' imprisonment) should the likelihood of committing a new crime stand a broader construction. The purpose of these limitations is to keep out of detention persons deemed to have committed ordinary, non-violent crimes, especially of theft of various objects, up to and including computers or cars.

Many of the persons who would avoid detention under this scheme might be subjected to other measures of restraint, such as agreements to stay in town and cooperate with the investigation and, in some instances, house arrest. Note that bail does not represent a real alternative to pre-trial detention when there is no easy way to borrow money; accused persons with the resources to pay bail often hail from the world of organized crime.[41] Moreover, using any measure of restraint other than detention involves a risk; one should be prepared for up to 10 percent of accused left at large to flee.[42] Furthermore, as we suggested earlier, investigators forced by a reduction in pre-trial detention to bring in accused persons on a frequent basis for questioning should be provided with staff support (a policeman or bailiff) to summon and fetch accused persons, and witnesses, when needed. The cost of this support would be far less than that of holding accused in detention. We would also urge that investigators and procurators be made responsible for developing and maintaining reasonable rates of detention—through both positive and negative incentives. As a rule, the rate of pre-trial detention should not exceed that of imprisonment after conviction.

Second, reducing the length of detention calls for a two-pronged strategy—reconfiguring the legal time limits on detention before trial to produce reasonable maximum terms; and taking steps to reduce delays in the process of investigation itself. The current set of time limits on pre-trial detention allows up to 18 months of detention for the investigation alone and another six months to enable defense counsel (in complicated cases) to read the one copy of the case file. Abuses of the prerogative of extending periods of detention to these maximum terms transforms the pre-trial process into genuine punishment.[43] We would urge the imposition of real limits of six months for most cases, with the possibility of an extra three months only in cases with multiple accused or of especially serious crimes.[44] These terms would not include the time of the trial itself. To keep detention to a reasonable duration will also require shortening the length of trials, wherever possible. (Several mechanisms for achieving speedier trials were discussed in Chapter 6.)

Eliminating common sources of delays in the pre-trial phase would make it easier to complete investigations according to this new timetable. One source of delay is the long wait for expert witnesses (psychiatric, forensic, specialists in explosions/fire etc.). Bottlenecks with expertise stem from a shortage of both funds to pay experts and qualified specialists in some fields.[45] We urge that both of these problems be addressed. Another source of delay stems from the traditional Soviet principle of criminal procedure (embodied in article 20 of the 1961 Code of Criminal Procedure) that investigations must be "complete" (*vsestoronnoe*) as well as objective. In practice, this principle requires investigators to waste time on full investigation of every incident in a multi-charge indictment rather than simply proceeding to court with the charges easily supported by sufficient evidence. If investigators fail to handle every incident, they face the prospect of a return to supplementary investigation by the trial judge; if that judge overlooks such an omission, the appellate court may choose to make the same return. In our view, the rigid requirement to investigate fully each incident of an offense should be eliminated, from law and practice.

Finally, another source of delay is the rules governing the access of defense counsel to the case file at the end of the preliminary investigation. As it stands, the defense counsel himself/herself must personally read the file and is allowed only to copy out by hand extracts from it. Upon the recommendation of Duma deputy Viktor Pokhmelkin, the latest version of the draft Code of Criminal Procedure allows defense counsel to make photocopies (a good idea), but due to strong objections from many quarters, another good idea—to permit counsel to send an assistant (another lawyer or a law student working as a clerk) to read and copy from the file—was removed from the draft. In our view, this objection was in error. Although counsel will in most cases need to see the file once, delegating further study and arrangements for copying to a subordinate would speed up the process; and the law could supply whatever protections or limitations on access seemed appropriate.

Let us be blunt. With its current rates, lengths, and conditions of pre-trial detention Russia has joined the company of Columbia, Chile, Venezuela, Argentina, and Uruguay; and Russia has far higher rates of pre-trial detention per capita than any country of Eastern Europe. Even Ukraine (in 1994) held in pre-trial detention half as many persons per 100,000 population as did Russia.[46] Part of the problem lies in Russia's propensity to lock up convicted offenders; only the United States, with its peculiar problems of race and drugs, rivals Russia in per capita rates of imprisonment. The overuse of all kinds of confinement, including pre-trial detention, costs a great deal of money that the Russian government can ill afford; it goes without saying that Russia would benefit greatly from the savings generated by lower rates of detention. In fact, the savings could well be reinvested—first in support for investigators, and second in desperately needed resources for the courts.

We have outlined a package of reforms of the pre-trial phase of criminal justice designed to reduce the accusatorial bias and pre-trial detention and focusing especially upon transforming the investigator and his/her role. The package would work best as a whole. For one thing, neutral investigators with a more adjudicatory role would not need to have so many accused held before trial. But if decision-makers proved loathe to proceed with a new separate agency for investigators (or even the creation of a separate hierarchy of investigators within the MVD), other parts of the package could be implemented separately. The elimination of supplementary investigation deserves immediate attention, as does the redesign of bureaucratic regulations on pre-trial detention to help the new Criminal Procedure Code reduce use of detention as a means of restraint.

Recommendations

7.1 Create a separate agency for investigators and adopt measures to encourage their autonomy and neutrality. Or, as a fallback, organize investigators within the Ministry of Internal Affairs into a separate vertical structure, eliminating all subordination of investigators to police chiefs.

7.2 Grant to defense counsel: (a) the right to conduct independent inquiries during the period of the preliminary investigation; and (b) access to the formal case file during the same period.

7.3 Ensure adequate representation for non-wealthy accused, especially during the pre-trial phase, through restructuring of the defense bars and their consultation offices and/or the establishment of duty counsel attached to the courts.

7.4 Eliminate the institution of "supplementary investigation" (with appropriate modifications to court procedures).

7.5 Reduce the use of pre-trial detention as a measure of restraint by changing the criteria for its use (in law and in regulations).

7.6 Decrease the length of pre-trial detention by setting shorter legal limits and by reducing delays in the pre-trial investigation, through: (a) eliminating the procedural requirement that all criminal incidents must be fully investigated; (b) expanding the pool of available experts and increasing the funds available to pay them; and (c) giving defense counsel the right to photocopy from the case file and to use assistants in the review of the file.

Notes

1. See Mirjan R. Damaska, *The Faces of Justice and State Authority: A Comparative Approach to the Legal Process* (New Haven, CN, 1986).

2. Peter H. Solomon, Jr., *Soviet Criminal Justice under Stalin* (Cambridge, UK, and New York, 1996), pp. 75-76.

3. I. L. Petrukhin, *Pravosudie: vremia reformy* (Moscow, 1991), pp. 68-75; B. N. Topornin, ed., *Stanovlenie sudebnoi vlasti i obnovliaiushchei Rossii* (Moscow, 1997), pp. 19-22 (section by A. Larin).

4. Eugene Huskey, "The Politics of the Soviet Criminal Process: Expanding the Right to Counsel in Pre-trial Proceedings," *American Journal of Comparative Law*, Vol. 34, No. 1, Winter 1986, pp. 93-112.

5. Solomon, *Soviet Criminal Justice under Stalin*, p. 282, and Chapter 11; *Ugolovno-protsessualnyi kodeks RSFSR* (Moscow, 1952), esp. article 398; *Ugolovno-protsessualnyi kodeks RSFSR: Ofitsialnyi tekst po sostoianiyu na 15 fevralia 1997 goda* (Moscow, 1997), esp. articles 232, 258, 339, and 378.

6. Todd S. Foglesong, "*Habeas Corpus* or 'Who Has the Body?': Judicial Review of Arrest and Pre-Trial Detention in Russia," *Wisconsin International Law Journal*, Vol. 14, No. 3, Summer 1996, pp. 541-78; Igor Petrukhin, *Neprikosvennost lichnosti i prinuzhdenie v ugolovnom protsesse* (Moscow, 1989), pp. 169-94, 249-53.

7. Peter H. Solomon, Jr., "Reforming Criminal Law Under Gorbachev: Crime, Punishment, and the Rights of the Accused," in Donald D. Barry, ed., *Toward the "Rule of Law" in Russia? Political and Legal Reform in the Transition Period* (Armonk, NY, 1992), pp. 235-56; Foglesong, "'Who Has the Body?';" *Kontseptsiia sudebnoi reformy* (Moscow, 1992).

8. "Istina—v zakone!" (Beseda s Vladimirom Alferovym), *Militsiia*, 1998, No. 4, pp. 20-22.

9. *Sostoianie zakonnosti v Rossiiskoi Federatsii (1993-1995)* (Moscow: NII Prokuratury RF, 1995), esp. pp. 142-46; "Materialy polozheniia k informatsionnoi zapiske 'Nekotorye voprosy realizatsii ugolovnoi politiki v sovremennykh usloviiakh'" (Moscow: Obshchestvennyi tsentr sodeistvii reforme ugolovnogo pravosudiia, 1997), esp. pp. 22-23.

10. See Peter H. Solomon, Jr., "The Persistence of Judicial Reform in Post-Soviet Russia," *East European Constitutional Review*, Vol. 6, No. 4, 1997, pp. 50-56.

11. Petrukhin, *Pravosudie*; *Kontseptsiia sudebnoi reform*, pp. 68-75; E. Dolia, "K voprosy sozdaniia Sledstvennogo Komiteta," *Sovetskaia iustitsiia*, 1993, No. 20, pp. 9-10; A. M. Larin, "Sledstvie—kakim emy byt," *Chelovek i zakon*, 1996, No.10, pp. 50-55; I. N. Kozhevnikov, "Kak sledovat sledovatelei," *ibid.*, pp. 73-78.

12. For example, Sibilev, the Director of the Main Administration for Criminal Investigations in Nizhny Novgorod, now reports directly *only* to the national-level committee for criminal investigations within the MVD, but informally, due to a combination of tradition and regular budgetary shortfalls, remains accountable to the Director of the Regional Administration of the MVD (UVD).

13. A. A. Rogatkin and I. L. Petrukhin, "O reforme ugolovno-protsessualnogo prava Rossiiskoi Federatsii," in *Problemy Rossiiskoi advokatury* (Moscow, 1997), pp. 100-155; R. Blanpain, ed., *International Encyclopaedia of Laws* (The Hague, 1998) pp. 284-85; Steward Field and Andrew West, "A Tale of Two Reforms: French

Defense Rights and Police Powers in Transition," *Criminal Law Forum*, Vol. 6, No. 3, 1995, pp. 473-506.

14. "'Ugolovno-protsessualnyi kodeks Rossiiski Federatsii,' proekt vnositsia deputatami-chlenami Komiteta Gosudarstvennoi Dumy po zakonodatelstvu i sudebno-pravovoi reforme," unpublished document (May 1997).

15. "Tablitsa popravok k proektu 'Ugolovno-protsessualnogo kodeksa Rossiiskoi Federatsii' vnositsia deputatami Gosudarstvennoi Dumy–chlenami Komiteta Gosudarstvennoi Dumy po zakonodatelstvu i sudebno-pravovoi reforme," (n.d.: winter 1998), pp. 332-45, esp. pp. 335-36.

16. For recent Russian discussions of these questions, see R. Lisitsyn, "Pravo na zashchitu: mezhdunarodnye standarty i rossiiskaia deistvitelnost'," *Rossiiskaia iustitsiia*, 1999, No. 6, pp. 8-10, and L. Vinnitskii, "Uravniat' prava storon v ugolovnom protsesse," *Rossiiskaia iustitsiia*, 1999, No. 6, pp. 43-44.

17. L. Tkachenkova, "Grustnye mysli o sledstvii," *Zakonnost*, 1998, No. 5, pp. 20-23.

18. "'Federalnyi zakon ob advokature v Rossiiskoi Federatsii,' proekt ko vtoromu chteniiu (25 maia 1999 goda)"; "Rezoliutsiii s'ezda Federalnogo soiuza advokatov," *Rossiiskaia iustitsiia*, 1999, No. 5, p. 11; Sergei Krivosheev, "Ne vsiak advokat advokatu brat," *Rossiiskaia gazeta*, 18 March 1999, p. 3; Gasan Mirzoev, "Getto dlia advokatov," *Nezavisimaia gazeta*, 14 April 1999, p. 3; Valerii Savitskii, "I advokat segonia prosit o zashchite," *Rossiiskaia gazeta*, 24 April 1999, p. 2; Aleksei Klishin, "Advokatov khotiat lishit nezavisimosti," *Izvestiia*, 29 May 1999, p. 6; Konstantin Katanian, "Zashchitniki otstaivaiut svoiu nezvisimost'," *ibid*.

19. See I. L. Petrukhin, ed., *Problemy rossiiskoi advokatury* (Moscow, 1997); Pamela Jordan, "The Russian *Advokatura* (Bar) and the State in the 1990s," *Europe-Asia Studies*, Vol. 50, No. 5, July 1998, pp. 765-91; *idem*., "Russian Advocates in a Post-Soviet World: The Struggle for Professional Identity and Efforts to Redefine Legal Serivces," unpublished doctoral dissertation, University of Toronto, 1997.

20. Iu. Shchadin, "Nuzhen li institut dopolnitelnogo rassledovaniia," *Zakonnost'*, 1995, No. 10, pp. 31-33; interview with G. Ponomarev, former procurator of the city of Moscow, 29 May 1997.

21. Peter H. Solomon, Jr., "The Case of the Vanishing Acquittal: Informal Norms and the Practice of Soviet Criminal Justice," *Soviet Studies*, Vol. 39, No. 4, Oct. 1997, pp. 531-55; Todd S. Foglesong, "The Politics of Judicial Independence and the Administration of Criminal Justice in Soviet Russia, 1982-1992," unpublished doctoral dissertation, University of Toronto, 1995, pp. 238-50, 470-72; "Tablitsy o dvizhenii ugolovnykh del za 1990-1997," Ministerstvo iustitsii, 1998.

22. Boris Iamshanov, "Novyi kodeks v starom mundire" (Beseda s Igorem Kozhevnikovym), *Rossiiskaia gazeta*, 17 Dec.1997, pp. 1, 4; Igor Kozhevnikov, "Uporidochit polnomochiia sledovatelia," *Rossiiskaia iustitsiia*, 1997, No. 12, pp. 22-24; "Istina—v zakone," p. 21.

23. "Postanovlenie Konstitutsionnogo Suda RF po delu o proverke konstitutisonnosti polozhenii punktov 1 i 3 chasti pervoi stati 323, chasti chetvertoi stati 248 i chasti 258 Ugolovno-protessualnogo kodeksa RSFSR v sviazi s zaprosami Irkutskogo raionnogo suda Irkutskoi oblasti i Sovetskogo raionnogo suda gorod Nizhnii Novgorod,"(20 aprelia 1999), *Rossiiskaia gazeta*, 27 April 1999, p. 4.

24. According to one informed estimate, only 6.5 percent of cases returned to police investigators in 1996 were stopped by them, something over 3,000 cases; this figure does not, of course, include the more serious cases handled by investigators in the procuracy. Marina Vasileva, "Igra v odni vorota" (Beseda s Igorem Kozhevnikovym), *Chelovek i zakon*, 1997, No. 11, p. 25. Official data for 1997 showed that 88.5 percent of cases undergoing supplementary investigation (by all investigatory agencies) were sent back to the court; these data suggest that investigators stopped on average 10 percent of the cases returned to them. "Tablitsy o dvizhenii."

25. See the report of the November 1998 hearings in the Council of the Federation, "Polozhenie v mestakh lisheniia svobody priznano kriticheskim," *Rossiiskaia iustitsiia*, 1999, No. 2, pp. 51-53. On 7 December 1999, the Prime Minister announced the release of 4,213 pre-trial detainees who were found to present little or no risk to the community. The announcement, made on the nightly television news (ORT) and coupled with a report about a program in Saratov for non-custodial measures of restraint for juveniles, suggests the present government deems the problem of pre-trial detention grave, and worthy of systemic reform.

26. As of 1 January 1998, the law requires that each detainee have 4 square metres of cell floor space, an increase of 1.5 square metres from the previous minimum. According to a Press release of the Chief Penal Board of the Ministry of Justice, 10 March 1999, at present, each detainee has an average of 1.73 square metres. This datum, which suggests that jail capacity is overstretched by more than 200 percent, contradicts the claim made elsewhere that present capacity is exceeded by only 142 percent.

27. Anatolyi Kucherena, "Arest kak mera ustrasheniia. Predvaritelnoe zakliuchenie v sovremennoi Rossii poprezhnemu iavliaetsia tiazheleishim fizicheskim i moralnym ispytaniem dlia zaderzhannykh," *Nezavisimaia gazeta*, 22 May 1998, p 3.

28. According to the Chief Medical Officer of the Main Penal Board of the Ministry of Justice, mortality rates in SIZOs nearly trebled between 1996 and 1997. Press Release; interviews with Iu. N. Labutin, Director, Main Penal Board, Nizhegorod Region, A. A. Serikov Vice Governor for Social Policy, Nizhegorod Region, and Iu. I. Kalinin, Deputy Minister of Justice.

29. In summer 1996 in connection with Russia's entry into the Council of Europe, the government started plans for a program of construction and repair of the investigatory isolators. See "O merakh po obespecheniiu uslovii soderzhanii lits, nakhodiashchikhsia v sledstvennykh izoliatorakh i tiurmakh ugolovno-ispolnitelnoi sistemy Ministerstva vnutrennykh del Rossiiskoi Federatsii,"

Postanovlenie Pravitelstva RF ot 27 iiuniia 1996, No. 760, *Rossiiskaia gazeta,* 20 July 1996, p. 4. On the situation in the isolators generally see "V etom godu v Rossii smertnuiu kazn ne primeniali," *Trud,* 25 Oct. 1997, p. 3; Petr Mishchenkov, "I v tiurme chelovek ne bespraven, *ibid.,* 12 July 1997, p. 3. See also, "Kapitany tenevykh kapitalov rvutsia k vlasti," *Rossiiskaia gazeta,* 1 Oct. 1997, p. 4.

30. In the course of preliminary research in Moscow and Nizhny Novgorod for a project on pre-trial detention reform sponsored by the Vera Institute of Justice, we heard many police and procuracy officials insist the "only solution" is to "build more prisons."

31. See the reports of Deputy Minister Justice Kalinin, and V. U. Yalunin, Head, Main Penal Board (GUIN), during parliamentary hearings, "Stenogramma zasedaniia 'kruglogo stola' na temu: 'o kritecheskom polozhenii v ugolovno-ispolnitelnoi sisteme RF'," 27 noiabria 1998 goda.

32. For the past five years, an average of 35 to 38 percent of all accused have been remanded into custody pending the outcome of trial. See Foglesong, "Who Has the Body?," and the annual reports produced by the Department of Statistics of the Ministry of Justice.

33. The data come from Form "V," produced by GUIN, the Main Penal Board of the Ministry of Justice.

34. Interviews with V. I. Radchenko, Deputy Chairman of the Supreme Court of Russia, and Tsyganov, Deputy Director of the Main Administration for Criminal Investigations, Nizhny Novgorod.

35. "Stenogramma parlamentskikh slushanii na temu: 'O sostoianiia borby s prestupnostiu i ob ukreplenii pravoporiadka v Rossiiskoi Federatsii v sovremennykh usloviiakh'" (1 June 1997), p. 9 (vystyplenie Zam.Gen. Prok. RF Chaika); "V Ministerstve iustitsii RF," *Rossiiskaia iustitsiia,* 1998, No. 4, p. 45 (vystuplenie S. Stepashina).

36. "Materialy prilozheniia, pp. 41-44; "Ob izbranii mer presecheniia," Ukazanie Generalnogo Prokurora R.F. i Minstra vnutrennykh del R.F. ot 17 ianvaria 1995 No. 4.15.1, *Kommentarii k Federalnomyu zakonu "O prokurature Rossiiskoi Federatsii" ot 17 noiabria 1995 goda, s prilozheniem vedomstvennykh normativnykh aktov* (Moscow, 1996), pp. 492-93.

37. According to I. A. Popov, Deputy Head of the Informational-Analytical Board for the Committee of Inquiry (*Doznanie*) of the MVD, detention was ordered in more than 50 percent of cases of "category 2" theft in Moscow in 1998. For "category 3" thefts, detention was ordered in 84 percent of cases. "Protokol zasedaniia palaty po pravam cheloveka Soveta Federatsii, 'O merakh preodeleniia kriticheskoi situatsii v ugolovno-ispolnitelnoi sistemy RF'," 19 marta 1999.

38. "O vnesenii izmenenii i dopolnenii v zakonodatelnye akty Rossiiskoi Federatsii."

39. "'Ugolovno-protsessualnyi kodeks Rossiiski Federatsii,' proekt vnositsia deputatami-chlenami Komiteta Gosudarstvennoi Dumy po zakonodatelstvu i sudebno-pravovoi reforme," unpublished document (May 1997), Chapter 12.

40. According to the recent legislative proposals of the Ministry of Justice, detention should be prohibited for juveniles in prosecutions of offenses carrying less than six years' imprisonment.

41. See, for example, the discussion in N. Kolokolov, "Mery presecheniia imushestvennogo kharaktera," *Rossiiskaia iustitsiia*, 1998, No. 12, pp. 41-42.

42. In the 75 most populous counties in the United States during May 1992 "about one-third of all released defendants with state felony charges were either rearrested for a new offense, failed to appear in court as scheduled, or committed some other violation that resulted in the revocation of their pre-trial release." U.S. Department of Justice, Bureau of Statistics, Pre-trial Release and Detention Statistics (BJS homepage: www.ojp.usdoj.bjs). For other estimates of arrest and release rates, see John Clark and Alan D. Henry, "The Pre-Trial Release Decision," *Judicature*, Vol. 81, No. 2, Sept.-Oct. 1997, pp. 76-81.

43. Iurii Feofanov, "Zek do prigovora," *Izvestiia*, 31 Oct. 1997, p. 2.

44. The current Ministry of Justice bill recommends a one-year maximum for adults, and a six-month limit for juveniles. The Ministry of Internal Affairs is adamantly opposed to these proposals. See the remarks of Popov, in "Protokol zasedaniia palaty po pravam cheloveka Soveta Federatsii."

45. See "Byt ili ne byt sudebnoi ekspertize," (Beseda s Tatianei Moskvinoi), *Iuridicheskii vestnik*, 1997, No.13, p. 12.

46. Mark Ungar, "All Justice is Local: Judicial Access and Democracy in Latin America," paper presented to the annual meeting of the Latin American Studies Association, Guadalajara, Mexico, 17-19 April 1997; Roy Walmsley, *Prison Systems in Central and Eastern Europe: Progress, Problems and the International Standards* (Helsinki 1996), pp. 24-29.

8

Civil and Commercial Judgments: The Problem of Implementation

In the new Russia, where the major players in the economy are now private firms, the handling of commercial disputes represents an important new function of courts. In the capitalist economies of the West, courts may not be involved in the bulk of such disputes, but they stand as a viable and respected last resort for many, and may act as well as a deterrent to breach of contract. Whatever the courts' impact on the overall process of commercial dispute resolution, their role in this process adds to their status and reputation. In Russia, too, courts deal with only small portion of commercial disputes, but for reasons peculiar to Russian economic realities. These reasons include the prominence of cash and barter transactions (which do not produce written evidence), the prevalence of hidden parts of businesses (to avoid taxation), and relationships with private protection agents (providing what Russians call a "roof"). All the same, a substantial number of commercial disputes do reach the courts in Russia, and there is an opportunity for the courts there to raise their profile by handling them well.

In post-Soviet Russia most disputes among private firms and between private firms and state bodies belong to the jurisdiction of the *arbitrazh* (or commercial) courts. Administratively separate from the system of courts of general jurisdiction analyzed in this report, the *arbirtazh* courts were established in 1991 as successors to the system of state arbitration bodies (*gosarbitrazh*) from the Soviet period. The full-time arbiters who staffed the state arbitration bodies dealt mainly with disputes between state firms from different ministries and became skilled at assigning blame for failures to achieve planned targets or fulfil delivery obligations. Transformed into the judges of the *arbitrazh* courts, the former arbiters shouldered new responsibilities for resolving disputes among private firms (disputes which often concerned failures to make payments); and the new judges learned to operate within a new set of procedural rules. The *arbitrazh* courts had no monopoly in business dispute resolution. Especially in Moscow, some commercial disputes were resolved through private mediation services (including the so-called *treteiskie sudy*).[1]

At the start of 1998, there was one crucial flaw in the judicial processing of commercial cases in Russia (its "Achilles heel," according to the Chairman of the Supreme *Arbitrazh* Court), and that was the low chance of getting court judgments implemented. The conventional wisdom was that well under 40 percent of the decisions of the *arbitrazh* courts in disputes among private firms achieved implementation.[2] Admittedly, this figure is only an estimate, which probably does not record subsequent negotiated settlements (e.g., when the winning side agrees to accept less than the full amount of the judgment in return for promises of future deals), and certainly does not include implementation secured with the help of private protection companies.[3] But there was a strong consensus in Russian legal circles at least that an unacceptably large proportion of judgments of the *arbitrazh* courts was not realized. To a degree, the low rate of implementation reflected problems beyond the control of the government, much less the courts, such as the weak viability (borderline bankrupt) position of some firms, and the capacity of many others to hide their assets. But it was also clear that the whole system of implementation, and the persons responsible for it, were inadequate to the task; that the resolution of at least some disputes and on occasion even the enforcement of court decisions was handled through private enforcers; and that, as a result, the reputation of the courts was suffering.[4]

In the mid– and late–1990s it became increasingly difficult to implement judgments in non-commercial disputes as well. On the one hand, such traditional problems as collecting alimony from alcoholics and unemployed men were aggravated by the growth of these conditions, and it was also hard to collect alimony from employed persons whose wages were delayed or paid in kind. Nor was it easy for a judicial enforcer to ensure that the victor in a dispute over unpaid wages got his or her due. (Note that in 1998, in contrast to the previous few years, the bulk of complaints from citizens received by the Ministry of Justice concerned failure of implementation of decisions in alimony and wage cases, rather than cases of commercial debts.[5]) On the other hand, new types of difficult-to-implement civil judgments also became commonplace, including decisions relating to claims in automobile accidents (most drivers have no insurance), compensation for investors deceived in fraudulent schemes (pyramids), and compulsory evictions in real estate disputes.[6]

The Bailiffs

In 1993 leading justice officials began considering the replacement of the existing judicial enforcers with a service of armed bailiffs, trained and equipped to execute commercial judgments—a variant of the service that had existed in Tsarist Russia, reportedly a "strong agency" revived and developed as part of the Judicial Reform of 1864. In planning the post-Soviet revival of the bailiffs, reformers studied the experience both of European countries such as France that contracted out implementation work and of the United States Federal Government, whose marshals combined the functions of guarding courthouses and securing compliance with judicial decisions.[7] In mid–1997 a law establishing bailiffs—to both enforce judgments and guard and service the courts—finally gained approval of the legislature and was signed by the President.[8] In our view, bailiffs of both kinds deserve major assistance.

In the Soviet period commercial disputes heard at the state *arbitrazh* pitted one state firm against another. Most disputes concerned the assignment of blame for failures to achieve planned targets (or related breaches, such as delays in the deliveries), and at most the judgments called for the transfer of assets from one state bank account to another. Compliance with these decisions was virtually automatic (it was not possible until 1990 to have more than one bank account) and did not require the use of enforcement agents or services. And, tellingly, the state *arbitrazh* did not need or have its own judicial enforcers.[9]

For their part, the judicial enforcers (*sudebnye ispolniteli*), who were attached to the district-level people's courts, were engaged mainly in the implementation of civil judgments from the general courts, covering such private matters as alimony payments (arranging garnishing of wages), labor disputes (ensuring payment of back wages after illegal dismissal), and conflicts over living space (arranging evictions). The enforcers consisted mainly of women, between 30 and 50 years of age, with low pay and low status. In the 1990s, as the legal private economy developed in Russia and the state arbitration tribunals were transformed into *arbitrazh* courts, these very judicial enforcers were for the first time charged with implementing commercial judgments.[10] A case would reach the enforcer in the absence of voluntary compliance (a rarity with financial judgments in Russia) and then only after an enforcement order obtained by the victorious petitioner from the *arbitrazh* court judge had failed to extract sufficient funds from the respondent's bank account. At this point, the petitioner, armed with the right documents, would turn to an enforcer, who was obliged both to find the defendant and to locate and seize (usually) physical assets equal to the judgment, which might mean used, even obsolete, industrial or office equipment. The enforcer then had to move and store the goods; get an agreement on their market value (sometimes with outside expertise); and finally, try to arrange their sale (if necessary at auction). For the most part, the beleaguered enforcers lacked cars and trucks and places to store the goods; and they were not authorized to carry weapons.[11]

In the summer of 1997 the Russian government legislated the creation of a new service of bailiffs, some charged with guarding and servicing the courts, others, the so-called bailiff-enforcers, replacing the judicial enforcers. Like their predecessors the judicial enforcers, the bailiff-enforcers have been placed within the Ministry of Justice, but have no administrative subordination to the courts. Instead, along with the bailiffs servicing the courts, the bailiff-enforcers form a part of a vertical hierarchy ultimately subordinate to a Chief Bailiff in Moscow and the Department of Bailiffs headed by his deputy. As of the middle of 1999 that Department had a staff of 300, engaged in developing the legal, financial, and administrative infrastructure of the service. The direct administration of the bailiffs is concentrated in a unit at the regional or republican level, itself divided into separate sections for the court bailiffs and the bailiff enforcers, and subdivided into district and increasingly interdistrict units. While most of the enforcement work is to be conducted by bailiff-enforcers in these units, the bailiff services in the larger regions will eventually have a staff of 20, enough to allow more than mere supervisory activity. The regional units may well include staff with more specialized expertise and credentials; the senior bailiff in charge of the regional units must be a jurist, and some of his/her colleagues should have specialized financial or business expertise, useful for the handling of large or complicated cases.[12]

As opposed to the old judicial enforcers, at least some of the new bailiffs engaged in enforcing court judgments will carry arms, and, according to the design, include more men. They are also supposed to be more knowledgeable about the realities of business and finance and as a rule better educated. In a published interview in November 1997 the new chief bailiff (for the whole country), Boris Kondrashov, stressed his service's need for economists and accountants, as well as specialists in various areas of law. The head of the Department of Bailiffs in the Ministry of Justice, Valentina Martinova, expects that eventually most bailiffs engaged in execution of judgments will have not only the required high school education but also secondary legal training. (Senior bailiffs are expected to have higher legal education, but as of 1999 one-third of them lacked that attribute.) Meanwhile, however, most of the current judicial enforcers have been retained; in the first part of 1998 the 10,000 judicial enforcers underwent a review (*pereattestatsiia*), and 9,000 of them passed and gained reappointment as bailiff-enforcers. The 1998 budget provided resources for the hiring of another 2,000 new bailiff-enforcers at the district level, and more than 700 to form the new departments in the regions. Chief Bailiff Kondrashov spoke to the press of his ambitious plan—to increase the service of bailiff-enforcers during 1999 and 2000 by another 14,000 persons, to reach a total of 25,000—but there was no indication that the government would provide this level of funding. In fact, on 20 July 1998 (as the financial crisis loomed), the government issued a resolution imposing a 20-percent reduction of the number of bailiffs.[13] Combined with the rising case load, the reduction ensured the continuation of backlogs and regular violations of the time periods set for various stages in the implementation process specified in the Law on Implementation Procedures.[14]

Even so, with each year a portion of the former judicial enforcers converted into bailiffs was likely to retire, opening the way for the phasing in of new staff. To perform well, most bailiff enforcers, new and old, will require training. The Russian Legal Academy has been ordered by the Ministry of Justice to create a special faculty for training bailiffs, but finding faculty and arranging the program represent challenges for the future.[15]

The judicial enforcers had suffered not only from inadequate qualifications but also from inertia and even despondency about the difficulties in fulfilling their responsibilities. Consequently, the designers of the new bailiff-enforcers tried to supply them with special incentives to work hard and well. Thus, in addition to a decent base wage the new bailiffs were to receive rewards of 5 percent of the total sum extracted, or

5 percent of the value of property seized, up to a maximum of 10 days' minimum wage. The law grants bailiff-enforcers free passage on all public transport (including trains), but strangely does not provide this benefit to the bailiff-guards, who often work with the bailiff enforcers on hard cases. Nor does the law make any provision to give bailiffs cars.[16]

Notwithstanding the shortage of funds (which we have discussed already), the draft budget of the Russian government for 1998 included a new allocation of 290 million rubles to support the service of bailiffs (both parts), and in the actual budget this figure was raised to 400 million—an indicator of the priority the government attaches to this initiative. Provision is also made for additional funding for the service based upon its productivity. Debtors are to pay to the government a collection charge of 7 percent of the debt, and 70 percent of the collection charges received will go into an extrabudgetary fund for "the development of the implementation process."[17]

Making a success out of the new institution of bailiff-enforcers should be a high priority for supporters of judicial reform in Russia. A significant improvement in the share of *arbitrazh* court judgments that get implemented could raise the prestige of the courts overall. It might also lead over time to an increasing reliance on the courts for the resolution of at least some kinds of business disputes. However, we worry lest the new bailiffs fail to live up to expectations at least in the short run. There is a danger that the initial investment in the bailiffs will prove insufficient to make them effective and that the new service will not enhance the status of the courts.

To begin, the training of the new bailiffs, first the senior ones (who are supposed to have legal education), then the rank and file, needs special attention. The Russian Legal Academy could use help, especially from foreign funders and experts, in developing and staffing a training program. Funds are needed to pay potential faculty, domestic and foreign, at rates that will make teaching bailiffs attractive. Expertise could be used to put together a useful combination of lectures and seminars. It might also make sense to train bailiffs in a number of centers outside of Moscow—probably the same places where training for judges might be organized, i.e., cities with strong legal faculties.

Moreover, the new bailiff-enforcers would gain in both effectiveness and prestige if they had access to cars and trucks. Nearly one-third of the respondents in our survey of judges cited provision of transport to the bailiffs as the single most important means of increasing the rate of implementation of court decisions. The Ministry of Justice, and the services of bailiffs of the subjects of the Federation, should make every effort to ensure that at least some of the bailiffs are provided with motor vehicles.

Another way to strengthen the hands of the bailiffs is to enhance their legal powers and make those powers real. In the past, the judicial enforcers experienced difficulty entering the premises of respondents (whom they were not allowed to bother on weekends or evenings) and were crippled by a lack of the right to bear and use weapons. The law establishing the post of bailiff-enforcers promises to bailiffs the rights to enter and search premises and seize goods as well, but it is vital that operating instructions clarify this power. The new law also grants bailiffs the right to use guns and promises that they will be supplied eventually. It is essential that the new bailiffs actually obtain guns without delay. The regulations of the Ministry of Internal Affairs that have impeded the acquisition of guns by judges must not be allowed to stand in the way of the bailiff-enforcers becoming armed officials capable of seizing property even in the face of resistance.[18] As of late summer 1998 the law on weapons had been amended to enable some, but not all, bailiffs to carry arms. Often, in practice, only the bailiffs guarding the courthouses had the right to carry arms, and the bailiff-enforcers had to recruit their colleagues to help them when they needed to "raid" an enterprise or warehouse. But this could not happen in most places, where the bailiff guard service had not yet been established for lack of budget.[19] Another problem encountered in practice was the failure of the law on bailiffs to entrust supervisory personnel such as the regional and even national chief bailiffs with the legal power to implement decisions. Yet, the active participation of the top bailiffs was necessary to secure execution of decisions against powerful officials or executives.[20]

Finally, the implementation of court decisions in business disputes would be improved by the development within the bailiff service of more specialization. Instead of the customary practice of the assignment of cases from the *arbitrazh* courts to bailiff-enforcers who also handle civil cases from the courts of general jurisdiction, the business cases could be concentrated in the hands of particular bailiff-enforcers, at least in any district where there are two bailiff-enforcers. Specialization of this kind does occur in some bailiff offices (especially in large cities), and it is being encouraged by the bailiff service in Moscow. Moreover, as more bailiff services are organized not in districts but in interdistrict formations, there tends to be a department or division specially to service the *arbitrazh* courts, sometimes located physically in those courts' own buildings. In at least one instance the initiative for specialization came from the court. In 1998 the *arbitrazh* court of Omsk region urged the Regional Justice Administration to organize a separate subdivision of the bailiff-enforcers to handle that court's decisions and concentrate in that unit the best qualified bailiff-enforcers. In return, the court itself promised to provide special training for the team of bailiffs assigned to the enforcement of its decisions. This arrangement strikes us, the authors of this study, as a good one on all counts. The execution of decisions in commercial disputes differs fundamentally from that in most ordinary civil judgments, and so do the skills needed to accomplish it. The combination of specialization with extra training—provided in this case by the *arbitrazh* court itself—makes sense and deserves to be pursued throughout the Russian Federation.[21]

A foreign funder intent on making an impact upon judicial resolution of commercial disputes might well consider supporting a demonstration project aimed at developing maximally effective bailiff-enforcement service in the shortest period of time, in, say, three cities or districts in different parts of the country. This would involve ensuring recruitment, specialization, and training, providing motor vehicles, guns, and other equipment, experimenting with other measures to improve the implementation process, and monitoring and evaluating the project.

In the long run, though, the bailiff service, like many other aspects of the administration of justice in post-Soviet Russia, needs a large infusion of new budget. For, as of mid–1999, the bailiff-guards were present in only a handful of courthouses (in no case on a permanent basis), and the bailiff-enforcers faced caseloads of more than three times the established norms. Even so, they reportedly improved the rate of implementation of court decisions (that is, "successful" processing of documents from 35 percent in 1996 to 42.9 percent in 1997, according to another source, to the 48–percent level by late–1998; but measured in monetary terms, the bailiff-enforcers delivered 38 percent of court-supported obligations in 1998[22]). Accounting and public relations aside, the Council of Judges resolved in October 1998 to complain to the government of the Russian Federation and to President Yeltsin about the underfunding and understaffing of the bailiff service.[23]

With more support and more staff the bailiff service could improve the implementation of decisions from commercial disputes resolved in the *arbitrazh* courts, but only to a degree. The difficult financial circumstances of many firms and the capacity of others to hide assets places limits on what enforcement officers can achieve.

The Role of Judges

Developing a reliable, armed service of bailiffs, with proper incentives, is one way in which the implementation of commercial decisions might be improved; another is encouraging changes in the conduct of judges at the *arbitrazh* courts. Judges should not treat execution of judgments as wholly beyond their responsibilities and should do what they can to facilitate enforcement, should the plaintiff prove victorious.

The 1997 Law on Procedures for Implementing Decisions gives *arbitrazh* court judges a new form of involvement in the implementation of their decisions, by allowing any affected actor (claimant, respondent, or third party) to complain to the court about any action or inaction on the part of the bailiff-enforcer (see especially article 90). Although the Law provided strict time limits, the exact procedures for handling these complaints had not been specified (as of mid–1999). But this appeal process promised both to make bailiff-enforcers accountable for their actions and to acquaint *arbitrazh* court judges on a regular basis with the difficulties in the implementation process. This might in turn encourage them to take preventive action more often.[24]

One form of preventive action would consist of paying close attention to the ability of the respondent to pay a judgment against him and being receptive to requests to freeze assets at the start of the trial. Too often in recent years, when the judicial enforcer finally locates the debtor it is only to discover that the firm has no money at hand, and sometimes no assets that can be sold without bankrupting the firm itself. To be sure, absent a well-documented request by one of the parties, judges would have difficulty discovering and evaluating what assets were available for freezing. Moreover, many plaintiffs may prefer not to endanger through an asset freeze the stream of income needed to pay a potential judgment in their favor. In fact, until recently, petitions by the plaintiff for even partial freezing of assets were uncommon, representing in Soviet business culture a sign of disrespect and lack of trust. Starting in 1995, it seems, petitions to freeze assets became more common, and in 1996 were made in approximately 11 percent of disputes between private firms heard at the *arbitrazh* courts in Moscow and St. Petersburg (with lower frequencies elsewhere). According to data compiled by Kathryn Hendley, judges in Moscow approved nearly 40 percent of these requests, and in some places the rate was even higher. It is hard to assess whether these approval rates were sufficiently high, and, more vitally, to determine the degree to which respondents complied with court orders to freeze assets. Rarely did judges apply fines to the delinquents for failure to comply with the orders, even when plaintiffs made complaints. But sometimes compliance was beside the point; merely obtaining an order to freeze assets might push the respondent into a negotiated settlement.[25]

The preservation of assets for potential payment of debts is too important a matter to leave in the hands of the parties themselves, even though they must bear primary responsibility. Judges in commercial courts should be encouraged to inquire into the matter at the start of trials, and invite the plaintiffs to initiate a freeze if appropriate. At the same time, respondents should be asked to report back to the judge about the implementation of any freezes ordered, and judges prepared to fine businesses for failure to implement freezes.

In general, we believe, judges should make more use of their existing powers to fine, not only with regard to asset freezes but also to improper conduct on the part of legal counsel and other participants in trials—e.g., lack of preparedness by counsel, failure to appear on the part of various persons, and even refusal to pay judgments. One reason that judges in Russia give fines so infrequently is the work involved in imposing this sanction.[26] In order to impose a fine a judge must prepare a detailed protocol and sometimes conduct a special hearing as well. We recommend simplification of the procedures for imposing fines. In our view, an increase in the use of fines against persons who fail in obligations to Russian courts would not only improve their performance (e.g., efficiency, likelihood of implementation), it would also enhance the authority, if not also the prestige, of those courts.

We recognize that there are occasions where petitioners sue respondents not with the hope of actually obtaining payment, but rather to establish a place in line in the case of a potential bankruptcy, or to demonstrate good faith efforts before writing off an unpaid obligation.[27] We recognize also that some respondent firms are so close to bankruptcy that any disruption in activities caused by freezing of assets or other forms of intervention might produce collapse. These issues should be taken into account by judges when considering whether an asset freeze is appropriate.

There may also be occasions when, to assure execution of judgments, judges need to apply some other kind of restraint upon a party to a case, for example, putting a hold on some business transactions until the dispute is resolved. As things now stand, judges in Russia lack the tools for intervening in the conduct of a firm's affairs, tools that are commonplace in some Western countries, such as the power to issue injunctions or temporary restraining orders. The new law on implementation procedures has not rectified this omission, but legislators in Russia might well consider amending it. To be sure, such powers would represent a novelty in the post-Soviet context, but they would add materially to the power of *arbitrazh* court judges and their capacity to deliver results.[28]

In the long run, the implementation of commercial judgments would become easier to ensure were firms to own the one asset that is difficult to hide, namely *land*. In Western countries, the ultimate threat which leads firms to come forward with other assets and pay off court judgments lies in the possible seizure of land and its forced sale. But in Russia, the question of land ownership, including the land on which industrial and business firms sit, has not been settled.[29] Land is leased, and in certain situations land may be "owned," but this is mainly land used for farming, and not necessarily with the full ownership rights to dispose of or sell the land to any comer. Of course, the whole issue of land is a controversial one, and will be difficult to resolve as long as the Duma has a large number of communist and agrarian party deputies. Furthermore, it is possible that businesspeople do not want the obligations and vulnerabilities that might accompany full ownership rights, and in a more favorable political environment would not press for them.

Recommendations

8.1   Encourage specialization among bailiff enforcers, so that a subset of them concentrates on implementing decisions in commercial disputes rendered by the *arbitrazh* courts.

8.2   Develop as soon as possible special courses—in Moscow and other parts of the country—to train bailiff-enforcers, especially those specializing in the decisions of the *arbitrazh* courts.

8.3   Organize demonstration projects in selected districts, in which the bailiff-enforcers would be provided with motor vehicles, weapons, and other support services; and evaluate the effects of full funding upon performance.

8.4   Encourage—through directives and, if appropriate, changes in the Arbitration-Procedure Code—an active approach by judges on the *arbitrazh* courts toward ensuring the enforceability of their judgments, including a readiness to freeze assets before trial, and to impose fines for non-performance of orders to freeze and other omissions.

8.5   Provide *arbitrazh* court judges with the power to issue injunctions and temporary restraining orders.

Notes

1. On the variety of dispute resolution mechanisms in post-Soviet Russia, including mediation (or what the author calls "tertiary courts") see Katherina Pistor, "Supply and Demand for Contract Enforcement in Russia: Courts, Arbitration, and Private Enforcement," *Review of Central and East European Law*, Vol. 22, No. 1, 1996, pp. 55-87. For analysis of dispute resolution by criminal organizations, see P. Skoblikov, "'Tenevaia iustitsiia,' formy proiavlenia i realizatsii," *Rossiiskaia iustitsiia*, 1998, No. 10, pp. 21-23.

2. Marina Vasileva, "'Nelzia zhit po zakonam dzhunglei'" (Interviu s V.F. Iakovlevym), *Chelovek i zakon*, 1996, No. 6, p. 57; Mikhail Nikolaev, "Sudebnyi pristav: On pristav k vazhnomu delu: okhraniat femidu i ispolnit ee resheniia" (Beseda s Valentinoi Martinovoi), *Iuridicheskii vestnik*, 1997, No. 22, p. 9. Skoblikov (in "'Tenevaia iustitsiia'") claims that only about 30 percent of *arbitrazh* court decisions sent to the judicial enforcers received "actual implementation" (meaning unclear). Note that this estimate refers only to the cases sent to the enforcers; it excludes court decisions marked by voluntary compliance, payment from the respondent's bank account through the enforcement order (*ispolnitelnyi list*), post-trial settlements, or the use of private enforcement. It would be helpful to obtain data on the proportion of *arbitrazh* court decisions that reached the judicial enforcers or their successors the bailiff-enforcers.

3. On the role of private protection companies in debt collection, with or without a previous court decision, see Vadim Volkov, "Violent Entrepreneurship in Post-Communist Russia," *Europe-Asia Studies*, Vol. 51, No. 5, July 1999, pp. 741-54.

4. A recent study of the ways more than 300 Russian firms handle contract disputes found that only three percent resorted to private enforcement (or mafia). This figure was much lower than the authors had expected. It is important to note that the study included many large and middle sized enterprises. There is reason to believe that small businesses make more use of private enforcement than the larger enterprises, which have their own legal staffs. See Kathryn Hendley, Peter Murrell, and Randi Ryterman, "Law, Relationships, and Private Enforcement: Transactional Strategies of Russian Enterprises," unpublished paper, 1998.

5. B. I. Skorobogatova, "Analiz raboty Departamenta sudebnykh pristavov s obrashcheniiami grazhdan po voprosam ispolneniia," *Biulleten Ministerstva iustitsii Rossiiskoi Federatsii*, 1998, No. 7, pp. 24-26.

6. Nikolai Nikinorov, "Pochemy neispolnitelen sudebnyi ispolnitel," *Rossiiskaia gazeta*, 5 Feb. 1997, p. 3; Dmitrii Sokolov, "Tikhaia grazhdanskaia voina," *Obshchaia gazeta*, 16-22 April 1998, p. 4; "Neispolnimyekh net, est neispolniamye," (Vitalii Volkov beseduet s Sergeem Pashinym), *Iuridicheskii vestnik*, 1998, No. 8, pp. 10-11.

7. O. V. Kononov and Iu. G. Kokarev, "Sudebnye pristavy: vchera, segodnia, zavtra," *Gosudarstvo i pravo*, 1999, No. 1, pp. 74-78.

8. Irina Lobova, "Zachem nam nuzhny sudebnyi pristav?" (Beseda s ministrom iustitsii V. Kovalevym), *Rossiiskaia gazeta*, 21 May 1997, p. 1; Marina Vasileva, "'Nelzia zhit po zakonam dzhunglei' shchitaet predsedatel vysshego arbitrazhnogo suda RF Veniamin Iakovlev," *Chelovek i zakon*, 1996, No. 6, pp. 54-59. See also Katherina Pistor, "Supply and Demand for Contract Enforcement in Russia."

9. See Stanislaw Pomorski, "State *Arbitrazh* in the USSR: Development, Function, Organization," *Rutgers Camden Law Journal*, Vol. 9, 1977, pp. 61-115; Heidi Kroll, "The Role of Contracts in the Soviet Economy," *Soviet Studies*, Vol. 40, No. 3, July 1988, pp. 349-66.

10. Nikinorov, "Pochemy neispolnitelen sudebnyi ispolnitel."

11. Kathryn Hendley, "Remaking an Institution: The Transition from State *Arbitrazh* to *Arbitrazh* Courts," *American Journal of Comparative Law*, Vol. 46, No. 1, Winter 1998, pp. 109-118.

12. "O sudebnykh pristavakh," Federalnyi zakon ot 21 iuliia 1997, *Iuridicheskii vestnik*, 1997, No. 17, *dos'e*: 1; Nataliia Vdovina, "Stavka na sudebnykh pristavov," (Interviu s Borisom Kondrashevym), *Rossiiskie vesti*, 22 Nov. 1997, p. 7; Vladimir Khitruk, "Delu—pomoshch, kazne—pribyl" (Beseda s Alekseiu Sarychevu), *Iuridicheskii vestnik*, 1997, No. 13, p. 8.

13. Vladimir Khitruk, "Kak dela, gospodin glavnyi sudebnyi pristav" (Beseda s Boris Kondrashovym), *Iuridicheskii vestnik*, 1998, No. 16, pp. 9-10.

14. The information on violations of time limits comes from monitoring of the work of the bailiff enforcers conducted by the procuracy in Primorskii territory. The same monitoring also revealed more substantive problems such as improper extraction of collection charges, misevaluations of property, illegal seizures of the property of third persons to disputes, and even inappropriate actions producing bankruptcy of firms. V. Kolesnikov, "Prokurorskii nadzor za ispolneniem zakonov sudebnymi pristavami," *Zakonnost'*, 1999, No. 7, pp. 25-30.

15. Khitruk, "Delu—pomoshch kazne—pribyl;" Nikolaev, "Sudebnyi pristav;" "S postanovelniem na pereves?" *Iuridicheskii vestnik*, 1997, No. 20, p. 4.

16. "O sudebnykh pristavakh."

17. Nikolaev, "Sudebnyi pristav;" Andrei Kamakin, "Boris Kondrashov: My meniaem 'iustitsiiu' kriminalnuiu na iustitsiiu bez kabychek," *Nezavisimaia gazeta*, 4 Feb. 1998, p. 8.

18. See "O postanovleniem napereves."

19. S. N. Ruban and V. V.Safonov, "Sudebnym pristavam nuzhna...pomoshch," *Biulleten Ministersva iustitsii Rossiiskoi Federatsii*, 1998, No. 10, pp. 15-17.

20. *Ibid.*; Khitruk, "Kak dela, gospodin glavnyi sudebnyi pristav."

21. Interview with Sergei Nikolaevich Ruban; "Uchitsia i ehche raz uchitsia: Oblastnoi arbitrazhnyi sud obobshchil 'opyt' raboty sudebnykh pristavov po ispolneniiu ego reshenii," *Sudebnye novosti: Obozrenie dlia SMI, vlasti i praktiku-iushchikh iuristov*, No. 3, Sept.-Oct. 1998), p. 17; discussion with Kathryn Hendley, 1 Nov. 1998.

22. Skorobogatova, "Analiz raboty Departamenta sudebnykh pristavov;" Maksim Glinkin, "Rol pristava v sudbe demokratii" (Interviu s Miniustom Pavelym Krashennikovym), *Obshchaia gazeta*, 12-18 Nov. 1998, p. 4; "Sostoianie ispolnitelnogo proizvodstva za pervoe polugodie 1998 g.," *Biulleten Ministerstva iustitsii Rossiiskoi Federatsii*, 1998, No. 10, pp. 14-15.

23. "Postanovlenie Soveta sudei Rossiiskoi Federatsii ot 30 oktiabria 1998 g."

24. T. V. Kuznetsova, "Nekotorye voprosy ispolnitelnogo proizvodstva po sudebnym aktam arbitrazhnykh sudov," *Vestnik Vysshego Arbitrazhnogo Suda RF*, 1999, No. 5, pp. 92-95; Vitalii Portnov, "Sud reshil. A kto isponit?" *Rossiiskaia gazeta*, 7 July 1999, p. 3.

25. Kathryn Hendley, "An Analysis of the Activities of Russian *Arbitrazh* Courts: 1992-1996," A Report Submitted to the National Council on Soviet and East European Research, Contract No. 811-18, 17-19; data supplied by Kathryn Hendley on petitions to freeze assets; comments on a draft of this section by Kathryn Hendley and Sarah Reynolds.

26. Memo from Kathryn Hendley, 2 Jan. 1998.

27. See Hendley, "Remaking," pp. 23-24.

28. Memo from Kathryn Hendley; "Ob ispolnitelnom proizvodstve," Federalnyi zakon ot 21 iiuliia 1997, *Iuridicheskii vestnik*, 1997, No. 17, *dos'e*: 5-16.

29. Conversation with Peter Maggs, 22 Nov. 1997. See Zvi Lerman and Karen Brooks, "Russia's Legal Framework for Land Reform and Farm Restructuring," *Problems of Post-Communism*, Nov.-Dec. 1996, pp. 48-58.

PART FOUR

Strategy: The Agenda For Reform

9

What Remains to be Done

This study has demonstrated that the realization of judicial reform in Russia, for all its accomplishments, remains in an early stage and requires many further initiatives to make Russia's courts autonomous, powerful, fair, and respected. We have identified more than thirty measures that would advance this goal.

Joining all of our recommendations is a perspective on the challenge of reforming justice in Russia. In general, we adopt a position that differs from those of both the radical minded scholars (some of whom seek to replace inquisitorial procedure with adversarial) and jurists in Russia who prefer minimal change. We, the authors of this study, stand strongly behind the *moderate reform agenda* (described in Chapter 1), as developed and supported by the judicial community in Russia since 1995. This agenda assumes the continuation in Russia of both the Civil Law tradition (including neo-inquisitorial criminal procedure, though with more adversarial imports) and a centralized judicial system (with only minimal elements of federalism). The moderate reform agenda does not stress the attainment in Russian justice of international standards of human rights, but it does not deny that goal. And, while supporting the moderate reform agenda, we also endorse some of the recommendations of bodies like the Council of Europe, Amnesty International, and Human Rights Watch concerning, for example, conditions of pre-trial detention.[1] Moreover, we stand firmly behind the efforts of the Russian judicial chiefs to avoid the potential tragedy of losing the reform gains to date as a result of systematic underfunding of the courts, significant decentralization within the courts and legal system, or a failure to reverse the decline in the quality of new judges.

To put it another way, we believe that judicial reform in Russia should focus upon the building and improvement of courts and legal practice rather than their transformation. We take this position because we believe successful courts in Russia must be grounded in Russian traditions and because modifying traditional ways is more feasible than their outright rejection. It will also prove advantageous, given the political uncertainties of the day, if judicial reform in the next decade can be pursued in a conservative political milieu; it should not depend upon the domination of "democratic forces" in Russian politics.

The recommendations that we have proposed fall into three groups. Some of them involve spending significant amounts of money, either at one shot or on an ongoing basis. Others call for changes in the structure of institutions or the procedural ground rules of criminal or civil justice, often requiring changes in law and therefore the approval of a variety of political actors. Still other potential changes fall within the competence of the judicial branch and its leaders to approve and realize, without significant financial investment or the consent of other politicians or officials.

In the final part of this study we analyze our recommendations within each of these groups and grapple with the difficult subject of priorities. We consider, first of all, the reform proposals that will cost money, especially large sums. Which should be addressed first? Where can foreign organizations, bringing only modest sums of money to bear, help the process most and make the greatest impact in the long run? Then we examine those of our proposals that call for changes in law and in regulations of agencies other than those in the judicial branch. Here we try to identify the main political actors whose consent may be needed and what kinds of trade-offs and appeals might be employed to mobilize their support. We also consider the obstacles to the implementation of controversial measures and the interconnections between different reform measures. From here we turn to the improvements that the judicial branch (Supreme Court, Judicial Department, Council of Judges) can realize on its own with neither financial investment nor the consent of outside political forces. In conclusion, we specify a time line for judicial reform, based on optimistic assumptions about the recovery of the Russian economy and the development of the Russian government's capacity to collect tax revenue. Absent these assumptions, we (and our Russian friends) will be forced to contemplate more modest and less effective approaches to the delivery of justice.

Spending Priorities

That significant reforms usually cost money is a truism. Moreover, even when the economy of a country is prosperous and uncommitted revenue available, there are as a rule many competitors for the funds. Post-Soviet Russia at the turn of the millennium did not have a well-functioning economy or a government that was capable of raising surplus tax revenues for new policy initiatives. On the contrary, the government of Russia experienced regular shortfalls of revenue collected, and held back from most government agencies and programs money already committed in the state budget. The government also managed to build up debts to many important players and constituencies—such as the military, the police, and the employees of state firms.

The courts, as we have seen, suffered in 1995–1998 from underfunding so significant as to jeopardize normal operations. Yet, the momentum of judicial reform required increases in government expenditures not just for recovering a normal level of operations but also for initiatives to transform the administration of justice. How to spend scarce resources and how best to make the case for new resources from a government under financial siege represented central dilemmas for judicial chiefs and reformers alike.

As a starting point for discussing these tradeoffs, it is useful to group new spending possibilities relating to judicial reform into five categories:

A. Increasing the budgets of all existing courts to cover administrative expenses and salaries of staff (pay raises and to hire additional persons, especially the new court administrator) OR an across-the-boards budget increase (5.2, 2.2)

B. Specific measures, of modest net cost, that could be funded separately or as part of an across-the-boards increase: the development of clerkships as a start in all courts with more than three judges (5.4); allocation of funds to develop and support more expertise in all areas where there is now a shortage (7.6b); support for the qualifications commissions and for the councils of judges (4.3); increasing payments to assessors (6.5); supplying bailiffs with vehicles (initially as an experiment based on cost recovery) (8.2).

C. Major funding initiatives: establishing a separate Investigatory Committee (in part a one time only expense) (7.1); establishing the justice of the peace courts, along with programs of training and support for the justices (6.4); expanding jury trials to more subjects of the Federation (6.6).

D. Special focused initiatives: establishing the Academy of Justice to train all new judges and with it a Research Center/Institute on the Judiciary and Administration of Justice (4.4; 5.3); establishing a journal and television programs on the courts (4.1); mounting training programs for new justices of the peace, for bailiff-enforcers, and for court secretaries, especially in the regions (5.1;8.1); mounting demonstration projects of well-funded district court/bailiff offices (2.3;8.3); supporting international conferences and consultations related to reform initiatives, e.g., on judicial misconduct/accountability or on appellate procedures and institutions (3.5); supplying technical support for courts, especially computers/modems to improve access to legal information and devices for recording trials (5.5b).

E. Related matters: developing legal services for non-wealthy persons (legal aid/compulsory service by legal defenders) (7.3).

The two largest expenditures on this list, both of which require substantial new investment, are the establishment of the justice of the peace courts (listed under C) and an across-the-board increase in support for existing general courts, including, if possible, the support of ancillary institutions such as the judicial qualification commissions and the lay assessors. All things being equal, it would be better if the across-the-board funding took precedence and occurred before the funding of the new peace courts. The logic is clear; the underfunding of today has reached such crisis proportions in many parts of the Russian Federation as to be counterproductive and wasteful. Courts are inefficient because witness notices do not go out by registered mail; cases wait for months in the regional capitals before being forwarded for review to the Supreme Court for lack of funds to forward the files; shortage of staff and low quality of staff contribute to the judges' falling behind with caseload, in turn keeping more of the accused for longer periods in pre-trial detention. Even relatively small increases in the base budgets of courts could yield important gains. At the same time, starting up any new institution, like the peace courts, always involves some disruption, unanticipated problems, and unplanned costs. No doubt, the peace courts will have to be introduced by stages in different parts of the country in any circumstance. But there is a danger that absent the obvious demands for creating a new institution backed by a legislative commitment, the Russian government will not be moved to supply additional budgetary resources to the courts. Although an across-the-board increase is the most rational course—and the step that would most improve the efficiency of

Russian justice in the short run—such an increase may not be politically feasible. It may be necessary to proceed with the new courts as the only way to leverage significant new resources out of the government's coffers. To be sure, the peace courts will eventually help the district courts, by assuming some 60 percent of the latter's current caseload. And as long as the district courts do not get swamped with appeals from the peace courts (and can escape the planned requirement of reviews by three judge panels), they should gain breathing room. Perhaps the combination of a lighter caseload with some of the simplifications of procedure widely supported by Russian judges today will prove sufficient to bring the district courts back to normalcy.

It is our view that even while justice of the peace courts are being established over the next decade, there must still be a general increase in the budgets of the regular courts—if only to counteract the loss of morale of their judges. The general courts must be receive at least 10 percent more real budget than what was allocated for 1999, and they must actually receive all the budgeted funds, avoiding the seemingly inevitable sequesters. The new 1999 rules for delivery of allocated funds to the courts (see Chapter 1) proved effective.

Apart from these two large expenditure items, top priority should be given as well to three other measures. The first is the provision of vehicles for at least some of the bailiff-enforcers. This may prove a low-cost initiative, for it is possible that the resulting improvement in the implementation of commercial decisions will generate additional revenue sufficient to offset the investment in motor vehicles. To determine the real costs and benefits, it would be advisable to mount an experiment in selected regions and districts. A second priority is the establishment of a separate investigatory agency. In this case, a substantial part of the costs would be incurred at the start-up, but the agency would require some budget above and beyond what would be extracted from the budgets of the Ministry of Internal Affairs (MVD) and Procuracy, say, to pay rent of premises. To function properly, the new investigatory agency should be provided with sufficient funds to cover costs of its work (e.g., payment of experts). If a new investigatory agency is not created soon, then it is imperative as a first step to place investigators working in the MVD into a separate administrative hierarchy independent of police chiefs at the different levels. Finally, a crucial area for investment is the development an adequate system of legal aid. The entire operation of the courts depends upon the presence and cooperation of competent defense counsel, but in the absence of laws widening the range of eligible jurists and guaranteeing legal defense for those who cannot afford to pay, defense counsel often are not available or are so busy as to cause delays in case processing. The need for more involvement of counsel in the pre-trial phase of criminal cases may require the establishment of some kind of duty counsel; this option deserves consideration. The current stalemate in the development of a law on the Bar (*advokatura*) needs resolution and with it investment in a new system of public defenders and legal aid. This will be especially vital should the new criminal procedure code require the presence of procurators (and therefore also defense) in all but the most minor criminal cases.

We should also stress that all of the special focused initiatives (listed in D) represent opportunities for tangible contributions to judicial reform in Russia at relatively low cost. Each of them would make a good choices for Western organizations that are prepared to invest in the improvement of courts and the administration of justice in Russia. For example, a research institute on the judiciary, attached to the Supreme Court and the Council of Judges, and staffed with social scientists as well as jurists, would provide the leaders of the judiciary and government alike with information and analysis about the actual work of the courts and help in mobilizing support for them. Note that both the Procuracy and the MVD have such research institutes; only the judiciary does not. Staff at the new institute could take responsibility for other special initiatives, such as the production of a popular journal and a television program on the courts, public relations efforts that are bound to give the courts new visibility and respect, especially if they emphasize the newer aspects of the courts' work. The Institute could also play a role in new programs for the training of judges.

Support for international conferences relating to crucial issues in judicial administration (such as evaluation and discipline of judges) and assisting with the mounting of training programs (for judges, justices of the peace, bailiffs, court secretaries) are natural projects for international cooperation. In fact, many of the activities of Western organizations to date have focused on training and consultations, and have led to the discovery of the often useful tactic of "training the trainers." In the absence of funds to train the large numbers of persons required to fill almost any role in Russia, some Western funders have focused on educating a small cadre prepared to take their learning to colleagues in the provinces.[2] The alternative approach of organizing training sessions throughout regional Russia has been adopted by the Russian Foundation for Legal Reform in its plan in the judicial reform area. The Foundation, which to date has received most of its funding from a World Bank loan, has announced its intention to conduct a series of regionally-based two-month seminars for new judges, regional seminars for mid-career judges on new legislation and the development of judicial style, and a series of six seminars of 100 judges each to discuss and gain support for reforming the judicial system of Russia. It is noteworthy that the Foundation has developed through other projects a presence and a capability in Volgograd, Nizhny Novgorod, Ekaterinburg, Saint Petersburg, and Saratov.[3]

Until now much of the foreign investment in Russian justice has focused on the development of jury trials and the *arbitrazh* courts. While valuable in their own right—and understandably attractive to Western funders—neither of these ventures represents in our view the top priority for the next ten years. At present it is the regular court system, rather than the commercial courts, which needs the attention of reformers, at home and abroad. The regular courts (almost entirely in non-jury trials) handle the overwhelming majority of criminal and civil cases and it is with these "courts of general jurisdiction" that most Russians come into contact. Only when these courts function fairly and well will the Russian public fully respect its courts and look consistently to courts and law for the protection of its rights. To be sure, the *arbitrazh* courts handle most of the disputes between private business firms, and their success has a bearing upon the development of the market economy. Moreover, improving the implementation of the judgments of the *arbitrazh* courts remains a pressing need. On the whole, though, the *arbitrazh* courts have been better supported than the regular courts (certainly than those at the district level) and have received more aid from the West as well. We are calling not for any desertion of the cause of the *arbitrazh* courts (which are also underfunded), but for some righting of the balance, such that the courts most Russian citizens encounter receive the attention that they deserve. Likewise, it is the core operations of the courts of general jurisdiction, rather than jury trials for a tiny number of the most serious offenses, that should assume priority for the time being. Admittedly, the expansion of jury trials to other regions and republics may depend entirely on the presence of significant support from abroad, and some investors may want to keep the momentum of the jury experiment going. While useful, this does not strike us as the best use for most of the money from abroad.

There are three further targets for foreign aid in the development of Russian courts that deserve special mention. One is the mounting of demonstration projects, with appropriate evaluations, to show what a well-funded district court or bailiff office can achieve. Such projects would have to be developed jointly with both local authorities and the judicial chiefs, not to speak of actual judges and court staff, but if done well, they could reveal which specific investments have the greatest impact. Another target that we wish to highlight is support for the Council of Judges and other institutions of the judicial community. Already, the Russian Foundation for Legal Reform, established to allocate funds from the World Bank loan, has contributed to the convening of one or more Congresses of Judges, and to a meeting of the heads of regional councils of judges. Such meetings—not only at the national, but also at the interregional and regional levels—represent important mechanisms in the development among judges of professional identity, not to speak of an ethos. Yet, without outside help the weakly funded bodies of the judiciary would not be able to hold many of these meetings. The various meetings of judges may provide opportunities for Western sponsors to encourage special sessions on matters such as judicial discipline, ethics, and the evaluation of judicial performance.

Finally, there remains the vital question of technical support for the courts. In our view, the operation of most courts would benefit greatly from the presence of computer access to legal data banks and equipment to record trials. Especially in provincial cities and remote parts of the country, judges typically lack access to the latest developments in law, decisions of the Supreme Court, materials in legal journals, etc. Yet, most or all of this material is now available electronically. To raise the legal literacy of judges, keep them up to date, and even reduce the frequency of appeals, each court should be equipped with a computer, modem, information on the various legal Web sites in Russia, and budget to cover access to those sites (i.e., the cost of an account and time charges, if applicable). Another piece of equipment that would improve the work of courts is recording devices (with a supply of tapes and storage facilities) to allow court stenographers to take down a full record of the trial, from which they could type out whatever portions, if any, were needed for appeals. Now the stenographers take notes (sometimes in shorthand) and produce summary versions of trials that are sometimes disputed by the parties.

Legal Change: Priorities and Political Challenges

Many of the recommendations developed in this study—aimed at improving the fairness and effectiveness of Russian courts—require changes in law (sometimes within codes), and often legal regulations as well. Here we examine these proposals as a group, and identify the main political forces and interests that have a stake in such legal changes and ready opportunity to voice their concerns. We go on to examine aspects of the political feasibility of legal change, including the variety of political appeals, the problems of securing implementation of changes adopted, and the coordination of changes in various areas of law.

Our proposals for legal change relate to six different subjects: civil procedure; the judiciary; constitutional review; criminal investigation; criminal trials; and appeals from criminal trials.

In civil procedure we support initiatives aimed at improving efficiency through the avoidance of unnecessary and wasteful activity and at raising the authority of judges. Thus, we have called for a major curtailment in the writing by trial judges of the explanations underlying their decisions (*motivirovochnaia chast*) by allowing delegation of this responsibility to clerks or secretaries (6.1a); and for the continuation (if not expansion) of recently introduced final decisions by appellate panels (6.3). While these proposals have strong support from judges, they face resistance from conservative academic jurists and politicians attached to traditional Soviet ways. Further, we support enhancing the power of judges to fine wayward participants in trials (6.7), and of judges in commercial courts to penalize noncompliance with orders to freeze assets (8.4). Finally, as judicial review of administrative acts grows more frequent and expands into new subject areas, it is important to refine the procedures for handling these cases (4.2a).

We endorse the proposal made by experts from the Council of Europe to treat newly appointed judges, who have not yet received life tenure, as probationers (2.1). This implies some limitations on their actual functions (for example, not hearing alone cases that bring more than two years' imprisonment, and not handling the most serious and controversial cases generally); some supervision and tutelage by the chief judge of their courts; and avoidance of statistical indicators in the evaluation of their work. Treating new judges differently from others might require some changes in the Law on the Status of Judges. There would be some problems with giving this special status to newly appointed judges in rural areas, where a court has only one judge (about 20 percent of courts); if necessary, some cases from those districts would have to be heard in a neighboring court.

In the constitutional realm we are concerned lest the Constitutional Court's decision of 16. June 1998 have the effect of shielding large categories of legal norms (including some bureaucratic regulations and normative acts of lower levels of government) from judicial scrutiny, and discourage citizens from challenging the constitutionality of legal norms in court. We urge the Russian government to develop and adopt legislation granting to particular courts the right to void apparently unconstitutional normative acts and regulations that are not now open to such action at the hands of the Constitutional or Supreme Courts of the Russian Federation (4.3).

The bulk of our recommendations for legal change are focused on the criminal process. To begin, we have endorsed a set of major changes relating to the pre-trial phase—creating a separate investigatory agency and reshaping of the mission of investigators (7.1); eliminating the requirement that all criminal incidents be fully investigated (7.6a); enhancing the rights of defense counsel to conduct inquiries and gain disclosure (7.2); and recasting of both the terms of and the criteria for using pre-trial detention (7.5). As a group these proposals promote adversarialness and fairness in the pre-trial phase, while at the same time retaining its inquisitorial structure and reviving its benefits. While the creation of a separate investigatory agency has broad support, our other proposals here are controversial and will require considerable persuasion of some potential opponents, especially from the world of law enforcement.

We have made a set of further proposals designed to improve criminal trials, most aimed at continuing or developing appropriate simplifications and increasing efficiency. Shortened trials after confessions (6.2c) and the resumption of adjourned trials where they left off (6.2a) make sense to virtually all judges in Russia, but may be opposed by jurists and politicians attached to Soviet traditions. The continuation and even extension of single-judge hearings also has support from most judges (6.2b), but faces opposition not only from traditionalists but also from some human rights quarters, who are concerned especially about accused persons not represented by counsel. We have stressed the need for new legal protections for the accused, including the taping of confessions and the mandatory appearance of defense counsel at single-judge trials with charges that could bring three years' deprivation of freedom. Strengthening the corps of lay assessors also requires legal change, necessary because this institution cannot survive without new bases for recruiting assessors, and many persons (most judges excepted) will not accept its demise (6.5).

Last, we have endorsed important recommendations relating to the outcomes of trials and the post-trial phases. These include elimination of returns to supplementary investigations (6.3); the shift from Soviet-style cassation to a proper appellate review (5.3); and the simplification of the appellate structure planned from reviewing decisions of the justice of the peace courts (5.4a). As changes bound to shorten the trial process and pre-trial detention, these proposals might gain support, but they go against the grain of Soviet traditions.

Although many of our proposals have considerable support within Russia, most also face opposition, real or potential, that will have to be confronted before they can be adopted and/or implemented. It is relatively easy in post-Soviet Russia for opponents to block proposed legal changes, temporarily and even for longer. On the one hand, there remains a longstanding Soviet tradition of giving special primacy in law and policy-making to the interests and opinions of the major bureaucratic players. In the process of consideration, proposals are sent out for comments to the leaders of the law enforcement and judicial agencies, not to speak of scholarly institutions. On the other hand, the legislative process established by the Russian Constitution of 1993 created instances specially suited for the expression and reflection of the interests of regional government (in the Council of the Federation) and of party political interests (in the Duma).

As a result, some seven different sets of interests are likely to come into play in decisions about legal changes relating to judicial reform. Along a spectrum one might place (1) the radical reformers (promoters of the radical agenda); (2) the legal officials of the Presidency (the State Legal Administration, Presidential Council on the Improvement of the Courts, legal advisor to the President)—which are as a rule favorably disposed to change; (3) the judicial chiefs (heads of the Supreme Court and other top courts, of the Council of Judges, and of the Judicial Department, formerly the Ministry of Justice), who tend to assess potential changes in pragmatic terms; (4) the "power ministries" (Procuracy, Ministry of Internal Affairs, Ministry of Justice in its new configuration—with prisons and bailiffs, but not the courts), who are concerned first and foremost with the needs of fighting crime and maintaining the face and power of their agencies; (5) the government, concerned mainly with financial questions; (6) regional interests, expressed in the Duma and especially the Federation Council; and finally (7) the interests of Soviet traditionalism (overlapping with the Communist Party), based in the Duma. On most matters of legal change it is difficult to gain adoption over the objection of even one of these sets of interests (although this does happen sometimes). On some issues, business, financial, and commercial interests represent another force (represented as a rule through the government and the Duma), but we have not yet seen signs of an interest on their part in judicial reform.

Getting the consent, however grudging, of most of these constituencies to an important legal change may involve appeals to more than one kind of logic or reasoning. Take, for example, the issue of "returns to supplementary investigation." Developed in the 1930s, this practice (as we discussed earlier) enabled judges to avoid handing out acquittals when the evidence was weak and to give the investigators and procurators another chance to build the case (or, if necessary, end the proceedings without the embarrassment of an acquittal). To any reformer committed to promoting adversarialism in Russian justice, "returns" represented a quintessential example of the Soviet tradition of placing the interests of the state ahead of the rights of the individual, and therefore deserved to be eliminated. In contrast, to many law enforcement chiefs and Soviet traditionalists as well, "returns" simply assured that "criminals" would not gain release because of the shortcomings of police and investigators, and thereby contributed to the larger goal of "fighting crime." Yet, there was another compelling reason for eliminating (or drastically reducing) returns to supplementary investigation: they had become extraordinarily wasteful. Two leading officials in the MVD's criminal investigation department have argued that the costs (in money and time) of reopening the investigations, not to speak of holding the accused in detention for lengthier periods, were not justified by the results. Either investigators should do the job correctly the first time, or an acquittal should follow. According to a former procurator of note, the elimination of supplementary investigations would improve the quality of initial investigations. For his part, one of the chiefs of the Russian Supreme Court has observed that judges often return cases to the investigators simply because of a failure to provide an expert assessment of the value of stolen goods— sometimes necessary for the proper qualification of the incident or sentencing. In a typically pragmatic way, the judge suggested that these returns could and should be stopped, as long as trials could be interrupted for a few days to obtain such expert judgments (not possible according to current procedural law). In our view, the elimination of returns to supplementary investigation must be based upon the joining of arguments of "conscience and convenience." Concerns with fairness to the accused alone are unlikely to sway the opponents of the change.

To achieve a reform goal through legal change also requires paying heed to the implementation of legal change—including how key players might react to the change. In the case of the elimination of supplementary investigations one would do well to ensure that trial judges felt free to give the acquittals that were deserved. This might require limitations on appeals from acquittals and/or changes in the evaluation of the work of judges (moving away from stability of sentences as an indicator of performance). Likewise, to achieve a real decrease in pre-trial detention (fewer accused, and for shorter terms) would require not only changes in the law but also the cooperation and commitment of key players, such as the chiefs of the Procuracy and the Ministry of Internal Affairs. The content of their directives to subordinates about the application of the law regarding detention shapes practice in decisive ways. There are indications that the persons actually running the institutions of detention (the investigatory isolators) support a reduction in the number of persons held, and with them some of the chiefs of the MVD, but that the heads of the Procuracy and now the Ministry of Justice (upon taking charge of prisons) prefer to maintain current rules and if necessary build more prisons. A real reduction in pre-trial detention will require the development of a lasting (rather than a temporary) commitment on the part of the leaders of law enforcement agencies to the principle of "economy of repression."

Finally, it is important to stress the interconnectedness of legal reform measures. To accomplish one measure of reform effectively may require a whole series of other changes, not necessarily in the same law. The continuation/expansion of trials by a single judge (without assessors or juries) supplies a case in point. The practical realities of Russian courts support the use of trials by a single judge for all offenses of moderate or average severity, if only because it is difficult to attract effective lay assessors without prohibitively high payments. The current practice is to allow single-judge trials for all charges of moderate severity (maximum punishment of five years' imprisonment), but the new Criminal Code has failed to include in this category the most common forms of theft—repeated theft and break and enter. Often these offenses do not involve goods of large value, and they may be committed by habitual petty thieves. Yet, because the maximum term is six years (rather than five), they are classified as "serious crimes," which must be heard with lay assessors. This makes no sense to many Russian judges, who recognize that these cases are routine and not really serious. Logically, extending single-judge hearings to the cases where they are most appropriate would require either raising the maximum penalty to six or seven years (the option favored by the Criminal Procedure Code drafting committee), allowing trials for these charges by a single judge while reducing the allowable sentence to five years in those particular cases, or, optimally, changing the Criminal Code to give qualified theft a new maximum in law of five years. But there is another problem. Does one want to trust any judge in Russia (given their motley experience and quality) to send an offender away for five years on his/her own say? The lay assessors may not add much to the decisions in most cases, but they do supply an element of accountability for the judge. In their absence, for cases involving more than two years' imprisonment, it is essential that the accused be represented by legal counsel during the trial. But with the shortage of counsel and the absence of adequate legal aid, many accused have trouble arranging legal representation. After all, according to the latest data, nearly half of all persons accused of theft lack any steady sources of income (more than 10 percent are officially unemployed). Should a person who steals out of need and cannot pay a lawyer be left to the mercy of a judge sitting alone? The point is that proper development of hearings by judges sitting alone calls for changes in the criminal law—which conservatives might oppose on principle—and for the establishment of a new system of legal aid—which the government might not be ready to pay for. Such dilemmas occur frequently for designers and advocates of judicial reform in Russia.

In short, improvements in the administration of justice in Russia require a variety of legal changes, many of which are controversial and require the careful building of support from diverse coalitions. They will require cooperation, if not commitment, from those charged with their implementation, and will prove counterproductive unless coordinated with other legal changes.

What the Judiciary Can Do

In addition to reforms that require new financing or legal change, there are some measures that the community of judges itself can undertake, especially to enhance the independence and autonomy of individual, trial-level judges. With the establishment of the Judicial Department, the administrative side of the work of the courts will more firmly than before be under the direction of the Supreme Court and the Council of Judges, and this should provide an opportunity for addressing a variety of issues. These include: protecting judges still on probationary terms from tough assignments and counterproductive forms of evaluation (2.1); issuing guidelines for multi-judge courts on the distribution of cases (3.1b); expanding the publication of decisions of the Supreme Court (3.3b); widening the process of selecting the issues for Supreme Court resolutions (3.3a); and making improvements in the judicial qualification commissions (3.4).

Beyond these useful but narrow changes, we identified three especially important issues that the judiciary in Russia must address in order to develop the autonomy of individual judges. At least from the beginning of the 1980s judges in the Soviet Union felt far more constrained in their judging by their vertical superiors, especially higher courts, than by any political officials or bodies, and all the evidence suggests that this remains the case. What to do? First of all, we believe that the power of the chairmen of courts over ordinary judges should be reduced, and that a key to this change is the removal of the chairmen from decisions about the acquisition for judges of key benefits, such as apartments (3.1). If the new court administrators, with help from the judicial department of a region, can perform this function effectively, judges will feel less dependent on their immediate chief.

Second, there is the problem of judicial discipline and the power over judges exercised, now and in the future, by the judicial qualification commissions (3.4). There are issues here to be addressed, but it is unclear what course of action would be best for Russia. While the availability of disciplinary measures for trivial infractions might reduce unjustified efforts to get judges fired, some judges fear that this tool might also be misused and serve as a new source of pressure to induce conformism on the bench. In our view, the problems of judicial misconduct and accountability deserve further study and the convening of additional conferences (with international participation).

Finally, we come to the crucial issue—eliminating or transforming the longstanding system of higher court guidance and evaluation of the work of judges below (3.2). There is nothing more destructive to the freedom of action of ordinary trial judges in Russia than the anticipation of negative assessments of their work on the part of their superiors. But the evaluation of the work of judges, and many aspects of their future careers, are based upon their records of stability of sentences, the product of the changes made by judges on the higher court who are responsible for guiding or educating them. The reliance on quantitative indicators and the tutelary approach to lower court judges date back some seventy years, and, however counterproductive, represent longstanding traditions. No doubt, when the quality of judges' preparation is low (as it was in the 1920s and 1930s, and again now to a lesser degree), the assignment of new district court judges to the tutelage of experienced judges of the regional courts may help them improve their performance on some dimensions.

We urge the leaders of the Russian judiciary to address these issues— by issuing new guidelines on evaluation that limit the role of statistical indicators and by actively exploring ways to decouple the existing system of mentoring and supervising of lower court judges by judges on superior courts (the *kurator* system) from the organization of cassation reviews. In this connection it would be useful to hold an international conference on how other countries, especially Germany, assess and manage judges.

Time Lines and Scenarios

The challenge of developing courts in Russia that are fair, effective, and respected requires a long-term perspective. Not only did the Soviet period leave Russia with administration of justice characterized by a strong accusatorial bias and little leverage against state officials, but also post-Soviet experience has impoverished the courts and produced a surge of crime that makes it more difficult to improve the position of the accused. All the same, there remained some commitment among politicians as well as legal officials to some kind of judicial reform, if only because the economy and government alike required better law.

How much judicial reform can be achieved and at what rate depends in part upon the speed of the recovery of the economy in Russia and the government's capacity to collect revenue. The political situation— including which political forces control the government—also influences the kind of legal changes that get serious consideration. If one makes optimistic assumptions on both of these counts, one can imagine a shorter time line than would otherwise be the case. In Chapter 6 we argued that it made sense to fix the operations of regular courts and support initiatives directly contributing to their effectiveness, such as the bailiffs and legal aid, before tackling the creation of the justice of the peace courts. An optimistic scenario would assign each of these phases a five year period—i.e., 2000–2005 and 2005–2010; while a more pessi-mistic (but equally teleological) one might treat each phase as a ten-to-fifteen year unit. The same reasoning might be applied to the realization of key legal changes. Only with propitious economic and political development can one imagine a rapid abandonment of traditional and conservative approaches to the administration of justice among key players, which would be necessary for the realization of the legal changes advanced in this report. The deep and multifaceted divisions over the draft criminal procedure code, which have existed for some years and are if anything sharper now, are a case in point.

The enormity and long-term nature of judicial reform in Russia suggests the need for all involved, including Western organizations, to take satisfaction in small steps and to pursue with vigor whatever can be done now to improve the performance of courts and their public image. In retrospect, the years 1991–1993 were a special time of achievements in judicial reform, but what made them possible were the struggles and smaller steps of the years that came before. Now, too, it is time to lay the ground for future breakthroughs, whose exact timing cannot be predicted.

Notes

1. In preparation for Russia's potential admission to the Council of Europe a joint team of Council-appointed scholars from Western Europe and Russian experts met a number of times and prepared recommendations for Russian legal reform. In addition, a number of general Council documents, for example concerning aspects of "Access to Justice," have been translated into Russian and distributed widely. Finally, the admission of Russia into the Council imposed a number of obligations on Russia, some of which relate to its courts. All of these developments add useful perspectives to debates over judicial and legal reform in the Russian Federation, but we do not believe that every practice used in Western Europe should be imported directly into Russia without careful consideration of its implications and feasibility. Thus, we have argued against the recommendation of the Council of Europe that the Resolutions (or Explan-ations) of the Supreme Court of the Russian Federation be eliminated. We agree with the majority of Russian judges that those resolutions play a largely positive role in the Russian judicial system. See, for example, "Konferentsiia po reforme sudebnoi sistemy RF," *Advokat*, 1996, No. 12, pp. 3-14; Inga B. Mikhailovskaia, "Problemy organizatsii sudebnoi sistemy v svete vstupleniia Rossii v Sovet Evropy," in "Kruglyi stol 'Sudebnaia sistema v Rossiiskoi Federatsii, Moscow, 14 marta 1997 g.'," pp. 1-14; "Dostup k pravosudiiu," *Rossiiskaia iustitsiia*, 1997, Nos. 6 through 11 (various pages); "Russian Federation: A Review of the Compliance of the Russian Federation with Council of Europe Commitments and Other Human Rights Obligations on the First

Anniversary of its Accession to the Council of Europe," *Human Rights Watch/Helsinki*, Vol. 9, No. 3 (D), Feb.1997, esp. pp. 13-15.

2. Robert Sharlet, "Bringing the Rule of Law to Russia and the Newly Independent States: The Role of the West in the Transformation of the Post-Soviet Legal Systems," in Karen Dawisha, ed., *The International Dimension of Post-Communist Transitions in Russia and the New States of Eurasia* (Armonk, NY, and London, 1997), pp. 322-49.

3. *Informatsionnyi biulleten Proekta Rossiiskogo Fonda Pravovykh Reform*, 1998, No. 1, p. 4; "Proekt Rossiiskogo fonda pravovykh reform 'Pravovaia kultura: Pravovoe prosveshchenie cherez SMI'," unpublished document, p. 7.

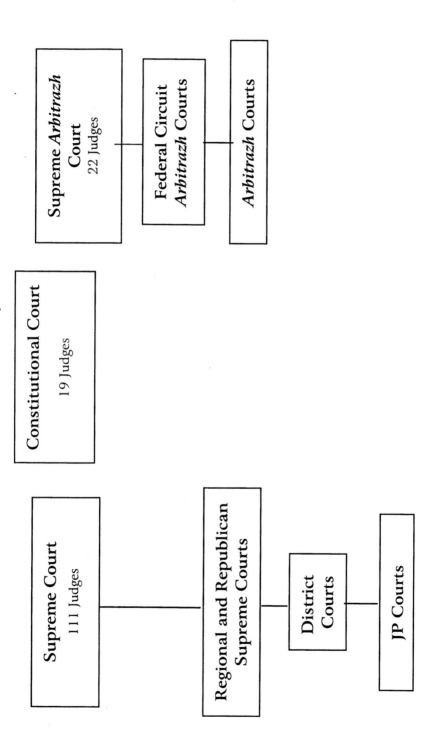

FIGURE 1: The Federal Court System of Russia

Figure 1: The Federal Court System of Russia

Constitutional Court judges are appointed by the Council of the Federation upon nomination by the President for a non-renewable term of 12 years. The Court reviews the constitutionality of legislation and other normative acts of agencies of the federal government and subjects of the federation, resolves jurisdictional disputes between government agencies and levels, and, upon request, interprets provisions of the Constitution. The 19 judges usually hear cases in panels of 10 and 9 but will sit as an entire court when asked to interpret the Constitution, review the constitutionality of laws and charters of the subjects of the federation, or certify the legality of impeachment proceedings against the President of Russia.

Supreme Arbitrazh Court judges (there are 22) are appointed by the Council of the Federation upon nomination by the President of Russia.

Judges on the 10 *Federal Circuit* (okruzhnye) *Arbitrazh Courts* are appointed by the President upon the representation of the Chairman of the Supreme Arbitrazh Court.

Arbitrazh Courts exist on the level of subjects of the federation, and their judges are appointed by the President of Russia upon the representation of the Chairman of the Supreme Arbitrazh Court with the consent of the legislative assembly of the subject of the federation. Arbitrazh courts resolve disputes between private firms and between private firms and government entities on the basis of their own code of procedure.

Supreme Court judges are appointed by the Council of the Federation upon the nomination of the President of Russia for life-terms. The Supreme Court is primarily an appellate court, although its trial court caseload is growing (see Figure 2). Whereas in most civil cases, trials are by a single judge, in criminal cases judges sit in panels of three or a single judge is assisted by two lay assessors. Panels of three judges consider appeals and protests in cassation and supervision.

Regional and Republican Supreme Court judges are appointed in the same manner as Supreme Court judges. These courts are primarily appellate courts, hearing protests and appeals of decisions made by district courts. They have a limited but important jurisdiction as a trial court - for criminal and civil cases of "special social significance." In civil cases, typically a single judge presides. In criminal cases, a single judge is assisted by two lay assessors or a panel of three judges deliberates together. Trial by jury is also available in 12 of the 89 regions.

District Court judges are appointed by the President from a list vetted by the Chairman of the Supreme Court, the local judicial qualification commission, and the legislative assembly. They try the overwhelming majority of civil and criminal cases, as well as all misdemeanors (administrative offenses). Most civil and criminal cases are tried by a single judge, although in serious criminal trials judges are assisted by two lay assessors.

Justice of the Peace Courts are hybrid federal-subject courts. JP court judges will be appointed or elected by regional legislative assemblies for five year terms, but their salaries will be paid by the federal government. They will try all misdemeanor offenses, all crimes carrying a maximum penalty of 2 years imprisonment, a substantial portion of all civil cases (esp. family and labor law), and all suits arising from legislation enacted by governments of subjects of the federation.

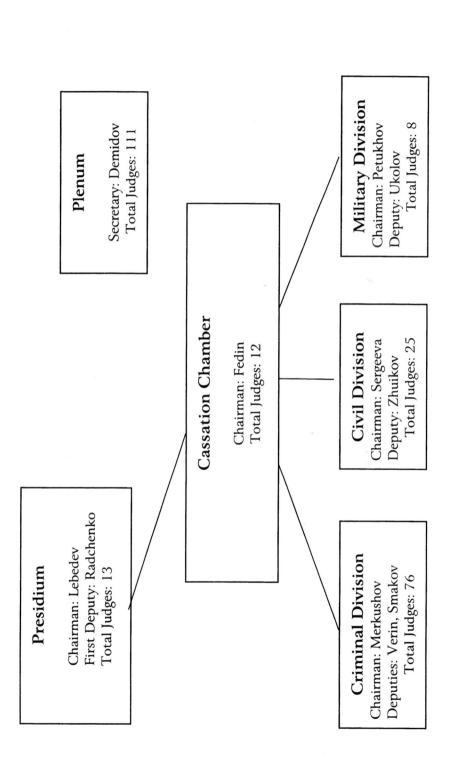

Plenum

Secretary: Demidov
Total Judges: 111

Presidium

Chairman: Lebedev
First Deputy: Radchenko
Total Judges: 13

Cassation Chamber

Chairman: Fedin
Total Judges: 12

Military Division
Chairman: Petukhov
Deputy: Ukolov
Total Judges: 8

Civil Division
Chairman: Sergeeva
Deputy: Zhuikov
Total Judges: 25

Criminal Division
Chairman: Merkushov
Deputies: Verin, Smakov
Total Judges: 76

Figure 2: The Supreme Court of Russia

The Presidium consists of 13 judges, including the Chairman, First Deputy Chairman, the six Deputy Chairmen, and five judges from the Supreme Court. The composition of the Presidium is proposed to the President of Russia by the Chairman of the Court and must be confirmed by the upper house of the Legislative Assembly, the Council of the Federation. The Presidium meets monthly, and is responsible for the general operation of the court, the analysis of the development of law and judicial statistics, and rendering "assistance" to lower courts in the appropriate administration of the law. The Presidium also acts as an appellate tribunal, reviewing in supervision decisions made by any lower court as well as rulings made by the Supreme Court's own various divisions.

The Plenum consists of all judges of the Supreme Court. It meets at least four times a year to discuss problems in the administration of justice, including draft legislation initiated by the Court, and to issue "explanations" (*raz"iasneniia*) on points of law. Representatives of agencies affected by the decisions of the Plenum, such as the Procuracy, MVD, and Ministry of Justice, are invited to make presentations during the deliberations, but the Court is not obliged to incorporate their views into its rulings.

The Cassation Chamber consists of 11 judges and one Chairman selected from among the judges of the three Divisions (Criminal, Civil, and Military). It hears appeals of decisions made by the three divisions of the Supreme Court when acting as a court of first instance. The Chamber was introduced in January 1999 partly in response to concerns voiced by the Council of Europe—namely, that the absence of a body for hearing appeals of Supreme Court decisions was a violation of human rights.

The Criminal, Civil, and Military Divisions act primarily as appellate tribunals, hearing appeals and protests of decisions issued by lower courts either in cassation or supervision. Their jurisdiction as trial courts is very limited, although the docket of the Civil Division (especially suits filed against federal agencies) has grown markedly in the last five years.

APPENDIX A

Key Laws in Russian Judicial Reform (1991-1998)

1. PRE-1992

4 July 1991:   Law on Arbitrazh Courts. (Zakon RSFSR, "Ob arbitrazhnom sude," *Vedomosti S'ezda narodnykh deputatov i verkhovnogo soveta RSFSR*, 1991, No. 30, st. 1013.) Replaced in 1995.

12 July 1991:   Law on the Constitutional Court of the RF. (Zakon RSRSR "O konstitutsionnom sude RF," *Vedomosti S'ezda narodnykh deputatov i verkhovnogo soveta RSFSR*, 1991, no.30, st. 1017.) Replaced in 1994.

21 Oct. 1991:   The Conception of Judicial Reform. ("O Kontseptsii sudebnoi reformy," *Vedomosti S'ezda narodnykh deputatov i verkhovnogo soveta RSFSR*, 1991, No. 44, st. 1435.)

2. 1992-1993: CORE INSTITUTIONS AND ROLES

23 May 1992:   Law on Judicial Review of Pre-trial Detention. (Zakon RF "O vnesenii izmenenii i dopolnenii v Ugolovnom-Protsessualnom kodekse RSFSR," *Vedomosti S'ezda narodnykh deputatov i verkhovnogo soveta RF*, 1992, No. 25, st. 1389.)

29 May 1992:   Law Establishing Single-Judge Trials in Criminal and Civil Cases. (Zakon RF "O vnesenii izmenenii i dopolnenii v Zakon RSFSR 'O sudoustroistve,' Ugolovno-Protsessualnom i Grazhdansko-protsessualnom kodeksakh RF," *Vedomosti S'ezda narodnykh deputatov i verkhovnogo soveta RSFSR*, 1992, No. 27, st. 1560.)

26 June 1992:   Law on the Status of Judges. (Zakon RF, "O statuse sudei v RF," *Vedomosti S'ezda narodnykh deputatov i verkhovnogo soveta RF*, 1992, No.30, st. 1792.) Amended 27 April 1993 and 14 December 1994.

27 April 1993:   Law on Judicial Review of Administrative Acts. (Zakon RF "Ob obzhalovanii v sud deistvii i reshenii, narushaiushchikh prav i svobody grazhdan," *Rossiiskaia gazeta*, 12 May 1993.)

16 July 1993:   Law Establishing Jury Trials. (Zakon RF, "O vnesenii izmenenii i dopolnenii v Zakon RSFSR o sudoustroistve RSFSR, Ugolovno-protsessualnom kodekse RSFSR, Ugolovnom kodekse RSFSR i Kodekse RSFSR ob administrativnykh pravonarusheniiakh," *Vedomosti S'ezda narodnykh deputatov i verkhovnogo soveta RF*, 1993, No. 33, st. 1313.)

12 Dec. 1993:   Constitution of the Russian Federation. ("Konstitutsiia Rossiiskoi Federatsii,"priniata vsenarodnym golosovaniem.)

3. 1994-1999: CORE INSTITUTIONS AND ROLES

21 July 1994:   Law on the Constitutional Court of the RF. (Federalnyi konstitutsionnyi zakon "O Konstitutsionnom Sude RF," *Sobranie zakonodatelstva RF*, 1994, No.13, st. 1447.)

28 April 1995:   Law on the Arbitration Courts of the RF. (Federalnyi konstitutsionnyi zakon "Ob arbitrazhnykh sudakh v RF," *Sobranie zakonodatelstva RF*, 1995, No. 18, st. 1589.)

31 Dec. 1996:   Law on the Court System of the RF. (Federalnyi konstitutsionnyi zakon "O sudebnoi sisteme RF," *Rossiiskaia gazeta*, 6 Jan. 1997.)

27 July 1997:   Law on Bailiffs. (Federalnyi zakon RF, "O sudebnykh pristavakh," *Sobranie zakonodatelstva RF*, 1997, No. 30, st. 3590.)

8 Jan. 1998:   Law on the Judicial Departments. (Federalnyi zakon RF, "O Sudebnom Departamente pri Verkhovnom Sude RF," *Rossiiskaia gazeta*, 14 Jan. 1998, p. 5.)

17 Dec. 1998:   Law on Justices of the Peace in the RF. (Federalnyi zakon RF, "O mirovykh sudiakh v RF," *Rossiiskaia gazeta*, 22 Dec. 1998, p. 4).

23 June 1999:   Law on the Military Courts of the RF. (Federalnyi konstitutsionnyi zakon, "O voennykh sudakh RF," *Rossiiskaia gazeta*, 29 June 1999, pp. 3-4.)

4. ANCILLARY INSTITUTIONS

17 Jan. 1992: Law on the Procuracy. (Zakon RF, "O prokurature RF," *Vedomosti S'ezda narodnykh deputatov i verkhovnogo soveta RF*, 1992, No. 8, st. 366). Replaced in 1995.

15 Nov. 1995: Law on the Procuracy. (Federalnyi zakon "O vnesenii izmenenii i dopolenii v Zakon RF 'O prokurature RF'," *Sobranie zakonodatelstva RF*, 1995, No. 47, st. 8330.)

There have been a number of versions of a new draft law on the advokatura, but none has been approved.

5. PROCEDURAL LAW

5 March 1992: Arbitrazh Procedure Code. ("Arbitrazhnyi protsessualnyi kodeks RF," *Vedomosti S'ezda narodnykh deputatov i verkhovnogo soveta RF*, 1992, No. 16, st. 836.)

5 May 1995: Arbitrazh Procedure Code. ("Arbitrazhnyi protsessualnyi kodeks RF," *Sobranie zakonodatelstva RF*, 1995, No. 19, st 1709.)

There have been many amendments to the Civil Procedure and Criminal Procedure Codes, but the new draft versions of each have yet to be approved.

6. DRAFT LAWS PENDING IN 2000

On courts of general jurisdiction (O sudakh obshchei iurisdiktsii).

On the Supreme Court of the RF (O Verkhovnom Sude RF).

The Criminal Procedure Code (Ugolovno-protsessualnyi kodeks).

The Civil Procedure Code (Grazhdansko-protsessualnyi kodeks).

APPENDIX B

Composite List of Recommendations

2.1 That to the extent possible judges serving their first and probationary terms (before life appointment) be protected from external influences through the avoidance of assignments of difficult or controversial cases.

2.2 That stable and adequate financing of the courts from the federal budget be guaranteed through a law on court finances.

2.3 That foreign supporters of courts in Russia consider providing small material benefits to many or all courts, items such as recording devices, fax machines, modems, and computers.

3.1 To reduce the power of court chairmen over other judges: (a) issues guidelines on case flow management; (b) establish the post of court administrator and empower him/her to handle to the extent possible the obtaining of benefits for individual judges.

3.2 To reduce pressures on judges to conform: (a) discourage the reliance in evaluations of judges' work upon quantitative indicators of performance, especially "stability of sentences"; (b) reorganize the system of *kurators* so that the same superior court judge does not instruct and review cases from any particular judge.

3.3 To refine, but not eliminate, the guidance provided by the Supreme Court to judges on lower courts: (a) keep the "explanations" issued by the Supreme Court, but widening the process of selecting issues to be covered; and (b) increase the number of Supreme Court decisions that are published.

3.4 To improve the Judicial Qualification Commissions: (a) clarify legal procedures; and (b) increase funding.

3.5 Convene a conference on judicial misconduct and accountability, emphasizing European approaches to these issues.

3.6 In establishing the Judicial Departments: (a) ensure that the court administrators serve as the representatives of their court chairmen rather than of the departments; (b) make sure that the departments are well funded and not forced to seek resources below the federal level.

4.1 Publicize the work of the courts (especially such new areas of activity as judicial review of administrative acts, direct application of the Constitution, and consumer protection cases) through a new popular journal (perhaps a revived *Sud idet*), a television program, and work with the Guild of Court Journalists.

4.2 Enhance the role of courts in holding government account-able through (a) legislation clarifying the rules of procedure in the judicial review of administrative acts; (b) strengthening the system for legal aid, in particular free consultations; and (c) studies of the variety of institutions handling complaints against officials.

4.3 Develop and approve legislation to fill existing gaps in the jurisdiction of the courts to void certain kinds of normative acts and bureaucratic regulations and ensure that some court is empowered to deal with any and all legal norms that violate the Constitution of the Russian Federation.

4.4 Improve and regularize financial support for the institutions of the judicial community—the Congress of Judges, the Council of Judges, the Supreme Judicial Qualification Commission, and similar bodies in the subjects of the Federation.

4.5 Establish and support, probably within the new Academy of Justice, a research center on the judiciary and the administration of justice.

5.1 Improve the recruitment of judges by: (a) simplifying the current system of rewards and ensuring that judges' salaries exceed those of procurators and police officials; (b) creating special judicial tracks in some law schools and supplying special stipends to future judges; (c) enhancing the work and rewards for student interns at the courts.

5.2 Revise the content of law school education to promote understanding of the socio-political context of law.

5.3 Establish a major compulsory training program for all new judges (presumably at the new Academy of Justice) and design that program to include innovations in both intellectual content and practical training.

5.4 Develop and expand the institution of clerkships (*pomoshchnik sudu*), especially to employ graduates of the new Academy of Justice not yet eligible to work as judges.

5.5 Improve judges' access to legal information by (a) sending to all judges on a regular basis a selection of newly published books (codes, commentaries, treatises); and (b) providing each courthouse with a computer, modem, and access fees for the major databases of Russian legislation.

5.6 Stimulate and improve the work of all judges by (a) upgrading and expanding the refresher courses; and (b) organizing local conferences, seminars, and other events.

5.7 Upgrade the training of other justice officials (court secretaries, bailiff-enforcers), paying special attention to the soon to be created justices of the peace.

6.1   Modernize civil procedure by: (a) allowing judges to delegate the writing of the detailed reasons for a decision in routine cases to a clerk or court secretary; and (b) continue the recent expansion of the responsibilities of the sides.

6.2   Improve the efficiency of criminal trials by: (a) eliminating the requirement of continuous trials, and allowing judges to adjourn trials, hear other cases, and reopen the adjourned trials; (b) expanding—with the addition of suitable protections—the practice of single-judge hearings; and (c) developing shortened trial procedures—again with appropriate protections (including the taping of police interrogations)—for cases where the accused does not contest the charge.

6.3   In both criminal and civil cases heard at all levels of the court hierarchy, replace the Soviet version of cassation with a full appeal, in which the higher court reviews the substance of the case and affirms, changes, or cancels the decisions of lower courts.

6.4   In establishing the justice of the peace courts: (a) develop a workable appellate process, using single judges and special appellate bodies to handle appeals relating to legislation of the subjects of the Federation; (b) set up at the level of the subjects programs to educate and support new justices of the peace, starting with a pilot program in a few regions.

6.5   Retain lay assessors for the most serious non-jury offenses, and improve their work through a new law and increased financial support.

6.6   Resume the expansion of the jury to other subjects of the Federation, while limiting somewhat the scope of their jurisdiction.

6.7   Enhance the power and opportunities for judges to fine persons who fail to appear in court without excuse (witnesses, experts, and perhaps procurators and defense counsel).

7.1   Create a separate agency for investigators and adopt measures to encourage their autonomy and neutrality. Or, as a fallback, organize investigators within the Ministry of Internal Affairs into a separate vertical structure, eliminating all subordination of investigators to police chiefs.

7.2   Grant to defense counsel: (a) the right to conduct independent inquiries during the period of the preliminary investigation; and (b) access to the formal case file during the same period.

7.3   Ensure adequate representation for non-wealthy accused, especially during the pre-trial phase, through restructuring of the defense bars and their consultation offices and/or the establishment of duty counsel attached to the courts.

7.4   Eliminate the institution of "supplementary investigation" (with appropriate modifications to court procedures).

7.5   Reduce the use of pre-trial detention as a measure of restraint by changing the criteria for its use (in law and in regulations).

7.6   Decrease the length of pre-trial detention by setting shorter legal limits and by reducing delays in the pre-trial investigation, through: (a) eliminating the procedural requirement that all criminal incidents must be fully investigated; (b) expanding the pool of available experts and increasing the funds available to pay them; and (c) giving defense counsel the right to photocopy from the case file and to use assistants in the review of the file.

8.1   Encourage specialization among bailiff enforcers, so that a subset of them concentrates on implementing decisions in commercial disputes rendered by the *arbitrazh* courts.

8.2   Develop as soon as possible special courses—in Moscow and other parts of the country—to train bailiff-enforcers, especially those specializing in the decisions of the *arbitrazh* courts.

8.3   Organize demonstration projects in selected districts, in which the bailiff-enforcers would be provided with motor vehicles, weapons, and other support services; and evaluate the effects of full funding upon performance.

8.4   Encourage—through directives and, if appropriate, changes in the Arbitration-Procedure Code—an active approach by judges on the *arbitrazh* courts toward ensuring the enforceability of their judgments, including a readiness to freeze assets before trial, and to impose fines for non-performance of orders to freeze and other omissions.

8.5   Provide *arbitrazh* court judges with the power to issue injunctions and temporary restraining orders.

APPENDIX C

Survey of Judges: Selected Questions

Between spring and fall of 1997 a questionnaire written by us was administered to judges throughout the Russian Federation as part of the program of the joint project "Reform of the Russian Judicial System," under the joint auspices of the Constitutional and Legislative Policy Institute (Budapest) and the Centre for Constitutional Research of the Moscow Public Science Foundation. Surveys were distributed to a meeting of the chairmen of the regional councils of judges, to a regional meeting of district court judges, and, most importantly, by mail for distribution by the chairmen of regional councils of judges to judges within their regions. Of the approximately 2,000 blank forms that were handed out, we received 321 completed questionnaires.

Although the distribution did not produce a random sample of judges across the Russian Federation, the characteristics of those that were completed give us confidence in the representativeness of our findings. Slightly more than half of the respondents were women (52.3%); slightly more than half had received legal education by correspondence or part-time (53.0%); about one quarter work as chairmen of (district) courts (the rest as judges mainly at district courts, but around twenty at regional courts). The respondents also cover the full gamut of experience as judges, ranging from persons who had worked only four years (25.5%) to veterans with more then fifteen years experience (26.2%), including at more than twenty years (10.7%); the median judge, however, had eight years experience. It is clear from the written comments, the occasional self-identifications, and the envelopes that reached us that the respondents hailed from many parts of the Russian Federation, and represented not only large cities but smaller towns and rural districts as well. In short, we can assert with confidence that the characteristics of our sample came close to those of the judicial corps as a whole.

Here we reproduce a selection of questions, especially those that produced results that we report in the body of this study.

1. Iavliaetsia li kvalifikatsionnaia kollegiia sudei v vashem regione ob'ektivnoi i bespristrastnoi pri (Is the Qualification Commission in your region objective and fair in):
   a) provedenii attestatsii kandidatov v sudi (in attesting candidates):
yes	88.3%	
no	4.1	(N=290)
not always	7.6	

   b) prisvoenii klassnykh chinov sudiam (in promoting judges to higher ranks):
yes	72.4%	
no	6.9	(N=304)
not always	7.2	
don't know	10.9	

   c) reshenii voprosa o prekrashcheniia polnomochii sudei (in dismissing judges)
yes	72.4%	
no	4.6	(N=283)
not always	7.1	
don't know	11.0	

2. Ushchemliaiut li nezavisimost sudei polnomochiia KKS otreshat sudiu ot dolzhnosti za narushenie protessualnogo zakonodatelstva, povlekshee volokitu? (Does the power of the Judicial Qualification Commission to fire judges for violations of procedure legislation producing redtape infringe on their independence?)
yes	32.6%	
no	64.5	(N=310)
don't know	2.8	

3. Sleduet li vvesti distsiplinarnuiu otvetsvennost sudei? (Should a system of disciplinary sanctions against judges be introduced?):
yes	29.9%	
no	65.3	(N=314)
don't know	4.7	

4. Chto stalo luchshe? (What got better?):
   v grazhdankom sudoproizvodstve (in civil trials):
   single judge trials
   (edinolichnoe rassmotreniia) 62.1% (N=87)
   v ugolovnom sudoproizvodstve (in criminal trials):
   single judge trials
   (edinolichnoe reassmotreniia) 63.8% (N=69)

5. Polzuet li vash sud uvazheniem (Is your court respected by):

sredi naseleniia? (among the public?)
```
yes             73.3%
no              13.3                        (N=255)
sometimes       13.3
```
so storony uchastnikov protsessa? (among parties to the case?)
```
yes             75.1%
no               7.8                        (N=281)
sometimes       17.1
```

6. Nuzhno li sokhranit institut narodnykh zasedatelei? Esli da, to v kakikh delakh i v kakoi forme dolzhny zasedateli prinimate uchastie v otpravlenii pravosudii (Is it necessary to preserve the institution of peoples' assessors? If yes, for what cases and in what forms must assessors take part in the administration of justice):
```
no                  61.4%
yes                 10.3
for juveniles        4.4                    (N=311)
for important cases 19.3
don't know/unsure    3.9
```

7. Igraiut li "raziasneniia" Verkhovnogo Suda polozhitelnuiu rol v regulirovaniia sudebnoi praktiki? (Do the Explanations of the Supreme Court improve judicial practice?):
```
yes             89.8%
no               3.5                        (N= 314)
sometimes        6.7
```

8. Vliiaiut li resheniia sudov ob osvobozhdenii iz pod strazhi nezakonno ili neobosnovanno zaderzhannykh podozrevaemykh ili obinvianemykh na uluch-shenii sostoianiia zakonnosti v deiatelnosti militsii i prokuratury? (Do the courts' decisions releasing suspects and accused from custody when their detentions are deemed illegal or groundless improve legality in the work of the police and procuracy?):
```
yes             65.9%
no              27.9                        (N=229)
```

9. Schitaete li Vy sebia nezavisimym sudei i podotchetnym tolko zakonu? (Do you consider yourself an independent judge, subordinate only to the law?):
```
yes                 72.1%
no                  15.2                    (N=315)
in part/not fully   12.7
sometimes            6.1
```

10. Iaviaetes li Vy bolee nezavisimym segodnia, chem v (Are you more independent today than in):

a) 1992:   yes   48.5%   (N=241)
                  no   51.0

b) 1987:   yes   52.4%
                  no   24.7   (N=166)
                  don't know   22.9

11. Ot kogo ili ot kakogo organa Vy naibolee 'zavisimy' segodnia? (On whom and on what agency are you most "dependent" today?):

none	34.5%	
next higher court	18.4	
department of justice	13.7	
local administration	16.5	(N=255)
funding agencies	9.4	
other	5.2	
don't know	2.4	

12. Pochemu vy naibolee zavisimy? (Why do you feel dependent?):

control over advancement	22.2%	
housing/perks	27.8	(N=108)
funding	47.2	

13. Poluchaet li Vash sud dopolnitelnye sredstva, lgoty ili uslugi ot organov mestnoi ili regionalnoi vlasti? (Does your court receive supplementary resources or benefits from local or regional power?):

no	41.5%	
yes	34.2	(N=284)
sometimes	23.9	

14. Esli da, to v kakoi forme predostavliaetsia takaia pomoshch? (If yes, what is the form of help?):

paper/postage/supplies	67.9%	
utilities/rent	20.4	(N=162)
typewriters/computers	2.5	
other	4.3	

15. Kogda vpervye (s kakogo goda) stali postupat takie sredstva ili byli predostavleny lgoty? (In what year were these resources or benefits first provided?):

before 1989	7.6%	
1989-91	3.8	
1992-93	9.5	
1994	7.6	(N=105)
1995	20.0	

1996   38.1
1997   12.4

16. Kak predostavliaetsia takaia poderzhka—po initsiative sude ili mestnykh/-regionalnykh organov vlasti? (At whose initiative was the support provided--the court or local/regional power?):

the court	90.4%	
local authorities	2.7	(N=146)
both	6.8	

17. Vliaet li podobnaia podderzhka na vozniknovenie chuvsta "obiazannosti" pered mestnymi/regionalnymi organami vlasti? (Did such assistance produce a sense of obligation to local/regional power?):

yes	55.3%	
no	44.7	(N=152)

18. Privodit li takaia podderzhka k poiavleniiu opredelennykh "ozhidanii" ot suda so storony sponsorov? (Did the assistance produce expectations from the court on the part of its sponsors?):

yes	52.6%	
no	44.7	(N=133)

19. Privodit li takaia podderzhka k poiavleniiu nedopustimykh trebovanii po razresheniiu tekh ili inykh del? (Did the support lead to improper demands in the resolution of particular cases?):

yes	16.4%	
no	83.6	(N=140)

20. Poluchal li vash sud kakuiu libo podderzhku ili pomoshch ot chastnykh organizatsii, vkliuchaia firmy ili predpriatiia? (Has you court received support or help from private organizations, such as firms or enterprises?):

yes	15.3	
no	84.7	(N=236)

21. Esli da, to kakogo roda pomoshch i v kakom obeme? (If yes, then what kind of help and on whata scale?):

paper/postage/supplies	50.0%	
rent/utilities	11.8	
computers/typewriters	11.7	(N=34)
cars	5.9	
other	14.7	

APPENDIX D

List of Persons Consulted or Interviewed

Included on this list are judges, officials, scholars, and others (journalists, activists) who were consulted or interviewed by either Todd Foglesong or Peter Solomon during their research for this publication between spring 1997 and summer 1999. The positions indicated are those held by our informants at the time of the interview. The authors are grateful to all of them for their cooperation and help.

A. JUDGES

Brykalova, Liubov. M.	Judge, Moscow Regional Court, and Deputy Chair, Judicial Qualification Commission
Chesnokova, Liudmila S.	Chairman, Soviet District Court, Novosibirsk.
Demidov, Vladimir V.	Secretary of the Plenum, Supreme Court RF
Lebedev, Viacheslav M.	Chairman, Supreme Court RF
Marasanova, Svetlana V.	Chairman, Moscow Regional Court
Maslov, Aleksandr M.	Judge, Supreme Court RF
Morshchakova, Tamara G.	Deputy Chair, Constitutional Court RF
Pashin, Sergei A.	Judge, Moscow City Court (formerly Chief, Department of Judicial Reform, State Legal Administration of the President)
Radchenko, Vladimir I.	First Deputy Chairman, Supreme Court RF
Razgulova, Tamara L.	Chair, Intermunicipal court, city of Moscow, Chief, Council of Judges, city of Moscow
Sabina, Iuryi	Chairman, Khimki District Court, Chief of Council of Judges, Moscow Region.
Serkov, Pavel	Chairman, Ulianovsk Regional Court

Shturnev, Aleksei L.	Chairman, Vyborg City Court, St. Petersburg
Sidorenko, Iurii I.	Member, Supreme Court RF, and Chairman, Council of Judges of the RF
Stakheeva, Natalya G.	Former Judge, Onega City Court, Arkhangel Region

B. OFFICIALS

Abrosimova, Elena B.	Senior Consultant, Constitutional Court RF (formerly at the State Legal Administration of the President)
Andriushchechkina, Irina N.	Deputy Head, Department of Statistics and Legal Information, Ministry of Justice
Cherniavskii, Valentin S.	Chief, Judicial Department of RF
Kaliagin, Vladimir A.	Member of the State Duma RF and its Committee on Legislation
Kiiamova, Alevtina N.	Senior Consultant, Supreme Judicial Qualification Commission
Koiliak, Anrei M.	Deputy Head, Department of Legal Information, Supreme Court of Russia
Kozhevnikov, Igor N.	Deputy Minister of Internal Affiars, Chief of Investigatory Committee of MVD
Krasnov, Mikhail A.	Presidential advisor on legal affairs
Levytskii, Viktor P.	Head, Department of Cadres, Ministry of Justice
Martynova, Valentina	Head, Department of Bailiffs, Ministry of Justice
Mazaev, Vladimir D.	President, Russian Foundation of Legal Reform
Nikitin, Iurii. N.	Head, Department of Generalization, Supreme Court of Russia
Orekhov, Ruslan	Consultant, Russian Foundation for Legal Reform (formerly Chief, State Legal Administration of the Presidency)
Pakholkov, Aleksei A.	Deputy Head, Department of Cadres, Supreme Court of Russia
Ponomarev, Gennadii S.	Former Procurator of the city of Moscow

Ruban, Sergei N.	Deputy Chief Bailiff RF and Head of Department of Bailiffs, Ministry of Justice
Semin, Iurii Iu.	Deputy Procurator, Moscow City Procuracy.
Shablinskii, Ilia G.	Legal Department, Federation Council
Shevchenko, Nikolai	Chief of Staff, Legislative Committee of the State Duma
Sidorenko, Evgenii N.	Deputy Minister of Justice
Shvartz, Olga	Staff, Committee on Legislation, State Duma
Survillo, Iurii M.	Chief, Judicial Department of Moscow Region
Tropin, Sergei A.	Former Deputy Minister of Justice
Zherebtsov, Anatolii V.	Chairman, Supreme Judicial Qualification Commission

C. SCHOLARS:

Alekseeva, Lidiia B.	Professor, Legal Academy of Ministry of Justice
Boikov, Aleksandr D.	Deputy Director, Research Institute on Problems of Strengthening Legality and Law and Order of the Procuracy RF
Iakovlev, Aleksandr M.	Professor, Institute of State and Law; formerly Presidential Representative to the State Duma
Kudriavtsev, Vladimir N.	Vice-President, Russian Academy of Sciences; Member of Presidential Council for the Improvement of the Judicial System
Larin, Aleksander M.	Professor, Institute of State and Law
Mikhailovskaia, Inga B.	Professor, Institute of the Advokatura
Petrukhin, Igor L.	Professor, Institute of State and Law,
Sirotkin, Sergei	Director, Centre for Legal Information, Moscow Public Science Foundation
Sukharev, Alexander Ia.	Director, Research Institute on Problems of Strengthening Legality and Law and Order of the Procuracy RF
Vitsin, Sergei T.	Deputy Chairman, Presidential Council on the Improvement of the Judicial System

D. OTHER

Maksudov, Rustem   Expert, Public Centre for the Reform of Criminal Justice

Rudnev, Valerii   Editor, *Rossiiskaia iustitsiia*, member of Presidential Council on the Improvement of the Judicial System.

Index